GOLD IN THE BLACK HILLS

GOLD IN THE

BLACK HILLS

Watson Parker With a New Introduction

SOUTH DAKOTA STATE HISTORICAL SOCIETY PRESS Pierre

This publication is funded in part by the Deadwood Publications Fund provided by the City of Deadwood and the Deadwood Historic Preservation Commission.

Library of Congress Cataloging-in-Publication Data
Parker, Watson.
 Gold in the Black Hills / Watson Parker ; with a new introduction.
   p. cm.
 Originally published: 1st ed. Norman : University of Oklahoma Press, 1966.
 Includes bibliographical references (p.) and index.
ISBN 0-9715171-2-6
 1. Black Hills (S.D. and Wyo.)—Gold discoveries. 2. Gold mines and mining—Black Hills (S.D. and Wyo.) I. Title.
 F657.B6 P32 2003
 978.3'902—dc21   2002036597

Printed in the United States of America

03 04 05 06 07 08 09 10 11 9 8 7 6 5 4 3 2 1

CONTENTS

ILLUSTRATIONS

ACKNOWLEDGEMENTS

There is no lack of books about the Black Hills. A glance at the bibliography will show that there is available much firsthand information about even the earliest settlements, and that from this primary material many useful and entertaining histories have been constructed. Yet none of these books has dealt with the central factor of early settlement—the Black Hills Gold Rush of 1874-79—as a unified historical phenomenon. The many writings have obscured rather than clarified this movement, and have fragmented rather than united the factors which produced its distinctive character. This book, therefore, attempts to weave from the delightful chaos of Black Hills history the story of the rush and the men who made it. If it has a lesson beyond the telling of a tale not told before, it is that no historical event is as simple as it seems, and that it takes more than gold to make a gold rush.

First among those without whose kind assistance this work could not have been carried forward is Professor W. Eugene Hollon, of the University of Oklahoma, who has been ever helpful with encouragement and emendation. Research Professor Gilbert C. Fite, Professor Donald J. Berthrong, Associate Professor Arrell M. Gibson, and Professor William E. Bittle have also contributed their comments, and many of the merits of the book are due to their suggestions. The faults and errors which it may embody, however, must be considered mine.

The assistance of libraries and learned societies has been of inestimable aid in assembling the materials for this work. Miss Opal Carr, of the Bizzell Memorial Library at the University of Oklahoma, was most helpful. Mrs. Boyce Timmons, of the university library's Phillips Collection, suggested many original sources. Mrs. Nan C. Gamble, of the inter-library loan service, found innumerable rare books and brought them to Norman for me. Rodney Reed drew the maps. Josephine Soukup typed the final copy with speed and judgment.

Miss Helen Hoyt, of the Rapid City, South Dakota, Free Public Library, has assembled a truly superior collection of Black Hills materials and greatly assisted me in their use. Mrs. Elmer Pontius, of the Deadwood Public Library, not only gave me a free hand among that institution's many rarities, but also secured many materials from private sources. The Adams Memorial Museum, also at Deadwood, was very helpful. Miss Dorette Darling, of the Homestake Library at Lead, made available without stint the large resources of Black Hills history in that collection. Mr. Gene M. Gressley, of the Western History Research Center at the University of Wyoming Library, pointed the way to much interesting material. The Coe Library of Yale University was generous in providing microfilm copies of rare books and documents. Mr. Carl Wiehe, of the Frontier Museum in Custer, South Dakota, provided access to documents and artifacts not otherwise available. The University of Nebraska Press at Lincoln kindly granted permission to use quotations from Martha Ferguson McKeown's *Them Was the Days*, which illustrate firsthand the way the rushers felt about the Hills.

Miss Ruby Mauch, of the library of the South Dakota School of Mines and Technology, was especially helpful in making available geological materials pertaining to the Hills. Mr. Don Howe, of the Public Relations Office of the Homestake Mining Company in Lead, gave me not only much printed material but many suggestions about finding more information on that famous mine. Mrs. Leo Ashland, of the Society of Minnelusa Pioneers at Rapid City, guided me to the Leedy Collection at that institution and kindly made its resources available. Colonel Will G. Robinson, secretary of the South Dakota Historical Society at Pierre, was of special assistance in my research among the many documents assembled there. Mr. J. Leonard Jennewein, at the Museum of the Friends of the Middle Border, Dakota Wesleyan University, Mitchell, South Dakota, was particularly helpful in providing access to rare Black Hills books, maps, and documents from the Jennewein Western Collection.

Among those individuals whose help has made my work a pleasure are Professor C. Albert Grimm, of the South Dakota School of Mines and Technology at Rapid City, whose knowledge of the Hills is encyclopedic; Hugh and Jacqueline Lambert, who aided with researches in the field and unearthed many forgotten mines and towns; Dr. and Mrs. Roland E. Schmidt, whose moral support and penetrating insight have clarified many perplexing problems; my parents, Mr. and Mrs. Troy Parker, of Hill City, whose library and encouragement have long sustained me; and my wife Olga, without whose help this book could never have been completed. I thank them all.

Watson Parker
Oshkosh, Wisconsin
October 17, 1966

INTRODUCTION TO THE NEW EDITION

The history of the Black Hills, once the gold rush to the placer mines subsided, has been complex and varied. The hard-rock gold mines, with their increasingly subtle ways of removing small amounts of gold from increasingly refractory ores, continued up into the late 1920s, when rising costs after World War I and a fixed price for gold gradually forced all but the mighty Homestake Mine at Lead and a few mines around Bald Mountain to go out of the business. The increase in the price of gold in 1933, from twenty dollars to thirty-five dollars an ounce coincided with the depression of the "dirty thirties" and brought hundreds, if not thousands, of unemployed workers and farmers to the Hills to scrabble in the creeks or to prod shafts and tunnels into even vaguely promising rocks. The coming of World War II shut down these hopeful enterprises, and even the Homestake closed down its mining operations and devoted its foundry to casting shells for hand grenades.

After the war, mining (except at the Homestake) became too expensive to be supported by gold at thirty-five dollars an ounce, but it boomed again in the 1970s when the price of gold was left to the free market—at one time it reached eight hundred dollars an ounce, and nowadays it is about three hundred dollars. Huge open-cut mines in the northern Hills tore down mountains, ground them up, stacked them into new and orderly hills, doused them with feeble cyanide solutions, and made a profit from ores that previously had been virtually worthless. These mines played out by the turn of the twentieth century, and in 2001 the Canadian company Barrick Gold had bought the Homestake and closed its mine at Lead, which was by then working at their eight-thousand-foot level.

Other mining also took place in the Hills. A tin boom flourished on British capital in the 1880s and was centered on Hill City when the Harney Peak Tin Mining and Milling Company bought some twelve hundred claims, built three big mills, and brought an evanescent boom to the central Hills. Alas, the tin deposits proved to be illusory, except for some meager ones in the northwestern Hills at Tinton (a mine that is still being worked for other minerals), and the peculations of the British promoters and their American henchmen brought disaster and disrepute to all of Black Hills mining.

Feldspar, used in ceramics, has flourished on and off, especially in the central Hills. Bentonite, a clay that can absorb enormous amounts of liquid, which gives it uses in everything from oil drilling to cat litter, is mined around Colony, Wyoming, and long trainloads of it pass through Rapid City every day. Lithium, which has many uses (one is in treating mental problems), boomed in the central Hills as part of the atomic-energy developments, as did beryllium, found in huge "logs" of spodumene embedded in the pegmatite of the central Hills. Arsenic was mined in Keystone in the 1920s for use in defeating a plague of grasshoppers on the farms of the Great Plains. The Bob Ingersoll Mine west of Keystone is said to have produced over fifty different minerals of commercial value, although not all of them at the same time, and mining continues for a variety of minerals throughout the Hills down to the present day.

Transportation, which made possible the gold rush to the Hills, flourished when the railroads reached the area in the late 1880s. The Chicago, Burlington & Quincy went up the center of the Hills (its roadbed is now the spectacular George S. Mickelson hiking trail); the Chicago & Northwestern moved northward along the eastern foothills; and the Milwaukee Road came in from the east. Railroads still serve the Hills, largely hauling out bentonite and lumber. Most materials, however, are now brought in by truck over Interstate 90, a route whose magnificence has been somewhat dimmed by the ghastly parade of billboards that decorate its margins all the way from Sioux Falls to Wyoming, signs which unfortunately prevent the modern travelers from seeing the Great Plains as their ancestors once saw them. Good highways now traverse the Hills, but only a few yards off the beaten path, the Hills are much as they ever were. Scenic beauty, ghost towns, and solitude soothe the eye and comfort the mind made weary by travel over the more congested major highways.

The lumber industry, utilizing the region's extensive stands of ponderosa pine, has long been controlled and guided by the Forest Service of the United States Department of Agriculture, which took over the Black Hills in the late 1800s and now controls about 90 percent of the area. Loggers complain about the restrictions placed upon their activities, and conservationists complain that the Forest Service does not restrict logging activities enough. When one looks at what private owners along the highways have done with private property, one tends to be grateful that the United States government owns the bulk of the Hills and now preserves them for present enjoyment and future use. A plague of forest fires in the summer of 2002 has brought about much rethinking of forest policies, for it is hard to reconcile human occupation with natural processes that are as destructive as forest fires.

Ranching, largely of cattle but with some sheep, has been a major Black Hills industry since the earliest days, when the miners needed beef. Ranging over the national forest lands—and over many of the highways—privately owned cattle have been the backbone of Black Hills agriculture, and the crops grown in the few level valleys have largely gone to feed the cattle in the wintertime. This grazing on the public land at least crops down the grasses, which, if allowed to dry, become in the fall a disastrous fire hazard. The short growing season—any night, even in the summertime, can bring a killing frost—has told against farming in the Hills, but for a while potatoes were grown with some success, though hay crops are more reliable.

Tourism has flourished in the Hills since their earliest days of settlement. Wild tales of mining riches have long lured investors (otherwise known as "suckers") to the Hills to pour money into various speculative enterprises, not all of them mines. Once here and swindled, these many visitors at least spread the word of the incredible natural beauty of the area. With publicity and pamphlets, the railroads did much to drum up the tourist trade, and nowadays the highways bring in visitors from all over the world to see the beauty of Black Hills solitude, now somewhat dimmed by the increasing multitudes, to hike the many mountain trails, and to gaze with awe upon the gigantic carvings of Presidents Washington, Jefferson, Lincoln, and Teddy Roosevelt on Mount Rushmore. A similar statue of Chief Crazy Horse is emerging from a granite mountain north of Custer, and it is hoped that the present century will see its completion. Custer State Park, one of the largest state parks in the nation, has four resorts for the comfortable accommodation of visitors to this wonderland of Black Hills scenery, and every town has good tourist accommodations. The number of so-called tourist attractions grows steadily, but it is to be hoped that these do not one day completely conceal the more natural attractions of the Hills.

The military presence continues in the Hills. At a 2001 Rapid City meeting of the Council on America's Military Past, two speakers were able to name more than sixty military posts that had at one time or another been located in the Hills. Perhaps the most astonishing one belonged to the Soviet Union, which was checking on the demolition of United States missile sites that had ringed the Hills with a rim of military might and potency during the Cold War.

Ellsworth Air Force Base just east of Rapid City had manned and serviced these sites and for nearly sixty years had housed the bomber squadrons that put teeth into America's military posture. The sites of many Civilian Conservation Corps camps of the 1930s, run by army officers with military discipline, dot the Hills from one end to the other. Veterans of these camps have recently succeeded in marking the sites of many of them with informative historical signs along the highways.

Like any other busy area, the Black Hills have their infrastructure of services and commerce. Many towns have hospitals, and the Rapid City Regional Hospital is a model center of good medical care. Banking is booming. Tourism, as mentioned, is well served by motels, restaurants, and a variety of entertainments and attractions, many of them worthwhile. The Black Hills have come a long way in the past 128 years, but once you get away from the cities, or venture off the pavement, you will see these Hills much as the early miners saw them: fertile, silent, and pristine, the home of winds and whispers that tell a tale of a happy present, a glorious past, and a future full of promise.

Watson Parker
Hill City, 2002

GOLD IN THE BLACK HILLS

GEOGRAPHY AND EARLY EXPLORATION

*Dakota comes! What varied wealth of mount and plains she
    brings!
How vast a golden light athwart the coming years she flings!
Her mines exhaustless, soil the richest, healthful, balmy air,
She holds to give and gives to bless—her bounties all may
    share.*[1]

Out of the sea of grass which waves from the Missouri to the Rockies rises an island of mystery, promise, and adventure, the Black Hills of Dakota and Wyoming. Embraced between the Belle Fourche and southern forks of the Cheyenne River, they rise more than four thousand feet above the surrounding plains, to tower nearly seven thousand feet above sea level. Their rocky slopes are covered with a thick growth of pine, which, seen from a distance, fades to a dusky purple and gives to the area the Dakota Sioux name *Paha Sapa*, the "Hills That Are Black."

The name Black Hills, however, was for years applied, not to the Dakota mountains alone, but to the general area from the North Platte to the Yellowstone rivers, and westward from the White River Badlands to the Big Horn Mountains. Lewis and Clark, in 1804, referred to the whole region as the Black Mountains, as they passed to the east and north of it. Later, the Laramie

[1] H. N. Maguire, *Black Hills Central* (Rochford), December 15, 1878.

3

Range in the southeastern corner of Wyoming was frequently called "the Black Hills," and it was not until the gold rush that the name was applied only to those mountains which lie between 103° and 104° west longitude and 43° and 45° north latitude in what is now southwestern South Dakota.

These mountains, formed by the thrusting up of various rocky strata and the subsequent weathering away of the highest points, resemble an elliptical layer cake through which some huge fist has been pushed. In the center, exposed by erosion, lies the granite Harney Peak Range. Surrounding it is a ring of schist and beyond that one of limestone, each cut into deep canyons which radiate from the center of the Hills. Farther still is the so-called Indian Race Track, a deep valley between the limestone and the red sandstone which appears at the outer margins of the Hills. The whole elliptical mass of hills runs roughly north and south, measuring perhaps one hundred miles in length and sixty miles from east to west. The uplift, however, does not taper uniformly downward from the center at Harney Peak, for the Hills slope from east to west, and as a result the towering limestone in the west in many places is nearly as high as the central granite.

These mountains presented a barrier to explorations, for their deep canyons were often filled with tangled thickets of aspen, birch, and willow, and flooded by the industrious beaver who fed upon these growths. The canyons were often so hemmed in by limestone or sandstone cliffs that once in them the traveler could not easily get out, while travel on the higher plateaus or on the mountains was constantly interrupted by these same impassable valleys. The mountain sides, covered with forests of pine interspersed with close-set jackpine, were no easier to traverse. Occasional open mountain meadows provided good grazing, while a profusion of wild fruit and berries supported birds and smaller animals. The mountain lion and the grizzly bear prospered in such an environment, and the latter, at least, made even the hardiest explorer pause before venturing where he might lurk.

The climate of the Hills is pleasant, with heavy spring snows, many thundershowers during the short and cool summer, a mild fall, and an open winter. Temperatures during the summer are mild, but the winters tend to be windy and bitterly cold. Like the Great Plains around them, the Hills are subject to wide yearly climatic variations—sometimes moist and fertile, sometimes arid and forbidding. In general, the southern Hills are warmer and drier than the northern, a phenomenon which was to produce some seasonal variation in mining and prospecting activities.

There is no doubt that some aborigines visited the Hills, drawing the pictographs in Craven and Whoop-Up canyons in the south and mining the flints of the nearby mountains. Old spear points and arrowheads are found even in the higher Hills around Harney Peak, and so-called tipi rings can be found in the meadows of the foothills from Hot Springs to Bear Butte. The outlying mountains—the Devil's Tower, Inyan Kara Mountain, and Bear Butte itself—were all considered sacred places, and often were visited by the Sioux, Cheyennes, and other tribes. The Indians, of course, say that the Hills were a favorite wintering spot for the Plains tribes, but these legends may have been prompted as much by the hope of government reparations as by the actual situation.

All early explorers in the Hills noticed signs of Indians, on occasion met with a few, and even used them as guides. They remained firm in their insistence that the Indians rarely visited the Hills, and then only for lodge poles, beaver, and a brief stay. The Hills, it was alleged, were "bad medicine" for the Plains Indians. Game, especially the buffalo, was not sufficient for a large group, the thickets were dense, and the violence of the thunderstorms, tornadoes, hail, and lightning were a frightening manifestation of the displeasure of the Great Spirit. These last phenomena were, of course, also present on the Plains, but perhaps in the Hills the reverberation of the thunder, the accumulation of hail in the valleys, and the destruction wrought by the wind among the pines were more fearsome than in open country.[2]

Legends about the Indian fear of the Hills were quickly seized upon and nurtured by white men who were eager to possess them. One story was told of a white giant held prisoner in a cavern

[2] Richard Irving Dodge, *The Black Hills*, 136–37.

under Harney Peak, whose struggles to escape and roars of anguish shook the Hills and boomed through the valleys. Another focused attention upon the frequent deaths by lightning, of which the Indians were presumed to be inordinately afraid. The Eden-like "Legend of the Rose" provided a semitheological background for these fears. According to this story, white men long ago came into the Hills and there succored a plague-stricken tribe. Recovering, the Indians ungratefully massacred the white men, and in turn were driven out by a rain of fire and stone, while the graves of the murdered whites were marked by the profuse growth of the wild rose so common in the Hills.[3]

The most likely answer to the question of the Indians in the Black Hills lies between the two extremes. They no doubt entered the Hills, but not in large groups which would move slowly and be vulnerable to attack in such difficult terrain. Superstition, as well as prudence, probably confined them to the foothills, away from the frowning granite of Harney Peak and the towering limestone plateaus to the west. The Black Hills, though lying in the land set aside for the Sioux in the Treaty of Laramie of 1868, were thus only partially used. Veneration rather than utility made the Indians cherish them.

The first white men to see the Black Hills were François and Joseph de la Vérendrye, sons of Pierre Gaultier de Varennes, Sieur de la Vérendrye, of Three Rivers, Canada. The Vérendrye brothers left Fort de la Reine, south of Lake Manitoba, on April 29, 1742, in search of a route to the Pacific Ocean. On May 19, they arrived at a village of "Mantannes," who furnished them with guides for a journey through the North Dakota badlands. On August 11, 1742, they arrived at a "Mountain of the Horse Indians," which many assume to have been Bear Butte on the northeastern edge of the Black Hills. Here the Vérendryes met a band of Beaux Hommes, and on November 9 traveled southwestward, apparently through the Hills. On January 1, 1743, they had a view of still further mountains, either a spur of the Rockies, or,

[3] Edwin Thompson Denig, *Five Indian Tribes of the Upper Missouri* (ed. by John C. Ewers), 6; Reverend Peter Rosen, *Pa-Ha-Sa-Pah*, 250.

6

if the Mountain of the Horse Indians was not Bear Butte, perhaps the Black Hills themselves.

On their way home the Vérendryes deposited a lead plate near Fort Pierre, South Dakota, on which had been previously inscribed "in the twenty-sixth year of the reign of the illustrious king and prelate, Louis XV, and while the Marquis of Beauharnois was viceroy, this was placed by Pierre Gaultier de la Vérendrye." On the back of this prepared plate they scratched the message "placed here by the Chevalier Vérendrye, witnessed by La Londette, Amiotte [two *voyageurs*], the 30th of March, 1743." The route of the Vérendryes, the place where the plate was deposited, and the message on it are all disputed. There is general agreement, however, that the brothers came near the Hills at some point on their journey and did bury the lead plate during their travels, although Indians may have discovered it and moved it to Fort Pierre where it was later found.[4]

The next purported visitor to the Hills was Jonathan Carver, who claimed that in 1766–68 he had made a seven-thousand-mile journey through the West in search of the mythical Straits of Anian. He brought back tales of marvelous "Shining Mountains," which sparkled and glowed when the sun shone upon them. Carver supposed that these might contain greater riches than India and Malabar, and though the bulk of his information came from other travelers, he told his stories so well that the legend of a crystal mountain in the West came over intact into frontier folklore. Actually, Carver may well have been speaking of the Black Hills, for when Lieutenant-Colonel George Armstrong Custer led his expedition there in the summer of 1874, Professor

---

[4] Nellis M. Crouse, *La Vérendrye, Fur Trader and Explorer*, discusses the problems involved in following the Vérendryes' trail; Pierre Margry (comp.), *Découvertes et Établissements des Français dans L'ouest et dans le sud de L'Amérique Septentrionale*, VI, 598–615, gives the original journals; Thomas E. Odell, *Mato Paha: The Story of Bear Butte*, 39–55, urges that Bear Butte was the Mountain of the Horse Indians; Charles E. Deland, "The Vérendrye Explorations and Discoveries," *South Dakota Historical Collections*, Vol. VII (1914), 262–84, discusses the finding of the Vérendrye plate at Fort Pierre; the plate can be found at The South Dakota Historical Society, Pierre.

A. B. Donaldson noted that the shales on the mountains glistened like silver and at times appeared transparent. One of the party claimed that he had found a mountain with a hole in its top. This error was discovered when the sun shifted.[5]

Meriwether Lewis and William Clark met the trader-trapper Jean Vallé near the mouth of the Cheyenne River on October 1, 1804. Vallé spent the previous winter in the Black Mountains, forty leagues above the forks of the Cheyenne. He reported that the mountains were very high, sometimes snow-capped all summer, and teeming with mountain sheep. He also told of mysterious booming noises like the discharge of cannon heard in the Hills. On November 3 they hired a French Canadian, Baptiste La Page. He, too, had spent a winter in the Hills and had seen the mountain sheep. Other *voyageurs* also told of the mysterious boomings and bangings, and on the whole endowed the Black Hills with an aura of mystery which would intrigue the curious.

Knowledge of the Black Hills appears to have been pretty reliable, even at this early date. Lewis and Clark carried a fairly accurate map showing their location. Even the gold later discovered with so much fanfare was already known, for a letter from Régis Loisel to Don Carlos de Hault de Lassus, lieutenant governor of Louisiana, dated May 28, 1804, mentions that nuggets might be found in the *Costa Negra*, or Black Hills, north of the *Rio Que Corré* (Niobrara).[6]

Wilson Price Hunt and the overland Astorians passed through or near the Black Hills on their way from St. Louis to Oregon in 1811. The area they traversed was composed of sandstone, broken into cliffs and precipices which resembled towns and castles. They, too, heard the booming known to Lewis and Clark. Their Indian guides attributed the noise to the bursting of rich mines of

[5] Jonathan Carver, *Three Years' Travels Throughout the Interior Parts of North America*, 76; A. B. Donaldson, "The Black Hills Expedition," *South Dakota Historical Collections*, Vol. VII (1914), 571.

[6] Reuben Gold Thwaites (ed.), *Original Journals of the Lewis and Clark Expedition, 1804-06*, I, pp. 175-77, 216; *ibid.*, II, p. 67; Pierre Antoine Tabeau, *Tabeau's Narrative of Loisel's Expedition to the Upper Missouri* (ed. by Annie Heloise Abel).

silver in the bosom of the mountains. Hunt found that going through the Hills required much exploration, for most of the valleys ended in a wild chaos of rocks and cliffs, impossible to either penetrate or avoid.

In one of these impassable canyons Ben Jones, a hunter, shot a Bighorn sheep, whose flavor was proclaimed to be of the best quality mutton. Less fortunate was the encounter of William Cannon with a grizzly bear, which chased him up a tree and kept him there for several hours.

The Hunt party eventually traveled around the Hills to the north and continued their trip toward Oregon. Many scholars are very dubious about their ever having been in the Black Hills and suppose that their adventures took place in the breaks and badlands of the Little Missouri, north of the Hills, on what is now the Montana–South Dakota border. Whatever the truth, the Hunt party's and Washington Irving's delightful accounts of their adventures publicized the area and so played an important part in its eventual settlement.[7]

Jedediah Smith, on his way to explore the Central Rockies in 1823, passed through the Hills from east to west. His party entered through the valley of French Creek, which his companion James Clyman overenthusiastically described as five hundred to one thousand feet deep and composed of black slate. Just before entering the Hills, Smith was attacked by a grizzly bear, and his scalp was half torn off. Clyman and other companions drove off the bear and sewed Smith's scalp together again, but he wore his hair long thereafter to conceal the scars. Passing on into the Hills, they went through an area of petrified wood, where Clyman noted that one stump was so tall he could barely reach the top of it while seated on his horse.

The whole story of Smith in the Hills is a difficult one to unravel, for Clyman wrote his account of it nearly fifty years later

[7] Washington Irving, *Astoria* (ed. by Edgeley W. Todd), 231–38; Philip Ashton Rollins (ed.), *The Discovery of the Oregon Trail: Robert Stuart's Narratives*, 282; J. Leonard Jennewein, *Black Hills Book Trails*, 12–13. Both Rollins and Jennewein suggest that Hunt did not visit the Hills.

and may easily have got his locations and descriptions so mixed up that no one can be sure of just where each event took place. Nevertheless, Smith's successful passage through the Hills was an accomplishment which no other explorer duplicated until 1875.[8]

With the growth of the western fur trade many trappers worked in and around the Black Hills. A brisk trade down the White River brought furs from the area to a trading post near Butte Cache, in present Shannon County, South Dakota. Thomas L. Sarpy had a fur post at the mouth of Rapid Creek, where it then joined the Cheyenne, which evidently drew its furs from the Hills. This post blew up on January 19, 1832, presumably as a result of selling gunpowder by candlelight. Old-timers in the Hills say that after the explosion "it rained bear traps for a week," but actually little damage was done to the post, and its abandonment was due more to Sarpy's death in the explosion than to material destruction.[9]

It was in the 1830's and 1840's, as the Hills became known to trappers, that the legend of Clyman's petrified forest became one of the traditional tall tales of the mountain men. George Frederick Ruxton puts the story into the mouth of old "Black" Harris, who claimed to have found a whole forest of stony wood, complete with petrified birds chirping petrified songs. Here, too, is found the legend of the stream which ran down the side of Harney Peak so fast it boiled away before it reached the bottom. The eight-hour echo which served as a reliable alarm clock is, however, generally attributed to the Rockies.[10]

Miners as well as trappers may have visited the Hills in the 1830's. A stone inscribed with this message was found in 1887 by

[8] Charles L. Camp (ed.), *James Clyman, Frontiersman, 1790–1881*, 17–19; Dale Morgan and Carl Wheat, *Jedediah Smith and his Maps of the American West*, 49.

[9] Lieutenant Gouverneur Kemble Warren, "A Preliminary Report of Explorations in Nebraska and Dakota in 1855-'56-'57," *South Dakota Historical Collections*, Vol. XI (1922), 194; Isaac H. Chase, "Our Fur Trader—The First White Man to Live in Pennington County," MS, Rapid City, South Dakota, January 10, 1962.

[10] George Frederick Ruxton, *Life in the Far West* (ed. by Leroy R. Hafen), 8–9.

Louis Thoen near Spearfish on the west side of Lookout Mountain:

> Came to these hills in 1833 seven of us DeLacompt, Ezra Kind, G. W. Wood, T. Brown, R. Kent, Wm. King, Indian Crow. All died but me Ezra Kind. Killed by Ind. beyond the high hill got our gold in 1834. [Obverse] Got all the gold we could carry our ponys all got by the Indians I have lost my gun and nothing to eat and Indians hunting me. [Reverse]

Thoen turned the stone over to John Cashner, who received letters, now lost, from a nephew of T. Brown who had left Missouri in 1832–33 with a man named Kent and was never heard from again. Mr. J. C. Adams of Ash Hollow, Pennsylvania, wrote Cashner that an uncle, Bela Kent, had disappeared with an adventurer named Kind in the 1830's, and it has been shown that the only family of Kinds in the United States came from Pennsylvania. Indian legends, recorded by William Gay (who appears to have been an unreliable source), tell of the massacre of a party of white men in the Hills during this decade. Frank Thomson of Spearfish has devoted years to the study of the Kind party, but so far has not presented enough evidence to verify its existence. Louis Thoen, the discoverer of the message, was a stonemason, and as such was not only the likeliest man to find the stone, but the likeliest one to have falsified its message. Many testimonials have been obtained regarding his upright character, but no one, so far, has come forward to swear that he was without a sense of humor.[11]

Whatever the authenticity of the Thoen Stone, there seems to be little doubt that some early miners came to the Hills for traces of their activities were found throughout the gold-rush period. The Gordon party, for example, coming to the Hills in 1874, reputedly discovered old sluice boxes, the remains of an

[11] The Thoen Stone is in the Adams Memorial Museum, Deadwood, South Dakota; "An Historic Stone," *Queen City Mail* (Spearfish, South Dakota), April 17, 1889, typescript copy, South Dakota Historical Society, Pierre, South Dakota, gives the Cashner letters; *Wi-Iyohi: Monthly Bulletin of the South Dakota Historical Society*, Vol. V (November, 1951), and "The Theon [*sic*] Stone," *South Dakota Historical Collections*, Vol. VIII (1916), 23–24, summarize the story.

old cabin, and a grave marked "J. M., 1846." In 1854 a party of French Canadians is believed by some to have made a successful strike on Castle Creek but were caught and massacred. Their gold was stored in a jug and buried by the Indians.[12]

It is often supposed that Lieutenant John Mullan, one of Isaac I. Steven's surveyors in 1850, entered the Black Hills, but a close reading of his reports indicates that in every case he refers to the Laramie Range, rather than the Dakota.[13]

During the 1840's and 1850's, Father Pierre Jean De Smet, the famous missionary to the Indians, was frequently credited with not only exploration of the Hills but with the sage advice to his Indian converts to conceal the gold which they found there. De Smet seems to have known of not only gold in the Black Hills, but of gold in California, in Idaho, and in several other places not yet identified. When this plethora of knowledge is coupled with his descriptions, which are obviously of mica rather than of gold, and when a close reading of De Smet's letters shows him to have never been in the Black Hills at all, one cannot help but discount his veracity, though not his influence, for his whispered cautions may have served to spread rather than conceal the golden rumors.[14]

De Smet's advice, however, may have contributed to a resolution passed by the Sioux Nation in 1857. Meeting at Lake Traverse, they decided that any Indians who showed the gold of the Black Hills to the white men should die, and any white men to whom they revealed the secret would, if available, die along with them. Even at this time the Indians could see clearly that miners rushing into the Black Hills should not only take possession of that

---

[12] Thomas G. Ingham, *Digging Gold Among the Rockies*, 146–49; Alfred Burkholder, "Another Hidden Treasure Story," *News* (Hill City, South Dakota), May 25, 1934.

[13] U. S., War Department, *Report of Explorations and Surveys to Ascertain the Most Practical and Economical Route for a Railroad from the Mississippi River to the Pacific Ocean*, Vols. I, II.

[14] Hiram Martin Chittenden and A. T. Richardson (eds.), *Life, Letters and Travels of Father Pierre-Jean De Smet, S. J., 1801–1873*, I, p. 51; *ibid.*, II, p. 622; *ibid.*, IV, pp. 1421, 1509–10, 1521–22.

area, but their passing across the whole of the Sioux hunting-ground would disrupt their way of life.[15]

The natives, however, did not keep their secret well, for by the 1860's they were trading gold for goods at Fort Laramie and at the Red Cloud Agency. At least one white man seems to have been caught by them, killed, and his gold hidden in a cave, where it would in later years prove an invaluable aid to ingenious swindlers who often tried to sell information about it to gullible treasure hunters.[16]

Certainly there was a need for watchfulness on the part of the Sioux, for parties bound for California were coming close to the Hills. In 1852 one or two seem to have actually entered them. In that year a group of about three hundred prospectors left Council Bluffs, Iowa, under the leadership of a Captain Douglas of Saint Joseph Valley, Michigan. Reaching Fort Laramie, thirty men left to prospect in the Black Hills to the northeast. Eight of them later overtook the Douglas party at the Humboldt River and reported that gold had been found in paying quantities in the northern Hills, but that since the Indians of the area were troublesome, it would be unsafe to return. The twenty-two men who remained in the Hills were never heard of again, except for the discovery in 1878 of some timbered shafts, a breastworks behind which lay two skeletons, and a notebook bearing only the date 1–52, which was presumed to have been 1852.

In the same year Thomas Renshaw, of Cincinnati, joined a party bound for California, and they, too, paused at Fort Laramie, heard rumors of gold in the Hills, went to them, and began placer operations which yielded one and one-half ounces of gold per day to each miner. One afternoon Renshaw returned from a long hunt to find his companions massacred and the camp burned. He made his way southward to the North Platte and safety, preserving thereafter a discreet silence regarding his discoveries. Renshaw, perhaps, was one of the Douglas party, or he may have been one of an independent group, though it seems rather a

[15] George W. Kingsbury, *History of Dakota Territory*, I, pp. 861–62.
[16] *Ibid.*, I, pp. 861–62; *Daily Leader* (Cheyenne), January 27, 1875.

coincidence that two separate parties would come to the Hills in the same year.[17]

In 1863, G. T. Lee, from Missouri, traveled with twelve companions toward Montana. Passing north of Fort Laramie, they entered the Black Hills, prospected and built sluice boxes, and in three days took out $180 worth of gold. Since an eighteen-inch snowfall not only threatened to interrupt their placer operations, but to trap them until late spring, they abandoned their claim and continued on to Montana. Returning in 1876, Lee was unable to find the spot where he had been.[18]

Another account, told by a prospector appropriately known as Crazy Hank Joplin, mentions a party that left Omaha in June, 1866. Near Fort Laramie they met an Indian boy whose arrows were tipped with gold, which he indicated had come from the Bear Lodge Mountains. Going there, the prospectors built a cabin and mined some $70,000 worth of gold, taking out $3,000 a day. This group, too, was attacked by Indians and massacred, except for Joplin, whose mind was so unsettled by his experience that he could not bring himself to tell the story until the gold rush to the Hills some nine years later.[19]

The frequent discovery of remnants of old cabins, sluices, and mining tools by the miners of 1875–76 does indicate that various parties had been in the Hills before them. An old hatchet was found on Whitewood Creek, buried deep in the ground. On the road between Rapid City and Galena old stumps, so fragile they could be kicked over, showed ax marks made long before. An oak tree near French Creek showed an overgrown blaze chopped, it was calculated, about 1855. On Battle Creek miners found a skull and a pair of silver-bowed spectacles. Nearby were a number of prospect holes with trees six inches in diameter growing in them. Near Montana City prospectors dug up an old hammer and a

[17] Robert Strahorn, *Handbook of Wyoming and Guide to the Black Hills and Big Horn Regions*, 200; *Daily Leader* (Cheyenne), July 18, 1877, March 6, 1878; H. N. Maguire, *The Coming Empire*, quoted by John S. McClintock, *Pioneer Days in the Black Hills*, 13–14.

[18] Strahorn, *Handbook*, 222–23.

[19] *Daily Leader* (Cheyenne), December 17, 1876.

rusted pick from fifteen feet beneath the surface. In early Deadwood a decayed house and small mine dumps indicated previous activity. A prospector in Custer in 1877 even found a quart bottle full of whisky at the bottom of an old shaft. Local experts pronounced it to have aged from ten to twenty years.[20]

All the early gold discoveries, with the possible exception of the Kind and Douglas parties, are considered as pure "hogwash" by John S. McClintock, who, during sixty-three years of residence in the Hills starting from gold-rush times, made a point of visiting supposed ancient sites. In no case did he either see the artifacts themselves or meet the men who had found them, and he believed that all of the stories of early gold miners rested on hearsay, wishful thinking, and subtle advertisement of the Hills.[21]

In 1855 an English sportsman, Sir Saint George Gore, guided by Jim Bridger, made an extended tour of the West. On the banks of Rapid Creek in the eastern Hills, one of his employees, Jeremiah Proteau, found great handfuls of glittering dust, which he stuffed into his shirt and showed to Gore, who only laughed at him, calling his find mica. After they had left the area, however, Bridger told Proteau, who later related the story to all who would listen, that Gore had admitted that the find was gold. It seems unlikely, for if Proteau had filled his shirt-front with handfuls of gold dust, he would have had to walk doubled over like a jackknife to keep the heavy dust from falling into his trousers, a posture which would have undoubtedly betrayed his secret and precipitated the gold rush which Gore wished to avoid.[22]

The first scientific expedition to the Hills followed Gore's closely, and, in fact, it obtained much of its equipment from him. On July 6, 1857, Lieutenant Gouverneur Kemble Warren and Ferdinand V. Hayden, accompanied by a military escort, left Sioux City for Fort Laramie. There the party divided, and Warren and Hayden, with seventeen men, made a northeasterly trip to

---

[20] Strahorn, *Handbook*, 223; William Littlebury Kuykendall, *Frontier Days*, 180–81; *Daily Leader* (Cheyenne), June 12, 1877.

[21] McClintock, *Pioneer Days*, 40–41.

[22] *Daily Leader* (Cheyenne), May 12, 1875; Strahorn, *Handbook*, 220–21.

the Hills. At Inyan Kara Mountain, west of the Hills, they met a band of Dakotas who were keeping a herd of buffalo in the area waiting for the winter slaughter. The Indians, whose attitude toward disturbing this herd was "what we should feel toward a person who should insist upon setting fire to our barns," demanded that Warren turn back and complained that if he explored the country further he would be followed by roads, military posts, and war. Warren, forced to admit the justice of the Indian position, prudently retreated, passing around the southern end of the Hills, up their eastern side to Bear Butte, and thence southward again.[23]

Although Warren did not penetrate deeply into the Hills, he went far enough to find gold, and to mention in his report that he had done so. In his opinion, however, the most important contribution of his expedition was military, for he believed that a war with the Dakotas was inevitable and that "The Black Hills is the great point in their territory at which to strike all the Teton Dakota." "The greatest fruit of the exploration I have conducted," he said, "[is] the knowledge of the proper routes by which to invade their country and conquer them." Because of the Civil War, Warren submitted no final report. One wonders if his recommendations were not later recalled by the War Department as the Indians became more and more restless and the gold of the Hills increasingly attractive.[24]

In 1859, Captain William Franklin Raynolds was sent to explore the tributaries of the Yellowstone, learn all he could about the Indians there, and assess the mineral and agricultural potential of the country. He set out from Fort Pierre, Dakota Territory, on June 28, 1859, with a small staff of scientists, a military escort, and seven young adventurers attached to the command by order of Secretary of War John B. Floyd. They camped near Bear Butte on July 11 and pressed on along the northern rim of the Hills via the Belle Fourche. Here several members of the party,

[23] Warren, "A Preliminary Report of Explorations in Nebraska and Dakota in 1855-'56-'57," *South Dakota Historical Collections*, Vol. XI (1922), 158-59.
[24] *Ibid.*, XI, p. 217.

including Jim Bridger and Lieutenant J. H. Snowden, found gold in modest quantities. Raynolds forbade them to seek further, believing that if paying quantities of gold were found, irresponsible members of the command might break away to prospect, leaving him and his officers to return alone. The party passed out of the Hills on July 14, 1859. Raynolds' report, including a mention of his gold discoveries, was published in 1867.[25]

More military than either the Warren or the Raynolds expeditions were the three prongs of the Powder River Campaign of 1865 under the command of Colonels James A. Sawyers, Samuel Walker, and Nelson Cole.

Sawyers, who was to lay out a wagon road between the Niobrara and Virginia City, Montana, passed south of the Hills, first sighting them on July 13, 1865. On July 22 and 29, he sent small parties to explore them. The undisciplined nature of his command and fears that his teamsters might desert the party to hunt for gold forced him to limit his exploration to scouting parties sufficient to guard the expedition from unexpected Indian attack from the Hills.[26]

Colonel Walker and his regiment left Fort Laramie on August 5, 1865 and headed northeast toward the Black Hills, where they were to rendezvous with Colonel Cole. A dry march of six days brought them to the South Fork of the Cheyenne, where several members of the command died, either from exhaustion or from drinking the brackish water of the river. Grass was so scarce that the horses had to be fed on leaves cut from the higher branches of

[25] U. S., War Department, "Report of Brevet Brigadier General W. F. Raynolds on the Exploration of the Yellowstone and the country Drained by that River," 40 Cong., 1 sess., *Senate Exec. Doc. No.* 77; *Daily Leader* (Cheyenne), January 12, 1875. Both Warren's and Raynolds' gold discoveries are mentioned in J. Ross Browne and James W. Taylor, *Report on the Mineral Resources of the United States*, 330 (published in 1867).

[26] H. D. Hampton, "Powder River Expedition of 1865," *Montana*, Vol. XIV (October, 1964), 2–15; James A. Sawyers, "Report on a Wagon Road from Niobrara to Virginia City," 39 Cong., 1 sess., *House Exec. Doc. No. 58*, 17–20; Albert M. Holman and Constant R. Marks, *Pioneering in the Northwest: Niobrara-Virginia City Wagon Road*, 14.

trees. Passing between the Bear Lodge Mountains and the Black Hills, Walker finally found both succor and Cole on the Belle Fourche, about forty miles north of the Devil's Tower.[27]

The largest of the three parties of 1865, that of Colonel Nelson Cole, contained about fourteen hundred men. It arrived at Bear Butte from the east on August 14 and then followed Raynolds' old trail west along the Belle Fourche to the rendezvous with Walker. One of Cole's guides found what he thought was silver-bearing ore, but Cole did not have sufficient training to judge its value. The net result of all three expeditions was to endow two or three thousand men with knowledge of both gold in the Hills and of the several routes by which it might be reached.[28]

The Black Hills, in short, though still unexplored, were at least well known, and the likelihood of gold in their forbidding fastness was widely publicized. Only the temper of the times, the distance to the Hills, the existence of other, more profitable gold fields, and the implacable hostility of the Sioux prevented a rush from following any one of the many gold discoveries made from 1804 to 1865. The temper of the times, however, was soon to be altered by subtle manipulation, distances reduced by modern transportation, and the Indians thrust aside. Only zeal and further exploration were required, and these were soon supplied by the ambition and the avarice of several interested parties.

[27] Colonel Samuel Walker, "Colonel Walker's Report," from *Misc. Ord, AGO, U. S. Army Records*, quoted by Leroy R. Hafen and Ann W. Hafen in *Powder River Campaigns and Sawyer's Expedition of 1865*, p. 93.

[28] Colonel Nelson Cole, "Reports of Colonel Nelson Cole" (The Powder River Campaign), in R. N. Scott, *et al.* (eds.), *The War of the Rebellion*, Series I, Vol. XLVIII, Part 1, pp. 366–83.

2

EARLY EXPEDITIONS TO THE HILLS

Down in a coal mine underneath the ground,
Where a ray of sunshine never can be found;
Digging dusky diamonds all the season round,
Down in a coal mine underneath the ground.[1]

The gold of the Black Hills might have lain for another generation in the fastness of the mountains if the hopes and ambitions of the people of Iowa and eastern Dakota had not urged forward the movements which revealed and publicized its presence. These pioneers, disappointed in their fortunes, sought, as frontiersmen have always sought, to enlarge their prospects by expanding their borders. Their efforts resulted in two exploring expeditions and the first authentic prospecting party to penetrate the Hills.

Yankton, Dakota Territory, was a bustling little Missouri River town in 1861, proud of its small progress and eager to make more. In January of that year a Black Hills Exploring and Mining Association was formed by Byron M. Smith, William P. Lyman, Moses K. Armstrong, Wilmot W. Brookings, Newton Edmunds, and J. Shaw Gregory. It so well fitted into the hopes of the Yankton citizens that it shortly enlisted over one-half of the town's adult male population. The association's principal contribution toward the exploration of the Black Hills was to request Congress for sur-

[1] Uncle Newt Warren's only song, David Aken, *Pioneers of the Black Hills*, 41.

veys and to supply the territorial governors of Dakota with frequent rumors of gold in the Hills for their annual messages. The Civil War and the Sioux uprisings prevented more vigorous activity.

Near the end of the war the association took on new life and issued an advertising pamphlet describing the Hills. Congress, sensitive to Western appeals, authorized the survey of a wagon road from Fort Pierre on the Missouri River to Bear Butte at the northern end of the Hills, and promised a military escort to protect the surveyors. However, the movement collapsed, presumably because the Army was more anxious to placate the Indians than Congress was to please the settlers. In this crisis the promoters turned to science in the hope that additional knowledge might influence the legislators.[2]

Dr. Ferdinand V. Hayden, who had accompanied Lieutenant Gouverneur K. Warren to the Hills in 1857, undertook a private expedition in August, 1866. He was escorted by a small detachment of soldiers from Fort Randall and by Charles F. Piccotte, a hunter who had lived with the Indians near the Hills. At Bear Butte, Hayden found gold, as well as many other geological curiosities. He returned to Yankton and in October raised the hopes of the Black Hills Exploring and Mining Association to wild excitement when he reported that "little particles or grains of gold can be found in almost any little stream in the vicinity." He refused to commit himself as to the exact quantity of gold available but his hearers were in no mood to quibble.[3]

The association under Smith's leadership again took heart. During the spring of 1867 one hundred ex-soldiers camped in tents near Yankton, eager to head for the Hills. To protect the party, Brevet Major-General A. B. Dyer, chief of the Ordnance Office at Washington, offered two mountain howitzers with two hundred rounds of ammunition. These were made available to the association at Fort Randall on June 11, but never picked up, for

[2] Kingsbury, *History of Dakota Territory*, I, pp. 861–63.
[3] *Ibid.*, I, p. 867; Ferdinand V. Hayden, "Address on the Black Hills," *Proceedings of the American Philosophical Society*, Vol. X (1869), 322–26.

Lieutenant-General William T. Sherman, commander of the Military Department of the Missouri, took a dim view of involving the Army with the Sioux in the Black Hills. Sherman instructed Brevet Major-General Alfred H. Terry to halt the expedition, pointing out that the Hills were the last refuge of the Sioux and that for Smith and his expedition to enter them might stir up an Indian war which would require more military protection than he was willing to provide. Terry transmitted Sherman's order to Andrew J. Faulk, territorial governor of Dakota, pointing out that the whites had no legal right to enter the Sioux territory and that for them to do so would seriously complicate already existing difficulties with the Indians. Smith's men had probably counted on stirring up trouble and forcing a military occupation of the Hills for they quickly disbanded when it became clear that the Army would neither countenance their folly nor rescue them from its consequences.[4]

Yet another group formed in November, 1867, under the leadership of Captain P. B. Davy of Blue Earth, Minnesota. Davy came to Yankton with grandiose plans, for he had passed near the Hills in 1866 on his way from Fort Abercrombie to Montana. He felt sure now that he could lead a party back in the spring of 1868 as soon as the grass was high enough for grazing. Davy lectured in Minnesota during the winter of 1867–68, and in response to his efforts more than three hundred men came to Yankton. The Hills, however, were at this time being considered as part of a proposed reservation for the Sioux, and Brevet Major-General D. S. Stanley, the commanding officer of the District of Southeast Dakota, received orders from the Department of Dakota "to prevent the proposed expedition, using force if necessary." Accordingly Davy abandoned his project. In 1868 the Hills were quietly incorporated into the Sioux reservation established by the Treaty of Laramie.[5]

Other groups turned their eyes to the Hills late in the 1860's, but were deterred as Smith and Davy had been. John S. Mc-

[4] Kingsbury, *History of Dakota Territory*, I, pp. 863–65.
[5] *Ibid.*, I, p. 871.

Clintock, traveling westward from Omaha had the Hills pointed out to him by an old-timer and was told that they were rich in gold and other precious metals. Thomas H. Russell, who later joined the Gordon party, first heard of Black Hills gold in 1868 at Cheyenne from Jack Jones, Chat DuBray, Jim Bridger, Jim Robinson, and old Papin, all mountain men of wide experience and talented imagination. Russell yearned to go to the Hills, and was sorry he had missed an expedition that had started for them that fall but which had been turned back by the Army.

During the winter of 1869–70 a Black Hills and Big Horn Association was formed at Cheyenne. Two thousand applications for membership were received, and 130 men actually showed up. The men, divided into two companies led by Billy Wise and Colonel Farrar, started out from Fort Russell under the command of William Littlebury Kuykendall, but were also stopped by the troops.[6]

Another unsuccessful move toward the Hills had its roots in the Fenian movement. Charles Collins, editor of the Sioux City *Times*, hoped to found an Irish colony in Dakota, opposite the mouth of the White River. There he would be ready for an invasion of Canada whenever England's peril might be Ireland's opportunity. The plan was submitted to the Fenian convention at St. Louis in the fall of 1869. The United States Congress authorized a colony corporation on the public lands. A committee appointed to inspect the site disagreed on its merits, and only a minority urged the establishment of the town of Limerick, near what later became Brule City.

The project collapsed, but Collins did not abandon his hopes. On February 27, 1872, he organized a Black Hills Mining and Exploring Association of Sioux City. Thomas H. Russell, who had read some of Collins' Black Hills articles, joined him in preparing publicity. Eminent Sioux City businessmen, including

---

6 McClintock, *Pioneer Days*, 1–2; Thomas H. Russell, MS on the Collins-Russell-Gordon Black Hills party of 1874, in possession of Don Clowser, 645½ Main Street, Deadwood, South Dakota, apparently a copy made by Percy Russell, T. H. Russell's son; Kuykendall, *Frontier Days*, 137.

Charles S. Soule of the Northwestern Transportation Company, Dan Scott, editor of the Sioux City *Journal*, and General A. C. Dawes, passenger-agent for the Kansas City and St. Joe Railway, joined in promoting the association. Meanwhile Russell toured the Missouri River towns distributing pamphlets and delivering lectures. The expedition proposed to start for the Hills on September 1, 1872, but Major-General Winfield Scott Hancock, commander of the Department of Dakota, warned that troops would be used to prevent any invasion of the Sioux reservation. Acting-Governor Edwin Stanton Cook relayed Hancock's order to the people of Dakota in a proclamation on April 6, 1872, and as a result, Collins' association became temporarily less active.[7]

The publicity which Yankton and Sioux City generated continued to have its effect. In 1872 eighteen soldiers from Fort Randall deserted in a body and formed an expedition to go to the Black Hills, but were captured and brought back. Agency Indians, returning from hunts, brought rumors of successful prospectors in the Hills. On January 24, 1873, the Legislative Assembly of Dakota Territory presented Congress with a memorial asking for a scientific exploration of the Black Hills. This was followed by another three days later urging that since the Indians used the Hills only as a retreat after hostilities, the government should confine them to a small part of their reservation and open the rest of the Hills to white settlement.[8]

General Phil Sheridan, who had heard of Father De Smet's dreamy rumors of gold in the Hills, in 1874 suggested to the War Department that the area be explored and a military post set up in it to protect the route to the Montana gold fields. Brigadier-

[7] Annie Donna Tallent, *The Black Hills*, 5, 7. Mrs. Tallent's book is widely used by Black Hills historians; much of it was taken from Rosen's *Pa-Ha-Sa-Pah* and A. T. Andreas's *Andreas's Historical Atlas of Dakota*. Hancock's order is given in Kingsbury's *History of Dakota Territory*, I, pp. 874-75.

[8] Legislative Assembly of Dakota Territory, "Memorial asking for a Scientific Exploration of that Territory," 42 Cong., 3 sess., *Senate Misc. Doc. No. 45*; Legislative Assembly of Dakota Territory, "Memorial in Reference to the Black Hills Country serving as a retreat for hostile Indians," 42 Cong., 3 sess., *Senate Misc. Doc. No. 65*.

General Terry relayed the order to Lieutenant-Colonel George Armstrong Custer, instructing him to leave Fort Abraham Lincoln for Bear Butte and to explore the country to the south, southeast, and southwest of that point. It was believed that whatever their gold content, the Black Hills would be the best place for a military post astride the Sioux war and hunting trails.

On July 1, 1874, Custer assembled ten companies of cavalry and two of infantry, totaling about one thousand men, equipped with 110 wagons, three Gatling machine guns, a three-inch Parrott rifle, and a sixteen-piece mounted band. The trip across the plains was uneventful. Custer's deer hounds ran after the antelope, and the commander bragged about his prowess with a rifle, without giving any convincing demonstration of it. Colonel Fred Grant, son of the President, accompanied the expedition and appears to have been drunk a good part of the time.[9]

Custer came southward toward the Hills, passing between them and the Bear Lodge Mountains. The party paused on July 23 at Inyan Kara Mountain, which Custer and his staff climbed. They then entered the Hills along Castle Creek, noting the richness of the soil, the pleasant climate, and the abundance of flowers in full bloom. Everyone commented on the beauty of the country, and the cavalrymen decorated their horses with nosegays. A small band of Indians was captured on July 26, and their chief, One Stab, was taken prisoner and used as a guide and hostage. The rest of the band, reluctant to remain near Custer's Ree scouts, abandoned their possessions and ran away. Camping three miles below what is now Custer, South Dakota, the Lieutenant-Colonel and his staff climbed Harney Peak, ascended nearly to the top, and there left a copper cartridge shell with their names enclosed on a slip of paper to mark the spot.[10]

[9] Captain William Ludlow, *Report of a Reconnaissance of the Black Hills of Dakota, Made in the Summer of 1874*; William H. Wood, "A Civilian with Custer in 1874," MS, Deadwood Public Library, Deadwood, South Dakota, mentions Grant's inebriation.

[10] Custer's own report was published as part of Henry N. Maguire's *Guide to the Black Hills*, 41–50, and in *South Dakota Historical Collections*, Vol. VII (1914), 583–94; Donaldson, "The Black Hills Expedition," *ibid.*, Vol. VII (1914),

During the expedition Custer killed a grizzly bear near what is now Nemo and contributed the carcass to his officers' mess. George Bird Grinnell, the party's zoologist, recorded that the gift was not appreciated, for the bear was old, tough, and rank.

Scouting parties were sent out to explore the southern Hills, but these were unable to reach the foothills because of the deep valleys and high cliffs which hemmed them in at every turn. On August 6 the expedition began its trip back to Fort Lincoln, passing northward up the center of the Hills to Bear Butte, which was reached eight days later. On the way home the expedition passed a large abandoned Indian camp. When the scout Luther North expressed relief that the Indians had not been encountered, Custer remarked that with the Seventh Cavalry he could whip all the Indians in the Northwest. He would soon be given the opportunity, for his expedition to the Black Hills opened the area to miners and precipitated the Sioux War.[11]

The traces of gold discovered by Custer's men while in the Hills were so little noticed that even the date of the original discovery was not recorded. There is also some controversy over the identity of the original discoverer. Indications of silver had been seen, and the Indian scout Red Angry Bear afterward claimed that he found gold in a spring and was the first to show it to the soldiers. Years later Horatio Nelson Ross, a professional miner who accompanied the expedition, showed Dr. Cleophas C. O'Harra the exact spot where he claimed he had found ten cents worth of gold on July 30. Probably there had been considerable prospecting and some "color" found long before any official notice was taken of the discoveries. On August 2, Ross and William T. McKay, another miner, washed gold in Custer's Gulch near the main camp. Ross collected some thirty to fifty specks, which could be identified with the aid of a strong reading glass and gave them to Custer. Another collection, given to Major J. G.

554–80, is another account of a participant. The cartridge was found in the 1930's by Troy L. Parker, of Hill City, South Dakota, but the message had vanished.

[11] George Bird Grinnell, *Two Great Scouts and Their Pawnee Battalion*, 242; Grinnell, who accompanied the expedition, did not entertain a high opinion of Custer.

25

Tieford, was gathered on August 5 by Ross, McKay, Mike Smith, and several others.

Everyone on the expedition noted the gold, more or less in passing, without attaching great significance to its discovery. Captain William Ludlow's report concluded that the real value of the Black Hills country was not mineral but agricultural. His opinion was supported by the expedition's geologist, Newton Horace Winchell, who steadfastly claimed that he had not seen any of the gold that had been discovered. Winchell's obdurate blindness gave rise to a newspaper discussion as to the merits of the trained "perfessah" as compared with those of the honest practical miner. In general the press preferred the miner, whose findings tended to be more sensational.[12]

If the reports of the expedition were modest in regard to gold, those subsequently published were not. On August 3, Custer sent the scout Charlie Reynolds to Fort Laramie with reports of the expedition, and these were rapidly spread over the nation. On August 11, the New York *Daily Tribune* spoke of the "New Gold Country." On August 12, the Bismarck *Tribune*, basing its information on Reynolds' letters, ran two columns on Black Hills gold. The Chicago *Daily Tribune* and the *Inter Ocean* on August 26 and 27 ran a series of letters and diary entries received from General George A. Forsyth which spoke of placers paying $10 a day to each miner. *Harper's Weekly* ran a full-page illustrated story of the expedition on September 12, mentioning $50 placers, and shortly thereafter it urged the purchase of the Hills from the Indians. Custer's own statements, however, remained cautious. Captain Ludlow urged that the best use of the area would be as an Indian reservation, where the rich soil might lend itself to the education of the natives in pastoral pursuits.

Even these modest estimates of the Hills' potential were dis-

[12] The gold discovery controversy is discussed in Cleophas C. O'Harra, "The Discovery of Gold in the Black Hills," *Black Hills Engineer*, Vol. XVII (November, 1929), 286–99, and in two letters from George Bird Grinnell to Doane Robinson, July 22, 29, 1924, Stack 6, Shelf 1, South Dakota Historical Society, Pierre; Major Tieford's gold is mentioned in the *Daily Press and Dakotaian* (Yankton), May 21, 1875.

paraged by the Reverend Samuel D. Hinman, whose expedition closely followed Custer's. Hinman, sent to find a more suitable location for the Spotted Tail Agency, left there on August 5, 1874, escorted by two companies of the Third Cavalry under the command of Captain Charles Meinhold and Lieutenant Emmet Crawford. Major E. A. Howard, the United States Indian agent at Spotted Tail, and several guides and miscellaneous employees also accompanied the party.

Approaching the Hills, the guides and teamsters all deserted, fearing either the mountain gods or the wrath of the Indians. Two Brulé chiefs, Spotted Tail and Two Strike, visited the party's camp outside of Buffalo Gap and endeavored to persuade the expedition to turn back. Hinman pointed out the exaggerated tales of the wealth and fertility of the Hills which were then current among the white men, and implied to Spotted Tail that the purpose of his expedition was to disprove these rumors and save the Hills for the Indians. Thus mollified, both chiefs then offered advice and information, all of which Hinman found helpful and accurate.

Entering the Hills, Hinman found the trails virtually impassable and was forced to abandon his wagons and break up his party into small groups. Some of his men were experienced California miners and searched diligently, but none found any trace of gold or any other valuable mineral. The Hills, he reported, were bleak, forbidding, sterile, useless for agriculture, and swept by fearful storms both in winter and summer. Black Hills timber, he admitted, might be useful for rough lumber and fuel when transportation made it more readily accessible. In short, he completely contradicted the report of Custer and his men and concluded that the Hills were not only useless to the white men, but unsatisfactory for even an Indian agency. The difference of opinion is doubtless due to two causes: Hinman had explored the drier, southern Hills, and he had come prepared to find them unpleasant. Custer had visited the more fertile northern and central sections with the hope of finding them delightful.[13]

13 Samuel D. Hinman, letter to Reverend W. H. Hare, chairman of the Sioux

The ease with which Hinman's report was ignored would be astonishing if one did not look at the source of the publicity given to the Black Hills. The western mining frontier had long suffered from a dearth of good fortune and adventure and was eager for a new bonanza. Frontier towns circling the Hills in a sweeping arc from Bismarck to Fort Laramie were eager for new and profitable excitement. Furthermore, the depression which began in 1873 was still in full swing, and the people of the United States welcomed any new opportunity to better themselves. These factors, combined with the wide appeal of the Black Hills, caused prospecting parties to move forward soon after Custer's report appeared.

Two minor parties may have started for the Black Hills from Sioux City in the fall of 1874. One, of which N. Johnson was a member, is supposed to have taken up five miles of claims. Another, led by a Colonel Grow, was said to have left for the Hills from Sioux City in October, and begun operations in the southern Hills until bad weather prevented profitable placer mining. Since neither party was heard of again, it is likely that both were the inventions of Editor Charles Collins' fertile imagination.

The manufacture of rumors did not interfere with the promotion of an actual Black Hills party. Collins and Russell, armed with the reports of the Custer expedition, concluded that if the Army could enter the Hills, a private enterprise might also be allowed to do so. Financed by Sioux City capital, Russell set up an office in Chicago from which he issued private circulars and letters to would-be adventurers. He estimated that new members with one hundred pounds of baggage could be brought from Chicago, via Sioux City, to the Black Hills at a cost of $50 each, and that two thousand men would join the party. Unfortunately Russell's office and activities were too close to General Sheridan's Chicago headquarters to be ignored, and within ten days Sheridan

Commission, November 10, 1874, in the *Annual Report of the Commissioner of Indian Affairs, 1874*, 90–97.

issued an order prohibiting the proposed invasion of the Sioux reservation.[14]

Russell and Collins at once announced to the press that the expedition had been canceled, but this was only a stratagem designed to placate Sheridan. Letters to some two hundred select adventurers secretly followed the announcement: "If you can raise $300, can handle a rifle, and mean business, be at Sioux City on or about the middle of September."[15] Obviously, such instructions were calculated to bring forth only those whose interest was at a fever-pitch. At the same time, Russell and Collins erected two tents at Sioux City with a capacity of fifty men each for the reception of the miners. Merchants there claimed that a man could be outfitted with rifle, revolver, ammunition, pick, shovel, gold pan, cooking utensils, blankets, and all other individual equipment for about $100. Collins estimated the cost of a complete outfit for a party of five, including wagon, horses, and provisions at $569.85. By September 3, 1874, one hundred frontiersmen were awaiting the departure of the expedition and presumably enriching the businessmen of Sioux City.

Sheridan did not content himself with mere disapproval. On September 3, he issued orders to General Terry at St. Paul and to General Ord, commanding the Department of the Platte, to stop the expedition and to "use the force at your command to burn the wagon trains and destroy the outfit and arrest the leaders, confining them at the nearest military post."[16] The order was no idle threat for detachments from the Lower Brulé Agency and Fort Randall were sent out immediately to patrol the routes leading to the Hills. The courage of all but the most foolish or most

14 *Daily Leader* (Cheyenne), November 4, 1874, January 23, 1875; the Russell MS and Erik McKinley Eriksson, "Sioux City and the Black Hills Gold Rush, 1874–1877," *Iowa Journal of History and Politics*, Vol. XX (July, 1922), 319–47, are exceptionally useful for Collins' activities.

15 Aken, *Pioneers of the Black Hills*, 8.

16 *Message from the President of the United States Transmitting information in relation to the Black Hills country in the Sioux Indian Reservation*, Special sess. (March 15, 1875), *Senate Exec. Doc. No. 2*, contains much of the Army correspondence relative to removing miners from the Hills.

determined of the Black-Hillers evaporated. When the expedition eventually materialized at nearby Covington on October 6, 1874, it consisted of only twenty-six men, one woman, and one boy.

Although sponsored by Collins and accompanied by his partner Russell, the expedition was from its beginning known as the Gordon party, taking this name from John Gordon, its guide and captain. The people of Sioux City paid Gordon $1,000 for his services and assumed that he had special knowledge of the trails to the Hills and sufficient powers of leadership to lead his party over them. He soon proved to be an inadequate and dictatorial leader but remained in command until he left the party in the Hills to return to Sioux City for more supplies and miners.[17]

Some of the Gordon party were raw tenderfeet like David Aken and John Boyle to whom everything was a new adventure. Others, like B. B. Logan's group, which included Black Dan and Red Dan McDonald, James Dempster, James Powers, J. J. Williams, and Thomas Quiner, were experienced woodsmen from Wisconsin, familiar with ax and rifle. Mr. D. G. Tallent was an ineffective sort, but his wife Annie was a great help in keeping up the spirits of the party. Lyman Lamb, who often helped the Tallents, was one of the most reliable of the group. Moses Aarons was always cheerful and uncomplaining, while J. W. Brockett deserted the party in Indian country leaving his hired gunhand, Charles Cordeiro, to make trouble along the way.

The expedition's equipment consisted of six wagons, each drawn by two yoke of oxen, five saddle horses, a burro, and two greyhounds. The group divided into five separate messes which cooked for themselves and, more or less, lived together and provided their own supplies. Enough staples were carried for eight months, with the expectation that hunting would augment the diet.[18]

To divert suspicion, the Gordon party painted the canvas

---

[17] A. J. Larsen (ed.), "Black Hills Gold Rush," *North Dakota Historical Quarterly*, Vol. VI (1932), 306–307.

[18] The accounts of Tallent, Russell, and Aken provide firsthand descriptions of the trip to the Hills.

wagon covers with the legend "O'Neill's Colony," in hope that any passing soldiers would assume that this Nebraska settlement was its destination. It seems to have been common knowledge, however, that the members were headed for the Black Hills gold fields, and, after arriving at O'Neill's settlement, they openly discussed their plans to press on to hostile territory.

Once in the Indian country and headed for the Hills, Gordon insisted that special precautions be taken to avoid discovery by either the Indians or the Army's patrols. All noisy camp duties were to be completed and all fires extinguished before dusk. No loud or unnecessary noises were permitted. On one occasion the burro, who brayed constantly, was muzzled. Three guards patrolled the camps until midnight, when they were relieved by three others. These duties were somewhat onerous and made Charles Blackwell, Eph Witcher, and Mrs. Tallent want to turn back, but a majority of the party voted against permitting them to do so since this only would further alert the military and give away their position.

Each day the Gordon party traveled from fifteen to twenty miles, then camped, ate quickly, and spent a couple of hours before bedtime telling stories and singing. Harry Cooper was the best performer, but all were required to participate. Mrs. Tallent usually told stories reflecting her fears, in which Indian massacres predominated. Uncle Newton Warren, whose one song has already been quoted at the beginning of this chapter, won applause no matter how often he sang it, each time giving new emphasis and meaning to the threadbare words. Occasionally, game was shot and cooked. Once Mrs. Tallent prepared an elk which all declared the most vile dish they ever had eaten.

On November 27, 1874, Moses Aarons died after a brief illness. Mr. J. J. Williams built a coffin nailed together with wooden pins. A grave was dug overlooking the Bad River and cribbed up like a mine shaft. Williams recited the Odd Fellows burial ritual and marked the grave with a cross. It was agreed that the symbol was inappropriate since Aarons was a Jew, but it was hoped that it might keep the grave from desecration by the Indians.

Gordon became increasingly despotic as the trip continued, and his orders were more and more resented. At last, reprimanding Cordeiro for being a little slow in coming to help fill in the road, Gordon was told by Cordeiro "to go to hell," to which he replied that Cordeiro was "a son-of-a-bitch." Cordeiro pulled his revolver and fired at Gordon but missed because his attention was distracted by Gordon's friend Russell Bishop. Bishop, who had his revolver trained on Cordeiro, stopped the shooting. Gordon, seeing his enemy disarmed, drew a knife and attacked Cordeiro, but he was prevented from killing him by Lyman Lamb. Opinion was divided as to who was right. Cordeiro apologized after a fashion, saying he had understood that Gordon wanted to settle the argument by an exchange of shots.

The party got its first glimpse of the Black Hills on the morning of November 30, and on December 9 entered them in a howling blizzard at a point about four miles south of present-day Sturgis. They camped two miles below Piedmont and then followed Box Elder Creek into the center of the Hills. Here they picked up Custer's trail and followed it to French Creek and Custer's old camp, which they reached on December 23. They at once began building a stockade some eighty feet square, made of thirteen-foot logs set three feet into the ground. Protective bastions projected from each corner to give flanking fire along the walls. The Army captain who later removed the party admitted that it would have been an impregnable defense against everything but artillery. Inside the stockade they built six cabins, dug a shallow well, and laid in a huge supply of firewood for emergencies, completing the entire operation by January 16, 1875.[19]

The log cabins were spaced about six feet apart. The Logan group's cabin was roofed with split-log tiles, a very workman-like affair. The most unpretentious cabin was the Tallents', which was

[19] The number of cabins in the stockade is variously given, but the diagram of it drawn by Captain John Mix and copied in the office of the chief of engineers June 18, 1875, shows only six, one a double cabin. Photostat, Jennewein Western Collection, Dakota Wesleyan University, Mitchell, South Dakota. The stockade has been rebuilt twice, in 1925, and again by the Civilian Conservation Corps in the 1930's.

roofed with poles covered with spruce boughs and earth. Mrs. Tallent assumed that the poles were of quaking aspen since they certainly "quaked" when the wind blew. Adjoining, but not connected, was Charles Cordeiro's shack, his violent nature having forced him to live alone. Evidently Mrs. Tallent got on amicably with him, for he had to borrow her pot to cook in and she his ax to chop firewood.

Life in the camp was uneventful. Once a tent burned to the ground, and another time the burro ate half a side of bacon—both having been left in charge of Mrs. Tallent. When queried by the suspicious owners on whether he ate it raw or fried it, she replied that "he didn't wait to cook it—he seemed to prefer it raw." To pass the time between such excitements, Mrs. Tallent read the two books that she had with her, *Paradise Lost* and a humorous *English Orphans*, until she could recite them by heart. The party laid out a townsite, named Harney City, near the stockade, and apparently another, at the present site of Custer, three miles above it, where Russell and Aken spent most of their time batching together under the protection of an overhanging rock.[20]

By the time the stockade and cabins were completed, the frost had penetrated from one to three feet into the ground and made prospecting difficult. Some gold was discovered in the stockade well, and other holes were put down, but both ice and excessive water kept most of them from showing more than "colors." R. R. Whitney wrote his wife that he had seen as much as twenty-five cents taken from a pan of gravel, but that it was so cold that he could only devote the middle of the day to prospecting and panning. The miners estimated that $10 a day could be made by men working full time with rockers, but they only washed out $40 worth of gold during the entire month of January, 1875.[21]

On February 6, 1875, John Gordon and Eph Witcher decided to make their way to civilization in the hope of bringing in more

[20] H. H. Anderson, "Gordon Stockade," *The Wi-Iyohi*, Vol. XV (February, 1962), 7, gives the texts of many Gordon party letters, which mention the upper town. Harney City is mentioned in the Russell MS, 24.

[21] Aken, *Pioneers of the Black Hills*, 128.

33

settlers and supplies. Twenty-three days later they reached Yankton, where their story created great excitement. With them went encouraging letters, one from T. H. Russell, which Gordon carried to Sioux City, saying that the gulch held plenty of gold and all that was needed were tools to mine it and lumber to build sluices to wash it out. On February 14, James Blackwell and Thomas McLaren built what Mrs. Tallent called a "contrivance," a combination sled and cart, and departed with it for Fort Laramie. On March 6, Newton Warren, Red Dan McDonald, J. J. Williams, and Henry Thomas took the burro and left for Fort Laramie. A letter from R. R. Whitney which they carried to Cheyenne said "I don't want to create any excitement . . . but if I was a young man I would emigrate to the Black Hills the first chance I had."[22] Whitney also advised his wife that he had set $150,000 as his goal before leaving the Hills and that he felt that, considering frozen boots, guard duty in the wind and cold, and the general discomfort of life at the Gordon Stockade, he would earn it.

The Army did not stand by idly while the Gordon party entered the Hills. General Sherman, writing from St. Louis, suggested that the season was too far advanced to send troops in pursuit, but General Sheridan overruled this cautious advice and insisted that the party be overtaken. Accordingly, a detachment of soldiers from Fort Randall under the command of Captain Thomas Murray Tolman followed the expedition into the Hills to within a day's journey from the stockade. Either the exhaustion of his troops or a kindly disposition toward the miners caused Tolman to abandon the pursuit. Indian Agent H. W. Bingham at the Cheyenne Indian Agency also sent out scouts and troops to intercept the Gordon party, but failed to make contact. Lieutenant William Henry Winters went out from Fort Laramie, only to be driven back by the severe cold.[23]

Captain Guy V. Henry, on December 24, 1874, received orders

[22] Russell's letter is quoted in the *Daily Leader* (Cheyenne), March 8, 1875; Whitney's letter is quoted in "The Gordon Stockade," *The Wi-Iyohi*, Vol. XV (February, 1962), 7.

[23] Eriksson, "Sioux City and the Black Hills Gold Rush, 1874–1877," *Iowa Journal of History and Politics*, Vol. XX (July, 1922), 329; *Daily Leader* (Chey-

from General E. O. C. Ord to go into the Hills and remove the miners. On December 26, he set out from the Red Cloud Agency with Troop D of the Third Cavalry, to which had been added fifteen men of the Ninth Infantry under Lieutenant Louis Henry Carpenter. Henry entered the Hills, but could not find the miners. On the return trip to the agency the soldiers were overtaken by a violent blizzard and were nearly frozen to death in the −40° F. weather before the command straggled into the Red Cloud Agency on January 8, 1875. The men were still on the sick list at Fort Laramie on February 22, when Captain Henry applied for sick leave because of frostbite and exposure.[24]

When the prospectors J. J. Williams and Red Dan McDonald arrived at Fort Laramie from the Hills, they were detained by the Army and used as guides for the one successful expedition against the Gordon party. On March 23, 1875, Captain John Mix, Lieutenant C. La Point, and Lieutenant Leonard Hay, with Company M of the Second Cavalry left Fort Laramie for the Hills. They passed around the southern end of the mountains, struck Hinman's trail, and followed it to a spot seven or eight miles southeast of the Gordon stockade. Here, on April 5, they set up what Mix called "Camp Success" and sent out scouts with Williams and McDonald. The miners were located and given two days to round up their stock and pack up their equipment, but since no wagons had been provided and most of the cattle had strayed, it proved impossible for them to take more than their personal belongings. Mining tools and heavy equipment were cached in the stockade, only to be stolen subsequently by Indians or by a later group of prospectors.[25] The sixteen remaining miners, Mrs. Tal-

enne), December 17, 1874; Message from the President, Special sess. (March 15, 1875), *Senate Exec. Doc. No. 2*, p. 10.

[24] Message from the President, *ibid.*, pp. 9–10; Brevet Brigadier-General Guy V. Henry, "A Winter March to the Black Hills," *Harper's Weekly*, Vol. XXXIX (July 27, 1895), 700; *Daily Leader* (Cheyenne), January 13, 21, 27, February 16, 22, 1875.

[25] Captain John Mix, "Report of Captain John Mix to the Post-Adjutant, Fort Laramie, Wyoming Territory, April 19, 1875," Photostat copy, File 13, Drawer 3, South Dakota Historical Society, Pierre. The date of departure from the stockade is given by Tallent and Russell as the sixth, by Aken as the seventh, and by Mix,

lent, and her son Robert left the stockade with Mix on April 10 and headed for the Red Cloud Agency. It was well that they did, for on the trip they encountered Indian parties coming into the Hills after them. The miners were released when they reached Fort Laramie, having been well treated by the troops.

The discoveries made by the Gordon party received wide publicity and soon started another rush. Letters brought to Sioux City by Gordon and Witcher and to Cheyenne by McLaren and Blackwell were widely published. The Sioux City *Times* at first preserved a discreet silence, but on February 20, 1875, it noted that the party had been heard from and was doing well. On March 4 the Cheyenne *Daily Leader* reported that gold had been found from grass roots to bedrock, as well as numerous silver- and gold-bearing quartz ledges. J. Newton Warren wrote that proper hydraulic equipment would pay $100 per day to each miner, and stressed the need for mining tools, provisions, and a sawmill. On March 10, three miners were reported to have left for the Hills—the first of the gold-rushers of 1875. The Cheyenne *Daily Leader* was quick to report Eph Witcher's recommendation that the route from Cheyenne, rather than that from Sioux City, be used by any miners going to the Hills.

Witcher did not follow his own advice, however, for he and Gordon soon organized a party of 174 men and 2 women, and planned to leave Sioux City for the Hills on April 20, 1875, with twenty-nine wagons. The party was captured on May 25 on the Niobrara by troops commanded by Captain Mark Walker. Unfortunately the expedition stubbornly refused to turn back and when Walker's superior, Captain Evan Miles, arrived on the scene, he ordered all their wagons burned, except for the one ably defended by Mrs. J. W. Brockett, the wife of the first man to desert the original Gordon party. Gordon, as captain of the second expedition, was arrested, tried at Omaha, and released.[26]

---

whose record was made at the time and was of some importance to his superiors, as the tenth. A photostat of Mix's map of his route to the Hills is in the Jennewein Western Collection, Dakota Wesleyan University, Mitchell, South Dakota.

[26] McClintock, *Pioneer Days*, 30.

Evidently he never prospered thereafter, for Mrs. Tallent met him in Deadwood a few years later, broke and in debt.

Witcher joined forces with Collins and left for Chicago to try to start a third expedition. After collecting some $3,000 from prospective members, they absconded, having bilked some six hundred adventurers of $5.00 apiece. Russell, disillusioned with Collins, later formed his own party in Pennsylvania and wrote at least one chiding letter to the Cheyenne *Leader* mocking Collins' continued efforts to establish a direct route between Sioux City and the Hills.[27] Tallent and his family returned to the Hills in 1876, where Mrs. Tallent taught school and prepared a notable history of the area and her adventures in it.

Although successful in starting a gold rush to the Hills, the efforts of Sioux City and eastern Dakota generally did not result in the hoped-for influx of business. Sidney, Nebraska, and Cheyenne, Wyoming Territory, gave a quicker and easier access to the Hills. A lively newspaper war followed, for each of the hopeful towns tried to encourage migration to the gold fields while disparaging its neighbors.

[27] *Daily Leader* (Cheyenne), March 19, 1875, June 3, 1876.

3

BOOMING THE BLACK HILLS

The roundhouse at Cheyenne is filled every night,
With loafers and bummers of most every plight;
On their backs there's no clothes, in their pockets no bills,
Each day they keep starting for the dreary Black Hills.[1]

To understand the Black Hills gold rush, it is necessary to examine the way in which it was advertised and the reasons why the nation responded so well. The rush, which began with the Gordon party in 1874 and continued until the Deadwood Fire in the fall of 1879, was not the result of any single cause, but of the interaction of several complementary pressures. The form which the rush assumed, the men who came to it, and the routes by which they traveled were all shaped by the publicity the Hills received from the surrounding towns. Furthermore, the wide acceptance of this promotion was due largely to conditions in the United States at the time.

In the 1870's the United States was ripe for a gold rush, and the promotional outpourings of frontier towns fell upon eager and receptive ears. As one pilgrim to the Hills said, a man can not "set comfortable by the fire when there's gold in the hills only five hundred mile from his door."[2] Young men who had missed the Civil War and older men who had never got over its excite-

[1] Traditional song of the period.
[2] Martha Ferguson McKeown, *Them Was the Days*, 167.

ment welcomed the opportunity for new adventures. Talk of successes in earlier rushes, exaggerated by time and distance, encouraged participation in a new one.

Not only did the gold beckon from the distance, but the dooryards of the nation were singularly unattractive. The farm and financial depression of 1873 was in full swing. For four years grasshoppers had swept over the Middle West. The damage they did was so severe that bills were introduced to Congress for the relief of settlers who had been forced to abandon their claims on public lands. Clouds of grasshoppers hung over Fort Sully, Dakota, "like coal smoke from a steamer." In some places the insects covered the ground three or four inches deep. The dismal story of Dan Cavanagh who was "eaten alive by Kansas grasshoppers" may not be true, but it did not seem fantastic at the time. As the plague continued, the governors of Missouri, Illinois, Iowa, Kansas, Nebraska, Minnesota, and Dakota joined in appeals to Congress for aid to suppress this "evil which has swollen into a scourge of national dimensions." When the Black Hills gold rush began in 1875, the farmers had already "raised three crops for the grasshoppers . . . and the men decided mining wasn't near as risky as farming."[3]

The distress of the farmers caused by the destruction of their crops was augmented by the financial panic. Farm prices dropped. Railways, whose branch-line building had offered employment, laid off construction crews. In Nebraska, as early as 1874, seven thousand destitute persons were threatened with starvation before the end of the winter. Crime rates went up all over the nation as jobs became scarce. Bankruptcies from coast to coast were daily news items. With failure facing him at home, a man did not need much encouragement to seek his fortune in the Hills.[4]

Other motives played their part. The varying fortunes of western mining camps released experienced prospectors for the Black

[3] *Harper's Weekly*, Vol. XIX (January 2, 1875), 3; *ibid.*, Vol. XIX (July 31, 1875), 615; *Daily Leader* (Cheyenne), February 4, 1877; 44 Cong. 2 sess., *House Misc. Doc. No. 10*; McKeown, *Them Was the Days*, 172.

[4] *Harper's Weekly*, Vol. XVIII (November 14, 1874), 938; *Daily Leader* (Cheyenne), December 12, 1874.

Hills rush. When Virginia City, Nevada, burned on October 26, 1875, many of its citizens decided to make their fortunes elsewhere. As the Nevada mines began to lay off their miners in 1877, Westerners were inclined to come to the hard-rock opportunities of the northern Hills. Many impoverished western prospectors lived high on the stories that they could tell of gold and adventure, and several ex-miners made their living spreading tall tales of golden opportunity throughout the frontier towns. The Molly Maguire troubles in the Pennsylvania coal fields doubtless brought still more trained miners to the Hills. Epidemics of yellow fever in the Mississippi Valley brought the fearful to seek a healthier climate. The extension of the Union Pacific Railway to Sidney, Nebraska, and to Cheyenne, Wyoming, made it easy to follow an inclination toward the Hills.

The publicity that the Black Hills received was not entirely favorable. Even Cheyenne at first disparaged stories of gold in the Hills as fabrications designed to bring unmerited business to Sioux City. The *Daily Leader* republished Lieutenant-Colonel Custer's unfavorable letter to the New York *World*, which predicted that many who came to the Hills would go away disappointed. The *Leader* also urged that no one go to the Hills at all until the Indian title to the area had been extinguished. General Sheridan, looking over Custer's report, said that as gold "colors" could be found anywhere in the western territories, it was folly to search for wealth in the Black Hills alone. Agent H. W. Bingham of the Cheyenne Agency tried to protect his Sioux charges from invading miners by predicting that prospectors would "return with much less wealth than they had when they embarked," even if they managed to evade the troops on the trail. Other mining areas, anxious to keep their population, attempted to deflate stories of Black Hills gold or stressed the growing danger from the increasingly hostile Indians.[5]

[5] *Daily Leader* (Cheyenne), January 25, 1875; Sheridan's report is given by Kingsbury, *History of Dakota Territory*, Vol. I, p. 883; Bingham is quoted by Larsen (ed.), "Black Hills Gold Rush," *North Dakota Historical Quarterly*, Vol. VI (1932), 306.

The *Scientific American*, at the very moment the Hills began to boom, urged that only men rich enough to work the quartz claims should go to them, and termed reports of rich placers "the most barefaced fabrications, got up by miners who wish to sell their claims." *Harper's Weekly* surmised correctly that much of the publicity came from the western communities which hoped to profit from a new mining fever, and suggested to its readers that "more money would be made by steady honest effort at home" than in the hazardous trip to the Hills. *Harper's* also urged that mines closer to home might be as profitably worked, and that, all told, Black Hills gold was found in such small quantities that gathering it would pay only low wages instead of the advertised fortunes.[6]

News from the Hills was often conflicting. Many inexperienced miners traveled a little distance into the area and then retreated, without either the opportunity or the ability to assess the value of the mines. Such greenhorns exaggerated the danger from the Indians and the poverty of the placers and ledges, often without seeing either. Failing to realize their glowing expectations, they denounced the Hills as a delusion and a snare. Richard B. Hughes, an early Hills journalist, noticed that most of the men who left the Hills went out through Buffalo Gap toward the East, and were probably tenderfeet from Iowa and Nebraska. One such group was thrown into a panic by the sight of some small prospect holes in the foothills, which they assumed to be newly dug graves for the victims of an Indian raid. Many similar tales of Indian atrocities, robberies, and hardship were concocted by tenderfeet and circulated as valid excuses for abandoning a trip to the mines.[7]

Newspaper articles were also often unkind to the Hills. An occasional correspondent, nettled by some imagined slight, often found revenge in debunking pretentious claims of gold in the Hills or the convenience of a particular route to them. One such writer,

---

[6] *Scientific American*, N.S., Vol. XXXIV (April 22, 1876), 262; *Harper's Weekly*, Vol. XX (March 11, 1876), 207; *ibid.*, Vol. XXXIV (April 15, 1876), 307; *ibid.*, Vol. XXXIV (May 6, 1876), 376.

[7] Richard B. Hughes, *Pioneer Years in the Black Hills*, 33–34, 40–41, 72.

who had insisted on the most comfortable seat in the stage from Rapid City to Sidney, was loaded with preposterous lies. Into his receptive ear the stage driver poured wild tales of road agents, Indian massacres, and vicious animals. At last the joke broke down when the driver tried to make the journalist believe that Pumpkin Creek was the Sweetwater, so called because there was a "sugar spring" at its source. Leander P. Richardson, mistakenly reported to have been murdered by Indians near Cheyenne, wrote an article critical of the Hills for *Scribners*. The Cheyenne *Daily Leader* retaliated by referring to him ever afterward as "L. Putty-head Richardson." Considering the stories which were sent to the eastern papers, it is more than likely that as many were "slain" by reports in the press as were actually killed by the Indians.[8]

Although eastern publicity for the Hills was sometimes unfavorable, that which was generated in the towns around the Hills made up for it. From Bismarck south to Sioux City and from Yankton westward to Sidney and Cheyenne, the outfitting towns clamored for the trade and attention of potential gold-rushers. Their efforts were soon aided by newspapers established in the Hills, each with its own tale to tell and route to promote.

Bismarck, Dakota Territory, showed an early interest in the Hills. Founded in 1873 with the arrival of the Northern Pacific Railway and until 1878 the western terminus of that line, Bismarck looked for a brisk flow of travelers, some from the East by rail and others from the South by Missouri River steamer. Custer's trail from Fort Lincoln, improved and relocated by Ben Ash in 1875, was the best-known route to the Hills. Bismarck's position seemed secure. Horatio N. Ross, the prospector who had found gold with Custer in 1874, led a party to the mines late in 1875. Other groups quickly followed. Stage and freight lines were organized, and, as late as 1878, Bismarck hoped for a major share of Black Hills travel. The trail, however, was a long one—220 miles from Bismarck to Deadwood—and led across hostile Indian territory. Travelers soon came to prefer points of de-

[8] *Ibid.*, 261–65; Leander P. Richardson, "A Trip to the Black Hills," *Scribners*, Vol. XIII (April, 1877).

The Black Hills of Dakota and Surrounding Settlements in 1875
with Present-day Political Boundaries

parture nearer the Hills, and roads which were easier and safer to travel.[9]

Sioux City, Iowa, whose schemes had helped precipitate the rush, also strove to attract outfitting business, but she suffered from an insuperable geographical handicap. The traveler who followed a direct trail from Sioux City to the Hills passed through Yankton and could as well buy his outfit there. To overcome this difficulty, Sioux City promoted the "sandhills route" which followed the Gordon party trail westward along the Niobrara River and thence north to the Hills. It was a long and difficult trail, and, like the Bismarck route, passed through rough country and the Sioux reservation.

Cheyenne interests quickly pointed out that the Gordon party had taken seventy-eight days to get to the Hills from Sioux City, but less than a month to come out to Cheyenne. Sioux City was accused of caring only for the outfitting business that the miners brought in, and of forming not mining expeditions to show their faith in the Hills but transportation companies to milk and bilk the travelers. Eph Witcher, who had accompanied both Gordon parties, hoped to haul freight into the Hills, but in July, 1875, he abandoned his plans, saying it was impossible to get wagon trains into the region. Unfavorable publicity, as well as natural disadvantages, soon reduced Sioux City's eminence as a jumping-off point.[10]

Yankton, the capital of Dakota Territory, met with better success. The town was on the Missouri River and connected to the Union Pacific Railway by the Dakota Southern. It had been promoting the Hills since 1861 and was fixed in eastern minds as a gateway to the gold fields. A traveler could come to Yankton from the South by boat, or from the East by train, outfit himself, and reach the mines in a few days. Steamers ran north to Fort

[9] Jennewein, "Ben Ash and the Trail Blazers," *South Dakota Historical Collections*, Vol. XXV (1951), 300–305; George Watson Smith, MS, diary of a trip to Bismarck, 1878, in possession of the author; *Daily Press and Dakotaian* (Yankton), December 11, 22, 1875.

[10] Eriksson, "Sioux City and the Black Hills Gold Rush, 1874–1877," *Iowa Journal of History and Politics*, Vol. XX (July, 1922), 319–47.

Pierre, a straggling village of twenty houses at the mouth of the Bad River, where the adventurer could take a stage or wagon westward. By early 1876, party after party was outfitting at Yankton. Two free reception centers were set up for miners, each with cooking, sleeping, and recreational facilities. Stationery and reading matter were also provided so that the traveler could read of the best routes to the Hills and then write home and tell his friends about them.

Yankton also worked closely with other towns to promote not only the Hills but the farming opportunities of eastern Dakota. It was hoped that the prospective immigrant who was unmoved by either perhaps might be won by both, and that which was a boost to Yankton and the Hills was a boost to the entire southern part of the territory.

Businessmen in Yankton were not only interested in outfitting the miners but often went to the mines themselves. Their letters from the Hills were passed on to the editor of the *Daily Press and Dakotaian*. Those which were enthusiastic about the gold prospects or the Yankton route were published, and copies of the paper were sent to other editors. Warnings, like that of young Don Shannon who told of an unfortunate traveler who spent six weeks on the Cheyenne trail, were also printed to disparage other frontier towns. When the *Daily Press and Dakotaian* heard of the arrest of the Gordon party, it feigned amazement. If the party had taken the sandhill route, said the *Dakotaian*, it could not have been arrested since it was in country which the troops had been unable to enter—a barren wilderness where "curlews and sandpipers have to carry rations."[11]

Even when the Army closed the route from Fort Pierre to the Hills on June 1, 1876, claiming that the troops could no longer protect the travelers, Yankton continued to prosper. The rise of two unexpected competitors shared but never captured her bonanza.

Several villages along the Union Pacific Railway in western Nebraska hoped to profit from the Black Hills gold rush. Only

[11] *Daily Press and Dakotaian* (Yankton), April 28, 1875, March 19, 1876.

Sidney, however, was able to capitalize on it fully. This town, of less than five hundred persons, owed its success as an outfitting point to its newspaper, its location, and its bridge across the North Platte.

Joseph Gossage, editor of the Sidney *Telegraph*, quickly saw what a Black Hills boom could do for Sidney. He praised the Hills, promoted the existing trail to Red Cloud, and boasted of Sidney's virtues as a mercantile center. His own advice proved too much for him. In 1878, he moved to Rapid City where he established the *Black Hills Journal*. There Gossage continued to boost Sidney, the nearest shipping point, hoping that anyone who outfitted there would come to the mines by way of Rapid City.

Sidney's location, about 180 miles south and east of the Hills, was another point in its favor. No town except Cheyenne was as close, and Sidney was nearer the East. Its trail toward the Hills, already well established as far as the Red Cloud Agency, had plenty of wood and water, as well as military protection from the agency troops. The only drawback was the Platte River crossing 35 miles north of town.

If the Old Platte did not have enough water on top to drown a man, said the old-timers, she would suck him down to where it was. The river, about six hundred yards wide, was dangerous when flooded and treacherous with quicksand when shallow. A government ferry and later a bridge at Fort Laramie at first drew many parties westward away from Sidney, simply to cross the river. All this was changed on May 10, 1876, when Henry T. Clarke completed his North Platte bridge and opened the way from Sidney to the Hills. The bridge was two thousand feet long, composed of sixty-one wooden spans. Materials for it had been carried to Sidney free of charge by the Union Pacific, and the government provided troops and a fort for its protection. Once the bridge was completed, Sidney began to boom.

During July, 1876, $5,869 worth of gold came down the trail to Sidney, and prospectors began moving northward over it. Two stage lines, Marsh and Stevenson, and Gilmer and Salisbury, were unable to carry the thirty to eighty miners who sought passage every day. Fifty to seventy-five freight wagons left daily for the Hills when weather permitted, and even these could not meet the demand for transportation. Sidney remained a major shipping point for the Hills until the railroad came to Rapid City in the 1880's.

Sidney's prosperity may be gauged by the virulence with which Cheyenne, her closest competitor, attempted to wrest away her business. Sidney, said the Cheyenne *Daily Leader* on July 21, 1877, had only three or four piddling merchants whose entire stock would not fill two wagons. The population was composed of border outlaws and escaped convicts. Even the briefest stop found the traveler surrounded and robbed by these ruffians. There were one hundred cases of smallpox in Sidney and no town government to prevent further spread of the disease. Transportation to the Hills consisted of worn-out wagons drawn by unmanageable mules. The few stations along the Sidney–Black Hills trail fed stage passengers at $1.50 a head on moldy hardtack and rancid bacon stolen from the government. Each passenger was charged $1.00 and emigrants $5.00 to $10.00 a wagon to use the bridge across the Platte, which was about to collapse. No wood or water was available along the trail, except for sagebrush and buffalo wallows. The few soldiers at Red Cloud could not control the thieves and murderers, red or white, who waited to pounce upon the traveler. This sort of diatribe is typical of the journalism of the period. Yet, in spite of it, Sidney developed a lasting business with the Hills.[12]

Cheyenne, in the southeastern corner of Wyoming, was, like Sidney, on the Union Pacific railroad. A well-traveled road led northward to Fort Laramie, where the traveler could cross the North Platte by government ferry, and after December, 1875, by the famous iron bridge. This combination of rail transportation, military protection, and a well-marked and convenient trail made Cheyenne the most successful town booming the Hills.

[12] Norbert R. Mahnken, "The Sidney-Black Hills Trail," *Nebraska History*, Vol. XXX (September, 1949), 203–25; *Daily Leader* (Cheyenne), February 21, 1877.

Western miners who turned toward the new mines were accustomed to doing business in Cheyenne and found it the nearest, as well as the most experienced, outfitting center.

Cheyenne at first was cautious about promoting the new gold discoveries. The Black Hills lay inside the Sioux reservation, and it seemed unwise to encourage an invasion of them which might precipitate an Indian war and cut off business altogether. The *Daily Leader* on one hand urged prospectors to wait until Indian title to the Hills was extinguished, and on the other ran an article day after day boasting of Cheyenne's advantages as an outfitting point. A committee, established by businessmen in the fall of 1874, answered inquiries, usually by sending issues of the *Daily Leader*. Editions of fifty thousand copies were printed on April 17 and 30, 1875. Since the total population of Wyoming at that time was about twenty thousand, it is evident that these were intended for advertising outside the state. The editor went into the horse business, advertising that "Black Hillers can now select a good team of horses at H. Glafke's," an enterprise which probably did not dampen his enthusiasm for the Black Hills.[13]

The ambivalence of recommending a gold rush to the Hills while urging the miners to keep out of the reservation was soon resolved. The *Daily Leader*, with the haziest idea of geography, insisted that the mines were not in Dakota but in eastern Wyoming, which was not reservation land at all.

During the spring of 1876 the *Leader* was faced with another difficult decision. Indian raids, reports of which could not be suppressed, increasingly threatened access to the Hills. To publicize these depredations further in the hope of obtaining more military protection might turn Easterners to Sidney or Yankton, or else discourage them altogether. Only the outbreak of hostilities broke this impasse. On May 18 the *Leader* brought itself to appeal for still more troops to protect communications with the Hills. De-

---

[13] *Ibid.*, May 13, 1875; Agnes Wright Spring's *Cheyenne and Black Hills Stage and Express Routes* tells Cheyenne's story in detail; Douglas Crawford McMurtrie's *Early Printing in Wyoming and the Black Hills* is based mainly on the files of the Cheyenne papers.

spite these Indian raids, which to some extent affected all the trails, Cheyenne became the leading outfitting town and point of departure for the Hills.

The columns of the *Daily Leader* reflect the growing impact of the gold rush on Cheyenne. Every arrival and departure of miners was recorded. A column of news from the mines entitled "Black Hills Items" became a regular feature, followed by a special weekly edition sent to the mines. In 1877 a correspondent, Mr. Rapherty, went in person, and ample space was given to his voluminous letters from the booming camps. For months the *Leader* ran an article on "The Black Hills—Information of Interest to Those Who Are Going to Them." This gave current prices of equipment and supplies, and a table of distances between stops along the trail. Advertisements of outfitters and ranches along the way appeared frequently, along with the news of the committee's activities and appeals for still more money for advertising. Letters from successful miners were published, and large shipments of gold, one worth nearly $250,000, were often mentioned, implying that there was still more where that came from.

Newspapers in the Black Hills continued the work of promotion which the frontier towns had so ably begun. The *Black Hills Pioneer*, a Deadwood weekly, appeared June 8, 1876. Within a month it had arranged to have from 150,000 to 200,000 stereotyped facsimile copies run off in Chicago for distribution on railroads and newsstands. Other weeklies followed quickly in Central City, Lead, Rapid City, Rockerville, Custer, and Rochford. Joseph Gossage's Rapid City *Black Hills Journal* ran a variously titled column for the outside world, which in one issue was labeled "Mining Mentions from All the Gelt Producing Localities—Come to the Black Hills and Partake of Our Wealth." News from other mining areas in the West, especially Leadville, Colorado, appeared frequently. This was doubtless for the benefit of western miners, and since it was generally bad news, it was probably intended to keep them in the Hills.

The miners who had joined the rush were of course unwilling to be thought fools for their efforts, and so wrote home glowing accounts of their own or their neighbors' successes. These letters were published in the writers' home towns, and, as was the custom of the times, copied as "exchanges" by other newspapers across the country. The number of successful miners who wrote home is probably a good deal larger than the number of successful ones who came home.

A more organized publicity effort was the Black Hills Mining Bureau set up at Deadwood in 1877 by Messrs. Woolley and Wilson. The bureau, intended to disseminate mining information, was also willing to transact real estate business, and, consequently, its advice may not have been totally unbiased.

An astonishing number of books and pamphlets were published to advertise the Hills and advise the miners. At least twenty appeared between 1865 and 1879, some with copious illustrations and detailed maps. Many contained advertisements for railways, stage lines, eating houses, and suppliers. These as a rule were aimed at promoting business in specific towns. Half a dozen maps of routes to the Hills and of gold fields within them were available. Frontier towns generally boosted the one that showed them in the most favorable light, and pointed out inaccuracies in the rest.[14]

The effect of these uninhibited publications was volcanic. Their advice was prudently directed to "the intelligent and diligent," but every reader assumed that they meant him. The son of a prospective miner tells the story:

> Taylor Brothers at Yankton had got out a hundred-page guide book that sold for fifty cents and it had two maps of the gold mines, and pictures, and everything a body would ever want to know about how to get there and what to take. Father got hold of one of them books, but when he tried to read to Mama about how "there was a fortune in gold nuggets waiting for every man brave enough to go after it," she just went right on talking about how we was all going to work hard and pay off what we owed on them cows.

[14] Jennewein's *Black Hills Book Trails*, 27–29, 46–54, is especially good on gold-rush books.

50

Nevertheless, "Father" went to the Hills.[15]

The written word was followed up by personal promotion. Mr. Z. Swaringen left the Hills for Washington, D.C., in December, 1875, with fifteen ounces of gold that he had taken from Castle Creek. Judge W. W. Brookings went to Boston in the spring of 1876 where he addressed large crowds and urged the poor of the East to migrate to Dakota. Mr. W. H. Wood sent a shipment of carefully selected ore from Custer to Omaha for smelting, and its value, $4,516.26 to the ton, received wide publicity. A good assay was always invaluable in promoting a mine, and any questions about its honesty were laid to rest by the thought that no one could really ask a miner to haul low-grade ore all the way to Omaha. Wood's selection, however, does seem to have been more than reasonably judicious.

A Dr. Nichols of Deadwood went to the Centennial Exposition at Philadelphia carrying seventy bushels of gravel and a string of sluice boxes, to show the Easterners how to wash out placer gold. A group of hard-rock miners went to Chicago with a ton of ore and "Smokey" Jones, a miner who proposed to grind out gold with a mortar, pestle, and pan. Mr. C. W. Meyer toured the country trying to publicize the Hills, but his efforts at least were a failure, for the *Daily Leader* reported in May, 1877, that he had made more enemies than friends.

From the beginning, the gold rush brought business to the towns around the Hills. Gun shops, hardware, and drygoods stores all prospered. Rubber boots, needed for the muddy placers, boomed as an article of commerce. A "complete camp chest," with compartments holding food for four for fifteen days, could be purchased; grocers were delighted to stock it, and to provide still more provisions. Wagons and the teams or yokes of oxen necessary to haul them to the Hills met with ready sale, but more than one eager prospector dispensed with business formalities in order to obtain immediate transportation to the Hills. A thoughtful Cheyenne barber ran an ad boosting the gold fields, but cautioned the prospector "before you start, go to Hardin's barber shop, on

[15] McKeown, *Them Was the Days*, 167–68.

51

Eddy Street, and get your hair cut." For those who had come to the frontier with misgivings, there was always Humphrey's Homeopathic Number 28, advertised as a sure cure for "nervous debility, vital weakness or depression, a weak exhausted feeling, no energy or courage, the result of mental overwork, indiscretion, or excess." The outfitters were ready for business.[16]

[16] *Daily Leader* (Cheyenne), May 14, 1875; *Daily Press and Dakotaian* (Yankton), March 24, 1876.

Custer Expedition of 1874. From left to right are Indian Scout Bloody Knife, Lieutenant-Colonel George Armstrong Custer, Colonel William Ludlow, and Private Noonan with grizzly bear killed near Nemo, South Dakota.

Courtesy Jennewein Western Collection

Stockade built by the Gordon Party in the spring of 1875 and later occupied by United States troops protecting the Hills from the invading miners.

The first placer miners lived in tents and worked the placer gold deposits with sluices (right foreground). Note venison on the keg tops.

Early Black-Hillers could sink shallow mine shafts with the aid of hand-windlasses. Note the collection of hand tools on platform.

Ore was brought out of mines on cars which ran on wooden rails covered with strap-iron strips. Note platform box (left foreground) used to sort ore.

Typical ore mill and shaft-house. The average mining promoter built these structures long before he was sure of the ore beneath them.

Courtesy Carper-Tscharner Photo Collection

*Sawmills sprang up throughout the Hills in response to the miners'
demands for lumber. Both oxen and mules were used to haul logs
to the mills.*

Deadwood, South Dakota, in 1876. Deadwood, like other early mining towns, boomed into a wild and crowded commercial center with one muddy thoroughfare.

Courtesy Deadwood Public Library

4

THE GOLD RUSH IN THE SUMMER OF 1875

In the valley of Custer, the park with its cluster
Of little log cabins spread out on the green.
'Tis the valley of Custer, where oft we did muster,
And drank to the brave from the soldier's canteen.[1]

Stimulated and supplied by the frontier towns, the miners began to head for the Hills during the early months of 1875. The well-equipped "pilgrim," as he was called, had a rubber ground-sheet, rubber hip-boots, two woolen blankets, and a rifle, pistol, and ammunition. Two tin plates, a dipper, knife, fork, and large spoon, some towels, and matches completed his personal outfit. Two men together might carry a round-pointed steel shovel, miner's pick, and other mining equipment. Messes of five or six shared a Dutch oven, frying pan, tin pail, handsaw, ax, and tent. Army-style provisions for three months cost less than $20 per man, and the entire personal outfit came to about $50. A mess might buy its own team and wagon or hire space in a wagon train already headed for the Hills. In either case, the men walked behind the wagon, for it was invariably full of food and equipment.[2]

Some of the early prospectors were experienced frontiersmen, like California Joe (Moses Milner) and his party, who came to

[1] Captain Jack Crawford, *The Poet Scout*, 143.

[2] This outfit was used by a Boston party and was described in the *Daily Press and Dakotaian* (Yankton), April 28, 1875.

the Hills in March, 1875, but saw so many Indian signs that they quickly left. Others, like Wade Porter, were guided by scouts and advised by old prospectors. Porter's experience is a typical one. He joined a group of prospectors at the Red Cloud Agency and in April journeyed with them to the Gordon party's diggings on French Creek. Here half the men were captured by the United States cavalry and removed from the Hills. Porter and the remainder of the party stayed on to assist the Jenney geological expedition in its assessment of the Hills, leaving in the fall of 1875. He later returned and played an important part in the discovery of gold near Deadwood. Not all the pilgrims were so successful. One disappointed German was overtaken by a freighter who offered to carry his pack out of the Hills: "No, no, I cary him, I valks," replied the German. "I learn this fool Dutchman somedings. Run around after ev'ry tam mining egzitements!"[3]

The weather in the Hills during the spring of 1875 also hampered the gold rush. Nearby Fort Laramie had rain on sixty-seven consecutive days. For three weeks the sun did not shine, and on June 2 it snowed for several hours. Terrific hail swept the whole area; one miner claimed it punched holes in a pan that he had left outside his shack. Nevertheless, miners continued to come to the Hills. By July, 600 men were prospecting on French, Rapid, Spring, and Castle creeks. Many of them followed the Jenney expedition hoping to profit from the professor's discoveries and to receive protection from his Army escort. By August 15, when the miners were expelled by General Crook, a newspaperman with Jenney estimated that some 1,500 men had entered the Hills.[4]

These early prospectors were equipped to extract only the placer gold from the gravel bars; the rich hard-rock leads were developed later in the rush. The experienced placer miner knew how to find a rich deposit where a stream had slowed down and dropped its load of gold. Some of these "bars" where the gravel

---

[3] William Rhoads, *Recollections of Dakota Territory*, 4–5.

[4] Spring, *Cheyenne and Black Hills Stage and Express Routes*, 65; other estimates of miners in the Hills are in *The Report of the Commissioner of Indian Affairs for 1875*, 7, and the *Daily Leader* (Cheyenne), July 27, 1875.

had been deposited were high on the rimrock, rich but dry, and excessive labor was required to haul the gravel to water. Others, in valleys, were so wet they could not be worked without first digging elaborate drainage ditches. French Creek, where Custer and the Gordon party had found gold, suffered from both defects: there was hardly enough water to work the placers, and the valley sloped so gently that the bedrock could not be drained.[5]

In addition to the alluvial bars were the "cement" deposits, a hardened conglomerate of earth and gravel held together in a matrix of iron rust or other "cement." These were found especially in the Deadwood area. Since they required some breaking up or weathering before washing, they were at first neglected.

Weather often influenced the choice of placer diggings. Shallow gravels might freeze solid, forcing the miner to stop work during the winter. Even if the streams did not stop flowing, washing out the gold was very damp work and nearly impossible in severe cold. In the winter a deep placer had its virtues for the miner could burrow into the ground and work protected from the weather. The gravel would in this case be put aside and washed out during one of the frequent Black Hills warm spells.

These underground placer mines were often elaborate. A shaft sometimes thirty feet deep was sunk to the bedrock where the bulk of the gold had settled. The shaft usually encountered water and had to be drained, either by a long ditch or by a pump powered by an adjacent stream. From the bottom of the shaft, tunnels or "drifts," as they were called, were run along the bedrock, and the richest gravels extracted. It was peculiarly dangerous work. Dry gravel would collapse like the sand in an hourglass, and wet gravel flowed like quicksand. Both required careful shoring with pole lagging supported by heavier caps and posts. The work of cutting and placing these timbers was onerous and was often neglected. The face of the drift was necessarily left unsupported, and when it was driven forward into a softer or wetter

[5] Eyewitness accounts of Black Hills placer mining methods include Rosen, *Pa-Ha-Sa-Pah*; Hughes, *Pioneer Years*; and George W. Stokes and Howard R. Driggs, *Deadwood Gold: A Story of the Black Hills*.

formation, it often gave way, pouring a torrent of mud and gravel into the tunnel. This flood usually pushed down the posts supporting the roof, and the whole drift then collapsed with results disastrous to the miners.

One such "run" of gravel in a Deadwood placer killed one miner and trapped his companion, Tommy Carr, flat on his back on the bedrock. The water-powered "China pump" draining the mine was also damaged. Carr could gauge the steps taken to repair it by the way the water rose or fell about him. He was rescued after twenty-four hours of harrowing confinement.[6]

Explosives, used to break up boulders, contributed their share of accidents. Prospector Frank Hebert, a thrifty soul, used fuses two inches long with a small fire built over them. As the fire burned down, the fuse eventually ignited and the charge would explode. One day, however, the fuse caught at once, just as Hebert's companion was hauling him out of the shaft. The explosion demolished the bucket and windlass, but fortunately threw Hebert clear.[7]

Once a gold deposit was found, the essential operation of placer mining was panning. Whatever method was used for the preliminary separation of gold from the gravel, panning was the final step. The gold pan was a sheet-steel basin about eighteen inches across the top with sloping sides two inches high and a flat bottom about fifteen inches in diameter. The gravel to be washed was put into the pan, which was immersed in water. That was where the prospector used his rubber hip-boots. He shook the pan and kneaded its contents, washing off the light dirt and throwing away the stones. The gold, if any, settled to the bottom along with any heavy metallic sands from the gravel. With a final dexterous twist of the pan the miner would spread its contents in a broad crescent across its bottom. At the convex edge appeared the flecks and flakes of gold, "colors," as they were called, which could be removed with a match stick or fingernail. This gold dust, often so

[6] Hughes, *Pioneer Years*, 142–44.
[7] Frank Hebert, *Forty Years Prospecting and Mining in the Black Hills of South Dakota*, 93–94.

fine that it would work through cloth, was stored in tin cans, quills, bottles, or, most commonly, in buckskin bags. A placer yielding three cents to the pan could be mined profitably with more efficient equipment, but the prospector who worked entirely by hand regarded ten cents to the pan as a minimum.

If a promising placer was far from water, or if only one or two men were available to work it, a rocker might be constructed. This consisted of a shallow sloping trough about two feet wide and four feet long, open at its lower end. It was supported on curved rockers so that it could be shaken from side to side. Its bottom was covered with removable transverse strips of wood called "riffles," and its lower end often lined with strips of carpet or sheepskin. A shallow box, floored with perforated sheet metal, was placed over the upper third of the trough.

In operation, one man shoveled gravel into the upper box while the other added water, sorted out stones, and shook the rocker. The resulting slurry of thin mud flowed into the lower trough where nuggets, sinking to the bottom, lodged behind the riffles, and the finer dust was caught by the carpeting at the lower end. Some of the water could be saved and used again when the mud had settled out of it. When the riffles were full of heavy sand, garnets, and gold dust, they were cleaned out and their contents panned.

If fine "flour" gold was encountered, mercury was put behind the riffles. This caught and held in solution light flakes which otherwise might have washed away. The gold was extracted from the resulting amalgam by putting it in a chamois bag and squeezing out the mercury, or by one of several crude processes of distillation. Old mercury tended to retain part of the gold it absorbed. When reused in a new placer, it indicated higher values in the gravel than were actually there, and often deceived tenderfeet into thinking that they had found a new bonanza.

When men and water were available, sluice boxes were used to wash out the gold. The demand for lumber to build sluices, as well as cabins, brought in the first crude sawmills. These whipsaw outfits were simple. A log was hewn flat on two sides with an ax or adz, then dragged over a hole seven feet deep. One sawyer stood beneath, the other above, and between them they pulled the saw up and down. The vertical motion of the blade meant a straighter cut, but the sawdust must have been unpleasant for the man below. Several such mills were in operation in the Hills by late May, 1875.

Six sluice boxes were the usual string. These were open troughs twelve feet long made of twelve-inch lumber. They were often tapered at the lower end, so each would fit into the next, but some miners preferred the extra turbulence that resulted from arranging them in a series of waterfalls. Each box was set to have a fall of exactly four inches from end to end. A steeper slope swept the gold along before it could settle, while a shallower gradient would not keep the gravel moving. The floor of the first box was covered with a riffle made by drilling a one-inch board full of one-inch holes. The rest of the boxes were floored with "Hungarian," or transverse riffles, slats behind which it was hoped the gold would come to rest. The whole purpose of the riffles was to tumble the mud as it passed and catch the gold as it settled. Some miners preferred lengthwise riffles made of poles. Others filled their sluices with a layer of heavy stones, which must have been rather ineffective.

Each ton of gravel washed in a string of sluice boxes required two thousand gallons of water to keep it moving. Fifty "miner's inches" of water, the amount that would flow through an opening one inch high by fifty inches long, were generally required to operate a sluice. Some of the water went through the boxes, while the rest was needed to carry away the gravel already washed. Usually a dam had to be built and ditches dug to supply this quantity of water to the sluices. Mining law required that the water be returned to the original stream channel, and this often called for even more ditching. By the time water reached the fifth or sixth miner downstream, it was so clouded with clay that gold recovery fell off sharply. This, combined with the many hands needed to set up and run the sluices, often forced a whole gulch to unite in a single sluicing operation.

Once sluices were set up and adequate water assured, gold washing began. Several miners carried gravel to the top of the sluice. There one man worked full time pitching stones off the board riffle with a specially shortened twelve-tined fork. Usually another patrolled the sluices, making sure that no large rocks got through to cause eddies, and that none of the riffles came loose and floated away. One unfortunate miner with two days' accumulation of gold in his sluices saw his entire string wash out, so this precaution was not an idle one. In addition, if too much iron or cassiterite sand clogged the riffles, the gold might wash on by, so a close check was needed to tell when to clean up. Usually the riffles were removed each evening, and their contents panned out. Not only did this keep them at peak efficiency, but it also reduced the temptation presented to one's neighbors.

As in the rocker, mercury was often put behind the riffles to catch the fine gold. In cold weather its action was sluggish, and the gold tended to escape. In warm weather, if the mercury was stirred too much by the passage of heavy debris, it was likely to "flour," or grow frosted in appearance, and then much of the gold passed over it. Even the most meticulous operation rarely got more than 65 per cent of the available gold. There was always some left in the tailings for the patient Chinamen who later made a business of reworking abandoned placers.

Even the lazy man could work riffles of a sort. By laying poles or rocks or boards in a creek below a sluice, some gold could be recovered. This device, often hidden in the muddy water of a ford, generally produced enemies for the man who had put it there as horses and wagons stumbled and jolted over it.

Hydraulic placer mining was not practiced in the summer of 1875 for there was neither time nor the equipment for it. Later it became the preferred way of dealing with large gravel or cement deposits. Dams were built, as at Sheridan, and the water flumed long distances to build up the required pressure. There was much dispute about whether wooden flumes or ditches were the more efficient way to move water. A ditch did not freeze so quickly, could not leak or burn in a forest fire, and it cost less in labor and materials, but sluggish flow and water lost by seepage tended to nullify these advantages. At least one operation carried water in a buried wooden flume, but that was admittedly overdoing it, for all the profits went to the crew that built the ditch and laid the flume in it.[8]

Visitors to the gold fields often were astonished to see the miners sitting beside their claims doing little or nothing. The reason lay in the miners' fear that the Army would shortly drive them out of the Hills and that while absent others might jump any claim that seemed to be paying well. Often groups of miners banded together and agreed not to reveal a rich deposit by working on it. Unity of purpose was sometimes further cemented by Masonic or other fraternal mummery which promised dire punishment to informers.[9]

Most of the miners also tried to protect their claims by the traditional American device of framing a constitution. These miners laws were surprisingly uniform for they were usually drawn up by old-timers from the California, Colorado, or Montana mines who knew the common problems and the traditional way in which they had been handled.[10] The first step was the district miners meeting, called by the captain of one of the prospecting groups or by a grizzled miner whose experience commanded the respect of his fellows. This worthy, who was usually voted into the chair by the assembled miners, presided over the election of a committee to draw up a mining code. The committee, often fore-

[8] Notable ditches can still be followed on the ground near Rockerville, at Big Bend on Rapid Creek, on Battle Creek above Hayward, on Castle Creek above Lookout, and, the buried flume mentioned above, on upper Spring Creek near the Grand Junction mine. Besides shafts and dumps, they are the most ineradicable evidence of mining.

[9] J. H. Triggs, *History of Cheyenne and Northern Wyoming, Embracing the Gold Fields of the Black Hills*, 75.

[10] Stokes and Driggs, *Deadwood Gold*, and Edwin A. Curley, *Guide to the Black Hills, Comprising the Travels of the Author and His Special Artist*, 114-15, are especially valuable for mining laws; examples can be found in the *Black Hills Pioneer* (Deadwood), March 10, 1877, *Daily Press and Dakotaian* (Yankton), June 15, 1875, and *Daily Leader* (Cheyenne) August 28, December 31, 1875; the laws of the Gordon party may be read in an unidentified newspaper clipping in the T. H. Russell file at the Deadwood, South Dakota, Public Library.

60

warned, sometimes had the code ready at hand, in which case it was adopted on the spot. A claim-recorder, the sole administrative officer of the district, was then elected, and the laws put into effect.

The first provision of a new mining code was to name and identify the district. The Palmer Gulch Mining District, for example, was named by the oldest man working in it, modest old George Palmer. The area was customarily defined as the drainage of the creek and its tributaries, extending to the tops of the ridges on either side.

Distribution of the mining claims was the next legal problem. When a placer had been discovered by a group working together, or where abandoned claims were being taken up again, distribution was often by lot, a method also used to divide land in potential town sites. More frequently possession came through individual discovery and location. The first miner to find gold on a creek was entitled to the "discovery" claim, which he located on what he hoped was the richest spot. He was also allowed to "locate" one or two adjoining claims as an added reward. Later claims were then numbered up and down the creek, like Deadwood's famous "Number Two Below Discovery." They extended across the valley from rim to rim, and three hundred feet along the stream. This size, large by California or Montana standards, occasioned some unpleasantness in Deadwood when late-comers agitated to have claims divided and one-half of each opened to relocation. Armed opposition ended the discussion.

Once located and marked, a claim had to be registered with the district recorder. For a dollar or two this official wrote in his notebook somewhat as follows: "Personally appeared before me James Andrews and recorded the undivided right title and interest to Claim Number 9, 'Above Bear Rock' of 300 feet for mining purposes. Recorded this 9th day of July 1875."[11] This record, together with the recorder's certificate issued to the miner, consti-

[11] Claim Recorder's Book, Cheyenne Mining District, Bear Rock, Dakota Territory, p. 44, in Stack 6, Shelf 5, South Dakota Historical Society, Pierre; this is perhaps the earliest surviving Black Hills claim record, and is reproduced in Appendix I.

tuted the whole title to the claim. After the Hills were opened to settlement in 1877, a government land patent could be obtained, but one cost about $1,000, and most of the placer miners believed that their claims would be worked out before one could be issued.

No claim could simply be recorded and held in perpetuity. It had to be worked, or, as the district laws put it, "represented," with fair regularity. One day a week during the mining season was a common requirement, although some districts permitted a claim to be held if it was worked as little as once a month. If a miner or group owned several contiguous claims, mining done on any one of them was usually sufficient for all. Near Deadwood one district allowed representation by labor on the wagon road which served the area. All of these provisions were aimed at preventing idle or absentee ownership which would tie up otherwise productive claims. Small, workable holdings meant that more men could share the wealth and be on hand to defend the area if occasion required.

The conflict between placer claims and town lots was never completely resolved. Every miner was happy to see a town established, even on his own claim, but he would not relinquish his right to mine the land. Even as the survivors of the Deadwood Fire of 1879 poked among the ashes, placer claim owners endeavored to reassert their rights. In general, the mineral claimant had the better of the argument for he could always commence "mining" operations under any building erected without his permission.

Mining disputes were settled by miners meetings, at least until regular courts were established. This assured that the verdict would be supported by a majority of those present, and so tended to reduce appeals to violence. Justice appears to have been done in most cases. For example, Joseph Sturgeon's Claim Number 12 below discovery on Deadwood Creek was jumped by three men who alleged that since Sturgeon was an alien, he was not entitled to mine. Sturgeon, however, swore that he had lived in the United States for twenty-nine years and had long ago declared his intention to become a citizen. The miners decided by a large majority that Sturgeon should regain his claim. In another case at Rochford, the town company demurred over the right of a claimant to his town lot, saying that although his house covered the specified area, it was not as wide as the town law required. A miners meeting decided that floor space, rather than shape, determined the value of the house, and that the miner had built sufficiently to "represent" his lot. These miners trials were certainly superior to the more regular court which once met at Rockerville. There, in a trial over a rich placer mine, the claimant in possession contributed so largely to the refreshment of the jury that they prolonged their deliberations until he had worked out the claim and departed.[12]

While the miners dug the gold, the Bureau of Indian Affairs tried to find out how much gold there was. If the Hills, then a part of the Sioux reservation, were rich, the miners could not be kept out, and some settlement with the Indians would be necessary. Neither the necessity for nor the size of settlement could be determined until the value of the Hills was known. Acting under the authority of the Secretary of War, the bureau appointed Walter P. Jenney and Henry Newton to conduct a geological exploration of the Hills.[13]

Jenney and Newton with fifteen assistants, escorted by four hundred soldiers under the command of Lieutenant-Colonel Richard I. Dodge, left Fort Laramie on May 24, 1875. They reached the base of the Hills near present Newcastle, Wyoming, on June 3 and camped along Beaver Creek. Jenney had hoped to establish a permanent base there, but the salty, purgative water which had previously wrought such havoc among Colonel Walker's command forced him to continue into the mountains.

Guided by California Joe Milner, the expedition got lost almost at once and spent two days trying to find a path to the gold fields. Milner, however, soon became accustomed to the Hills and was

[12] *Black Hills Pioneer*, February 24, 1877; *Black Hills Central* (Rochford), December 15, 22, 1878; Tallent, *The Black Hills*, 471.

[13] Because of the authorship of its final report, the expedition is commonly known as the Newton-Jenney exploration. See Henry Newton and Walter P. Jenney, *Report on the Geology and Resources of the Black Hills of Dakota* (hereafter cited *Report*), for the most detailed account.

usually able to find a trail that the wagons could follow. He also advanced the cause of science by telling Jenney of a zoological anomaly, the "camelk," which resulted from crossbreeding elk with camels previously imported by the War Department. He substantiated his story with the skeleton of a gigantic bull elk, and the tale has since been adopted into Western lore.[14]

Calamity Jane Cannary, the notorious harlot, also accompanied the expedition, disguised in soldier's clothing. Neither Colonel Dodge nor Professor Jenney mention her, so she may have been able to preserve her disguise successfully. However, two other eyewitnesses assert that her sex was discovered, and only the great distance to civilization prevented her being sent back.[15]

Jenney first investigated the placers on French Creek, which he found unpromising. He then explored the delightful area which is now Custer State Park, south of Harney Peak. Moving northward to Rapid Creek and its tributary, Castle Creek, he found increasing amounts of gold. Many prospectors joined the expedition and shared their information about the mines with Jenney. In return, the military escort provided protection from the Indians and did not interfere with the gold digging. The soldiers themselves spent most of their time panning gravel, but without any great success.

Jenney frequently wrote letters, which were widely printed, describing his meager finds. His brief initial report published in the fall of 1875 also was discouraging. Since the expedition had not carried equipment to test the quartz lodes, he had ignored them completely. It has been suggested that the Bureau of Indian Affairs had urged Jenney to play down the gold deposits of the Hills to prevent a mining rush which would upset the Sioux. On the other hand, he may easily have missed the best diggings for no

[14] California Joe's true name was Moses Milner. Joe E. Milner, *California Joe*, 225–28; *Daily Leader* (Cheyenne), June 14, 1879; Curtis D. MacDougall, *Hoaxes*, 23, quotes an 1875 story in the New York *Herald* on the camelk.

[15] Milner, *California Joe*, 230; Harry (Sam) Young, *Hard Knocks: A Life Story of the Vanishing West*, 170. Neither Milner nor Young appear to be entirely reliable. Julia McGillicuddy, *McGillicuddy, Agent*, tells the story of V. T. McGillicuddy, Jenney's topographer.

single expedition could hope to strike very many rich bonanzas. It is likely, too, that the prospectors with whom he talked concealed their best claims from him for fear that others might jump them.[16]

Whatever the reason, Jenney did not speak highly of the Black Hills. In French Creek, for example, he pointed out that the failing water supply and gentle slope of the valley made the gold deposits difficult to work. Spring and Rapid creeks were richer, but nowhere, he said, would the placers pay more than a good day's wages. Colonel Dodge was equally pessimistic. He, too, had seen no placers that would repay the effort needed to work them, unless a large investment in hydraulic equipment reduced the required labor. Dodge predicted that nineteen out of twenty prospectors would do better to stay at home, and that the main value of the mines would be to bring in a population which eventually would turn to farming. California Joe agreed with this, saying, "there's gold from the grass roots down, but there's *more gold* from the grass roots *up*." He bore out Jenney and Dodge's prediction, for although he staked out many claims, he ultimately settled on a ranch in Rapid Valley.[17]

Neither the miners nor the frontier towns were discouraged by Jenney's modest reports. Newspapers derided the educated opinion of "the perfessah" and encouraged the prospectors to go into the Hills. A rumor circulated that Jenney himself had referred to one placer on Rapid Creek as being rich enough to pay off the entire national debt, then about two billion dollars, while less enthusiastic but more factual estimates from miners in the Hills were widely published.[18]

The federal government did its best to keep prospectors out of the Sioux reservation. Federal law at that time provided a fine of

[16] Walter P. Jenney, "Report of Geological Survey of the Black Hills," *Report of the Commissioner of Indian Affairs for 1875*, 181–83; Jenney's letters are found in the *Daily Leader* (Cheyenne), June 24, July 6, 8, 1875; Kingsbury, *History of Dakota Territory*, I, p. 873.

[17] Colonel Richard I. Dodge, *The Black Hills*, 105, 107; Newton and Jenney, *Report*, 300.

[18] McClintock, *Pioneer Days*, 3–4.

up to $1,000 for unauthorized entry on Indian lands, and the Army vigorously patrolled the trails leading to the Hills in hope of catching offenders in the act. Indian scouts from the agencies joined in the hunt and did their best to make life miserable for the trespassers. Only Lieutenant-Colonel Dodge and Professor Jenney remained aloof, countenancing the presence of the miners in return for the aid they gave to exploration.

As early as January, 1875, Brigadier-General E. O. C. Ord suggested that an eight-company military post be built in the Hills, for he believed it impossible for the soldiers to operate there during the winter without permanent shelters. In March, General William T. Sherman ordered that regardless of the weather, the miners should be expelled. This move was backed up by Secretary of the Interior Columbus Delano, who on May 7 wrote that "the Sioux Reservation is guaranteed by solemn treaty to the Sioux Nation and any invasion of it by the white people until the present treaty is modified is unlawful, and cannot be permitted."[19]

Meanwhile, the Army did its best. Dozens of miners were caught in or near the Hills and ceremoniously escorted back to civilization, where they were released, often to return to the Hills again. One said that he had been run out of the Hills four times, and that he "figured he could stand it as long as they could." These scattered efforts were not enough to remove the trespassers. In July, 1875, General Phil Sheridan ordered Brigadier-General George Crook to go to the Hills in person, with sufficient men and authority to do the job.[20]

Crook, whose sympathies lay with the miners, considered the assignment a waste of time, especially as Lieutenant-Colonel Dodge was already in the Hills and should have been busy capturing miners. Crook saw, however, that at least a temporary evacuation of the Hills was essential before the Sioux would negotiate for their relinquishment, and on that understanding, he man-

---

19 "Message from the President of the United States Transmitting Information in Relation to the Black Hills Country," 43 Cong., special sess. (March 15, 1875), *Sen. Exec. Doc. No. 2*, p. 13; *Daily Press and Dakotaian* (Yankton), May 15, 1875, contains Delano's letter.

20 *Daily Leader* (Cheyenne), July 15, 1875.

aged to carry out his orders with a large degree of success. On July 30, he arrived at Camp Crook on Rapid Creek, today under the waters of Pactola Lake, where he issued a proclamation combining firmness with understanding. He made clear his intention to remove the miners by force if necessary, and also his desire to protect the mining claims which had already been established. Finally, he asked all the miners in the Hills to meet with him near the Gordon Stockade on August 10 to discuss means of achieving his aims with the least amount of friction.[21]

The miners, delighted to find consideration where they had expected coercion, happily co-operated with the General. Several meetings were held in the various mining districts. Only the most ardent prospectors hid in the high mountains and refused to leave the Hills. The town near the stockade, formerly known as "Stonewall," was platted out on a piece of birch bark with Crook's approval, renamed "Custer," and its lots distributed to the miners before they left. The only requirement for ownership was the completion of $50 worth of improvements by May 1, 1876, by which time it was supposed the Hills would be open to settlement. The Cheyenne District recorder, W. Harrison, with A. Garrison, A. D. Trask, Samuel Shankland, A. Thompson, C. Allen, and J. Sanders were elected to stand guard over the departing miners' rights. It was agreed that every man who returned to his lot or claim within forty days after the Hills were opened should continue in possession.[22]

Several hundred miners accompanied General Crook out of the Hills on August 15. All but one were released on promising that they would not again trespass on the Sioux reservation. The

[21] General George Crook, *General George Crook: His Autobiography* (ed. by Martin F. Schmidt), 158; a facsimile of the proclamation is in "Adams Memorial is a Black Hills Institution," *Black Hills Engineer*, Vol. XVIII (January, 1930), 42, and is reproduced in Appendix II.

[22] The names of the miners remaining in Custer is from the Claim Recorder's Book of the Cheyenne Mining District; Tallent, *The Black Hills*, 136, gives Shankland, Trask, Thomas Hooper, Robert Kenyon, W. H. Wood, Alexander Thompson, Alfred Gay, and H. F. Hull. The difference may arise from her listing, not those elected, but those clandestinely remaining in the Hills nearby.

dissident, Charles E. Solis, was prosecuted, but Attorney General Edwards Pierrepont decided that the statute against unauthorized entry on the reservation did not apply to citizens of the United States. Long before this decision the miners were returning to the Hills in ever larger numbers.

5

THE RUSH TO THE CENTRAL HILLS

Throughout the land, in every state,
Old miners with impatience wait
To see what Congress means to do,
And if the last reports be true.

. . . .

And when the way at last is clear
A mighty throng from far and near,
Of brave, determined men will seek
The country 'round old Harney's Peak.[1]

The number of men entering the Hills steadily increased as it became clear that the miners might be expelled but would not be prosecuted. These newcomers, many of whom had visited the area before, joined those who had evaded General Crook during the summer of 1875. By the end of the year they had discovered most of the important placers. Unfortunately, the rich gold deposits around Deadwood Gulch in the north were inaccessible because of snow and ice, and the bulk of the mining activity during the winter of 1875–76 was confined to the central Hills.[2]

[1] *Daily Leader* (Cheyenne), March 30, 1875.
[2] The heavy snow in the Hills is for some reason confined to the northern Hills; the dividing line, which in winter is sharp and obvious, lies a few miles north of Pactola.

The newly created town of Custer, although in the center of these early placers, was not a suitable base for mining since the Army maintained a post there expressly to capture and remove trespassers. This post, commanded by Captain Edwin Pollock, an officious and efficient officer, naturally kept down the mining population of the town and reduced it to a community of camp followers catering to the soldiers. Pollock had arrived from Fort Laramie during the fall of 1875 with a company of the Ninth Infantry and a troop each from the Second and the Third Cavalry. He set up his headquarters in a log cabin begun by Dr. D. M. Flick, established Camp Collins on the site of Custer City, and for the next three months scoured the Hills for gold hunters. Reinforced with additional troops as the size of his task became apparent, Pollock arrested dozens of miners, confined them to a notorious "bull-pen" in Custer, and later sent them under guard to Fort Laramie where they invariably were released without punishment.

Pollock, however, met with three serious impediments to the execution of his duties. First, the miners sneaked past him, often with the aid of friends in Custer, and hid in the fastness of the Hills. Mr. V. P. Shoun, for example, arrived near Custer in October, made friends with miners left behind by General Crook, and was warned away. Shoun and his friends camped high on the side of Harney Peak, pastured their horses in a meadow ten miles distant, and were never discovered. Their tiny cabin roofed with slate was not found until the Civilian Conservation Corps built a horse-trail into the area in the 1930's. Second, Pollock's soldiers compared their meager wages with the golden hopes which mining offered and deserted in droves. Their erstwhile comrades, moreover, assisted them in avoiding capture and gave them warning of impending raids. Third, as winter grasped the Hills, it seemed likely that even with the utmost preparation Pollock's soldiers could accomplish little more than survival.[3]

Despite these handicaps Pollock did remove miners from the Hills while he prepared shelters and laid in provisions for a stay

[3] Tallent, *The Black Hills*, 139, 179–81.

through the winter. President U. S. Grant, however, did not view the protection of Indian reservations as a proper duty for the Army. He called Secretary of War William W. Belknap and Secretary of the Interior Zachariah Chandler together, added Generals Sheridan and Crook to the meeting, and quickly reached a sensible if ungallant decision. The miners, Grant's conference agreed, were still forbidden to enter the Sioux reservation. The soldiers, however, would be taken out of the Hills, and no further military opposition would be offered to the miners. This policy, which was not publicly announced, might for a time remain concealed from Indian sympathizers in the East, while the absence of the troops would be noted immediately in the West. Thus both sections of the country would be pleased, honor preserved, and the soldiers stationed comfortably in established winter quarters at Fort Laramie.[4]

This pusillanimous policy was carried out at once. On November 17, 1875, Captain Pollock and his troops left Custer for Wyoming, leaving the Hills in fact, if not in theory, open to the miners. Such pangs of conscience that might have troubled Grant and his advisors were assuaged when the President, more than a year later, admitted in his annual message that "an effort to remove the miners would only result in the desertion of the bulk of the troops that might be sent there to remove them."[5]

Once the soldiers no longer barred their way, the miners began to come to the Hills in larger numbers. By Christmas, 1875, five hundred had arrived, and some of them were panning out $30 to $40 per day. By mid-January, 1876, it was estimated that there were four thousand men in and around the Hills. Custer had boomed to a town of a thousand, and Hill City, fourteen miles to the north, was nearly one-half as large. Miners pushed through

[4] *Daily Leader* (Cheyenne), November 17, 1875.
[5] James D. Richardson, *Messages and Papers of the Presidents, 1789–1897*, VII, p. 401; the date of Pollock's departure is disputed for Tallent gives it as December 1, but A. J. Jacobs, writing from Custer on November 27, 1875, and quoted in Larsen, "The Black Hills Gold Rush: Letters from Men Who Participated," *North Dakota Historical Quarterly*, Vol. VI (July, 1932), 309, had to wait until Pollock left before entering town, and says it was November 17.

the snow to the northern Hills to find the rich diggings on Negro Hill, Deadwood Gulch, and at the site of Dr. Hayden's old discoveries in Bear Butte valley. By April, J. W. Lytle, leaving the Hills for Cheyenne, passed fourteen hundred men and two hundred wagons on the trail to Custer. Not all the pilgrims were confident, but they were all determined. A letter written from Cheyenne suggests the prevailing attitude:

> My dear wife Mary, I wish to let you know that I am leaving here today for the Black Hills or death. Mary, there is at present a great war between the white men and the injuns. If they will leave me my scalp I will be satisfied. I will lose my life or find out what there is in the Black Hills or die, you bet.[6]

Now the chronological history of the gold rush must yield for a moment to a geographical description of the more prominent mining camps of the central Hills. The story of Custer, Hill City, Sheridan, Pactola, Rapid City, Hayward, and Rockerville, among others, centers in this area and occupies mainly, though not entirely, the fall of 1875 and the spring of 1876. Thus it seems appropriate to discuss briefly their entire history before examining the more varied account of richer and wilder mines of the northern Hills.

Custer, the first of the central Black Hills towns, was laid out on August 10, 1875, and its town lots were distributed to the miners prior to their removal by General Crook. A town in the Hills, one should note, was not merely a gathering of men at a certain spot, but generally a formal settlement with a town company in charge, a regular system of streets and avenues, and a set procedure for distributing lots. This ceremonious arrangement sprang, not from the miners' love of order, but from the hope that it would result in a grant of government land which would lead to secure land titles. Custer was just such a town.[7]

[6] *Daily Leader*, (Cheyenne), March 29, 1876.

[7] The assignment of "firsts" is always tricky. Harney City, at the Gordon Stockade, was undoubtedly the first town in the Hills, but is not often thought of as such. The town laid out by the Gordon party on the site of present-day Custer must then be the second town, but as it was not then occupied, perhaps it

The representatives of the miners who remained at the Gordon Stockade to protect the interests of their departing companions were neither careful nor successful in guarding the property left in their care. Returning prospectors found their equipment missing or stolen and tended to complain bitterly about the negligence of the guardians. They soon saw, however, the folly of antagonizing the claim recorder who was their sole source of clear land titles, and resigned themselves to their losses in the hope of recouping them from what was left of their claims. The miners' anger was eventually dissipated by running out of town five or six Chinamen who were suspected of having committed the thefts.

As might be expected the earliest business in Custer was a bar, said by Harry Young, one of its proprietors, to be "the best equipped saloon that was ever conducted in Custer City."[8] This enterprise, which at first relied mainly upon Captain Pollock's soldiers for support, was opened about November 1, 1875. In December, W. H. Cole brought three wagonloads of merchandise to Custer and began a general store, but as late as March of the next year, it was said that the ratio of whisky barrels to flour sacks in town was still two to one.

The winter of 1875–76 was mild in the central Hills. Even in January the hardier miners sometimes panned out gold in their shirt sleeves during the midday hours. Some eight hundred men were in the Hills, washing out from $5 to $7 a day with hopes of more when the weather improved. One enthusiastic prospector, perhaps with claims to sell, wrote to the Cheyenne *Leader* urging that "all the boys who are not making more than $10 per day [should] come to the Black Hills." During the depression years of the mid-1870's, that was pretty much of a blanket recommendation.[9]

Custer grew rapidly. During the first three months of 1876 someone, probably an optimist, estimated that from six to ten

cannot be counted, and in any event it yielded place to Custer, which was founded August 10, 1875.

[8] Young, *Hard Knocks*, 187; it should be understood that whenever Young is used as a source it is for local color rather than reliability.

[9] *Daily Leader* (Cheyenne) January 22, 1876.

thousand men had come into the area. A small smelter was built, and an assay office was set up during February. These two aids to promotion also must have helped to advertise the Hills. A sawmill run by Dave Ducent and Pat Murphy was set up early in the same month to provide lumber for sluices and for houses. Town lots fifty by one hundred feet sold for $25 to $500, the higher price being charged along Crook Street, the main thoroughfare. Crook Street had been laid out two hundred feet wide to permit a bull team to turn around in the middle of the business district. The same month saw the first hotel built by a Mr. Druggeman. Custer was on the boom.

Such a thriving community needed a municipal government, especially as the federal government refused to recognize the miners' presence in the Hills or appoint United States marshals to keep the peace. In March, 1876, a mass meeting set up a provisional government. Tom Hooper was elected "Supreme Judge" of the Black Hills, and E. P. Keiffer and H. F. Smith justices of the peace. Joseph G. Bemis was elected mayor of Custer, with a town board of twelve to give him moral support, which he evidently needed.[10] John Burrows was appointed town marshal, and Harry Young, the saloon-keeper, selected as his deputy, probably on the supposition that since much of the trouble in town originated in his place, the least he could do was help to suppress it.

Burrows and Young handled criminal cases with resourcefulness and aplomb. Serious malefactors were sent to Cheyenne for trial, and petty criminals were fined locally to finance the city government. The first real criminal trial was that of C. C. Clayton who had murdered Mr. Boueyer, a half blood. The miners, hesitant about their authority and rather sympathizing with Clayton, merely expelled the murderer from town. The earliest civil cases were over land. Mr. William Coad, for example, secured possession of a town lot from Mr. Swartout, an adverse claimant. Next, Captain Jack Crawford, the poet scout, sued Dr. Flick for having thrown him out of a cabin. Flick testified that he had built

---

[10] Curley, *Guide to the Black Hills*, 48, 70–71, speaks quite disparagingly of Joseph Bemis.

the cabin in question with his own hands during the summer of 1875, then left with General Crook. In his absence Captain Pollock had occupied the premises, and when he left, Captain Jack had moved in. Returning, Flick seized an opportunity to reoccupy the cabin when Captain Jack was absent. Crawford's lawyer claimed to the five-man jury: (1) that no land titles were good on the Indian reservation; (2) that Flick had obviously abandoned the building; (3) that Crawford was in legal possession and had been forcibly evicted. The miners, sensitive to the attack upon Black Hills land titles, hastily found for Flick.[11]

By March, the town of Custer had a population of five to six hundred, among whom were at least twenty persons referred to rather slightingly as "females." These doubtless helped to swell the number of business establishments in town, which also included six general stores, two bakeries, and numerous saloons. There were about three hundred houses with as many more under construction, but not many were worth bragging about. The roof of one collapsed, killing Charlie Holt of Sioux City and seriously injuring his partner. Captain Jack, who never learned the victim's last name, wrote:

> Poor Charlie braved the wintery storms,
> And footed it all the way;
> And now he is a bleeding corpse—
> He died at dawn today.[12]

This somehow says much, one way and another, about life in a mining camp and the way the miners reacted to it.

As the spring thaws began, one of the first significant gold shipments left the Hills: Emil Faust and D. G. Tallent carried $1,000 worth of dust from Custer to Cheyenne, where it created an understandable commotion. Better weather, however, also allowed migration to the richer placers in the northern Hills, and by mid-March, Custer had started to decline. Mr. J. M. Ward, who

---

11 Jesse Brown and A. M. Willard, *The Black Hills Trails*, 342; Tallent, *The Black Hills*, 265.

12 Crawford, *The Poet Scout*, 130.

arrived in Cheyenne on March 11, reported that he had passed 978 persons, including 27 "females," headed for the Hills—but most of them passed through Custer and kept on going. In April, Jerry Bryan, an Illinoisian, paused in town, where he was told that Custer contained four hundred houses. Bryan agreed that the estimate was correct, if it included "all kinds of Houses." Bryan ended his stay in a hurdy-gurdy saloon filled to capacity with miners being entertained by half a dozen games of chance and "4 or 5 Blisters." He concluded that "A Ruff crowd is Custer," and he was probably right.[13]

In late April, 1876, increasing Indian hostility began to disturb the Custer citizens. A company of two hundred militiamen was formed under Major Wynkoop to protect the town, along with a smaller party of scouts under the command of Captain Jack. The company and scouts were commanded by Mayor Bemis, and was referred to collectively as the "Custer Minute Men," perhaps due to a fancied similarity to the patriots of Lexington and Concord, or because they never got so far from town that they could not return in a minute.

Custer quickly recognized the further threat to her prosperity posed by the boom in the northern Hills. In April a committee compiled a list of unlocated mines and placers in Deadwood, in order that "when people arrive in Custer they may be conducted to any part of the country they prefer, and know before they start from here what they will find." Too many pilgrims, the Custer businessmen decided, had come to town, hung around without any definite objectives, and then gone home broke and disappointed. Custer might not be able to equal the Deadwood gold, but the town was at least a well-established supply base and fought to stay in business. The town, however, continued to decline. The difficulty of working the French Creek placers, which required a large investment in ditching and hydraulic equipment, combined with the lure of richer harvests farther north to depopulate Custer. During the summer of 1876 the sole income of the town was derived from "fleecing" rather than supplying miners. One cor-

[13] Jerry Bryan, *An Illinois Gold Hunter in the Black Hills*, 25.

respondent barely escaped a $5 fine for discharging his gun within the city limits. He thought this a little grasping since there were not then twenty-five persons in Custer for him to have hit.[14]

Custer was never completely deserted, and by the fall of 1876 it had begun to grow again. The sixty families in the area supplied twenty-five children to Miss Nellie Scott's school, which opened in J. W. Lytle's house of August 7. In November the town government was reorganized with J. W. C. White the Supreme Court judge and G. W. Rothrock president of the town board. Mr. A. R. Kennedy published the Custer *Herald* in January, 1877, but soon sold out to James Bartholomew. Bartholomew, eager to better himself, loaded the press and type on a wagon and left town headed for Deadwood. Irate citizens who wanted the paper to continue rushed after him, seized his property, and forcibly returned him to Custer. There he was compelled to stay in spite of his spirited requests for military aid. Bartholomew was later given the postmastership of Custer, but even this political plum could not hold him long, and in August he escaped with his equipment to Central City. The *Herald* was soon followed by the Custer *Chronicle*, which continues to the present day.[15]

The hard-fought Custer election of 1877 involved a contest over the Custer county seat as well as other public offices. Potential voters were recruited all over the Hills, refreshed at local bars, and hauled to the polls as often as the opposition permitted. When the town of Hayward emerged the victor, resourceful Custer patriots stole the county records, but it was all in vain, for Hayward remained firmly in control until 1879.[16]

In 1878, Custer mining began to flourish again as the northern

[14] Joseph G. Bemis, quoted in Larsen, "Black Hills Gold Rush: Letters from Men Who Participated," *North Dakota Historical Quarterly*, Vol. VI (July, 1932), 317; Richardson, "A Trip to the Black Hills," *Scribner's*, Vol. XIII (April, 1877), 754; Curley, *Guide to the Black Hills*, 72.

[15] The *Daily Leader* (Cheyenne) speaks of Nellie Scott, August 15, 1876; Tallent, *The Black Hills*, calls her Carrie. Neither source is noted for getting names correct. McMurtrie, *Early Printing in Wyoming and the Black Hills*, 63, although compiled solely from Wyoming papers which mention Black Hills items, is an invaluable guide.

[16] *Daily Leader* (Cheyenne), November 17, 1877.

placers and hard-rock claims were worked out or taken up by eastern investors. The whole of the central Hills experienced a second boom as new deposits were discovered. As late as August, 1879, one of the placer camps in the central Hills sent five hundred ounces of gold dust to Deadwood for deposit. The rush to these placers coupled with renewed interest in hard-rock possibilities brought renewed prosperity to Custer. The story of the Grand Junction and the Atlantic mines, which unfolded a little later than the period covered here, is typical of the area: A modest find, boomed by interested parties, was unloaded on unsuspecting East-erners. These speculators temporarily brought prosperity to Cus-ter as they endeavored to develop the properties into a paying proposition, but the failure of the mines resulted in eventual de-cline and renewed depression. The Black Hills habit of swindling eastern investors soon cut off this previously lucrative source of income, and gave the Hills a deserved but unwelcome reputation for ingenious mining swindles.

Custer's history is indeed the story of most of the Black Hills towns—a brief, tempestuous early rush, followed by migration to richer, farther gold fields. Then, sporadic returns to open up new prospects, followed by another depression when the new discoveries proved fruitless. No town in the Hills, except for Lead with its mighty Homestake ore body, has prospered to the present on the "diggings" which brought it its initial prominence.

Hill City, or Hilyo, at the confluence of Newton Fork and Spring Creek, was the second major town established in the Hills. The nearby Jenney Mining District was rich, and its gold seemed a likely base on which to build. Mark V. Boughton, former mayor of Cheyenne, shipped in a sawmill, and James W. Allen, a pros-pector on Spring Creek, brought in a wagon-load of mining tools. By January 22, 1876, there were thirty houses in Hill City and logs on hand to build seventy more. A group of Bismarck investors were building two stores and a hotel and urging their fellow townsmen to migrate to Hill City. There was little actual gold production for the cold weather hampered panning, but the miners spent the winter roaming the nearby hills and valleys look-

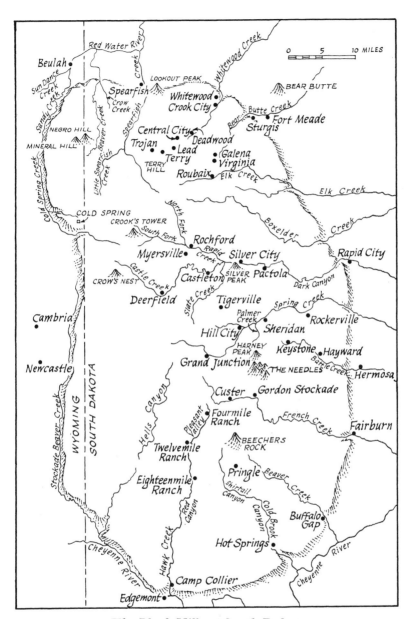

The Black Hills of South Dakota

ing for the richest deposits which they hoped to work in fairer weather.

The town site was organized and platted in February by Robert Florman, Thomas Harvey, John Miller, and Hugh McCullough. Mr. W. G. Hormins was elected secretary and recorder of a new Hill City Mining District along Spring Creek. Evidently town government brought prosperity, for by February 27 there were 250 houses. Many of the houses must have been torn down for firewood as the miners left, for on April 15 only 50 remained. Even though Hill City placers had steadily produced from $3 to $8 per day, news of the Deadwood strikes and the threat of Indian hostilities emptied Hill City, which soon was reduced to a population of one man and a dog.[17]

Hill City prospered again in 1877 when the miners returned to the meager but tested placers. Little towns like Newton Fork and Nugget Gulch sprang up, while hard-rock leads like the Bengal Tiger, Golden Summit, Grizzly Bear, and Saint Elmo brought new activity. It was not until the late 1880's, however, that the arrival of the railroad and the discovery of promising tin mines brought another boom.

Sheridan, or Golden City as it was then called, was a few miles down Spring Creek from Hill City. Here A. J. Williams found one of the first rich placers in the Hills when on August 18, 1875, he took $2 worth of dust out of a single pan of ore from Stand-off Bar. The bar was so named because he had to "stand off" the other miners with a shotgun. In October a group of Montana men set up camp on the lower end of the bar and in six weeks took out nearly $3,000, including one $23 nugget. Other claims yielded from $12 to $20 per day to each miner. In the fall of 1875 a town was laid out, which by February boasted four stores and several houses. As in Hill City, Indians were a problem, but the citizens of Sheridan seem to have been of sterner fiber than their neigh-

[17] The problem of determining the number of houses in the early towns is perplexing; it depends on what sort of a structure one calls a house, including floored tents, dugouts, and hovels generally. In addition, any house which was deserted soon disappeared, forming part of the homes and fires of the other miners nearby.

bors, for the outlying houses were built with loopholes all around and shelves under the windows where the women and children could hide in case of attack.[18]

One Sheridan miner, Norman McCully, is said to have mined $3,000 worth of dust and attempted to carry it alone to Rapid City. Waylaid on the trail by a drunken soldier, he was murdered and the gold hidden nearby. Since the soldier's guilt could not be clearly established, he was merely sentenced to imprisonment at Fort Benton, Montana, where he was put to work in the prison sawmill. Chided one day about the murdered miner, he thrust his tormentor into the circular saw and "parted his hair clear down to his navel." The rest of the sawmill gang, justifiably outraged, hanged him from the rafters without an inquiry about the missing gold. It is still missing.[19]

Sheridan, like the other central Hills towns, was deserted in the spring of 1876 when the miners rushed to Deadwood, but by the next year new placers had been found and the town revived. Some of the bars yielded $5 to $25 per day to each miner, even though much of the miners' time was taken up hauling the gravel as far as a mile to water. There was a good market in town lots, and placer claims sold for $15 a foot. When Pennington County was organized in April, 1877, the commissioners, R. H. Vosburg, M. M. Fuller, and Sam Coats, first met at Rapid City, but by May 7 they had decided that Sheridan was the more promising town. A log cabin there served as the territorial circuit court when Judge Granville Bennett presided over the first legal session held in the Black Hills. Rapid City, however, grew faster and on November 21 replaced Sheridan as the county seat. Some nearby hard-rock mines, like the J. R. and the Queen Bee, later brought a little business to Sheridan, and hopes of a copper strike at the Blue Lead were often revived. None of the mines prospered, and the town

[18] Andreas, *Andreas' Historical Atlas of Dakota*, 121; Mrs. E. B. Hulze, who lived in one of the cabins during the Ghost Dance uprising, recalled the defensive measures.

[19] Lee (Leland) Case, *Lee's Official Guidebook to the Black Hills and Badlands*, 63.

eventually dwindled to a few farms which in the 1940's were covered by the waters impounded by Sheridan Dam.[20]

Prospectors found gold on upper Rapid Creek, near what was to become Pactola, during the summer of 1875. This area, where General Crook had camped when he issued his proclamation to the miners, was at first called "Camp Crook" in his honor. It was here that a few of the miners hid and evaded the searches of both Crook and Captain Pollock. The spring of 1876 saw an increase in mining activity when James C. Sherman and several companions opened up and advertised the gold deposits. Miners rushed in—often 250 or 300 attended miners meetings—and the town grew rapidly. Sherman managed the local hotel, a general store served the miners, and both the Cheyenne and the Sidney stages brought in new prospectors. Camp Crook, too, suffered from the rush to the northern Hills, but, like the other mining camps, recovered as further placers and lodes were found. The Rapid Creek Mining and Manufacturing Company employed 80 men under the direction of Judge H. N. Maguire in an attempt to build a six-mile flume to the gravel at the Philadelphia Bar, below town. When confusion arose between Camp Crook and Crook City to the north, Maguire suggested the name Pactola, based on Pactolus, the Lydian river of golden sands. The miners, pleased with this apt and classical imagery, heartily agreed to the proposal. The flume scheme collapsed, and though others followed, Pactola never became a prosperous town. It now lies beneath the waters of Pactola Lake.[21]

The story of John R. Brennan, founder of Rapid City, is typical of the way the Hills were settled. Brennan, George W. Stokes, George Ashton, and W. Hawley came to Fort Laramie in October, 1875, where they joined California Joe Milner, George Palmer, and others on the way to the Hills. The party journeyed first to Custer, then pushed on to Hill City where it followed

[20] Carl H. Leedy, *Golden Days in the Black Hills*, 8–9; Leedy and his wife, the daughter of an early Sheridan settler, lived in the town for years. Further information is found in Tallent, *The Black Hills*, 418–19, 457–58.

[21] *Ibid.*, 462–65; Andreas, *Andreas' Historical Atlas of Dakota*, 113; Brown and Willard, *The Black Hills Trails*, 426–27.

Spring Creek to the mouth of Palmer Gulch. Here, on November 3, the party found evidence of rich placer deposits, and decided to stay for the winter. They built two cabins and on December 10 held a meeting in one of them to name the gulch and draw up a code of laws to govern the miners in it. Life in the gulch was pleasant. There was ample game—so much that by Christmas the frozen carcasses of twenty-one deer hung about the cabins as insurance against starvation. Nor were the amenities of life entirely lacking. Stokes ingeniously whittled a washboard by scoring the surface of a flattened log; his companions found it so useful that they washed clothes continually for the next several days. For Christmas, Stokes attempted an apple pie, using dried apples and deer fat, but this was not as successful as the washboard.[22]

The bedrock in Palmer Gulch seemed rich in gold, but the deposits lay deep and were flooded with ground water to within four feet of the surface. Palmer, an experienced prospector, suggested a long, deep ditch to drain the gravel, and work was begun accordingly. The ditch diggers ruined two axes chopping out the frozen sod so others with pick and shovel could reach the unfrozen dirt lower down. The work was arduous, and the miners quit one after another. One morning Brennan climbed out of the ditch, threw his shovel on the ground, and swore he would never lay hands on another mining tool. He departed to begin the town of Rapid City. Stokes and Palmer continued working the gulch and took out $1,000 each, to become the most successful miners in the area. Palmer Gulch, although thoroughly prospected from end to end and surrounded by hard-rock claims, was spotty and never became a prosperous mining district.

Brennan left Palmer Gulch in February, 1876, and on February 25, he and W. P. Martin, J. W. Allen, James Carney, William Nuttle, Sam Scott, and William Marston laid out the town of Rapid City on Rapid Creek just outside the mountains. Scott sur-

22 John R. Brennan, MS, "Some Early History of the Black Hills of South Dakota," n.d., Shelf 2, Tier 6, South Dakota Historical Society, describes the party in detail; Stokes and Driggs, *Deadwood Gold* and Stokes' article in the Casper, Wyoming, *Daily Tribune*, July 27, 1922, as quoted by Spring, *Cheyenne and Black Hills Stage and Express Routes*, 72–73, are also firsthand accounts.

veyed the town with a pocket compass and tape measure, which is one reason why the old part of town does not run due north and south. Six blocks in the center of town were divided up into lots and distributed among the founders, each man receiving five. Two days later a small party from Yankton arrived in Rapid City and urged that a wagon road be laid out through the Bad Lands to Fort Pierre. Brennan and Frank Conely agreed to return with them and mark a trail on the way. At Fort Pierre, Conely met General Campbell with one hundred prospectors, and guided them to Rapid City, while a few days later Brennan brought in another hundred men commanded by John Dillon.[23]

While Brennan and Conely were away, a party of two hundred Bismarck men came into Rapid City and offered to settle there if given every other block in the new town. The town's founders refused to do business, and the Bismarck group moved up creek three and one-half miles where they founded Upper Rapid for themselves.[24]

The spring and summer of 1876 was no time for internal division among the miners. Indian raids became increasingly frequent on the easern side of the Hills near the reservation. By May, deaths and desertion had reduced Rapid City to a population of nineteen men. They built a two-story blockhouse thirty feet square at the corner of Fifth and Rapid Streets and dug in for a fight. Their determination soon paid off and attracted other settlers. When Upper Rapid had to be abandoned on August 27 due to continued Indian attacks there were enough men in Rapid City to come to the Bismarckers' assistance and provide protection during the move.[25]

[23] Rosen, *Pa-Ha-Sa-Pah*, 259; Brennan, "Some Early History of the Black Hills of South Dakota," MS, n.d., Shelf 2, Tier 6, South Dakota Historical Society, 12-21.

[24] *Rapid City, South Dakota* (n.p., n.d., circa 1891 [?]) contains another account by Brennan of the founding of the town; Rapid City and Upper Rapid were separated from Pactola by the tortuous length of Rapid Canyon.

[25] A. C. Townsend, Rapid City, September 1, 1876, to I. C. Develling, Springfield, Massachusetts, typescript copy, Rapid City Public Library, Black Hills File Cabinet, Drawer 3.

In spite of Indian troubles the Rapid Creek placers prospered. Nels Velstrom, two miles above Rapid City, washed out one pound of gold a week, and many others did nearly as well. Allen and Conear with four helpers took out $2,000 in a single day, evidently from a rich pocket. In June, 1876, five hundred miners were working up and down the creek above Rapid City. Bedrock, however, was twenty-eight feet down. Pumps and drainage ditches were needed to free the workings of excess water, and dams were built to keep it from flowing back into the mines again. Rapid Creek placers were often valuable, but like most of the central Hills deposits, they were no place for the poor man who had to work alone.

By the end of 1876, Rapid City had a population of about three hundred, not counting the miners up and down the creek. Two general stores did a modest business, while Brennan's two-room hotel thrived. In the dining room, the genial host took his patrons' orders and shouted toward the kitchen. He then went to the kitchen himself, cooked the meal, and served it to his customers, maintaining the illusion of a bevy of servants at his beck and call.[26]

Brennan did not really need to go to all that trouble, for Rapid City was not yet a metropolis. Two stage lines had tried to come in from Fort Pierre during the summer of 1876, but Indian attacks had forced them to suspend operations. It was not until March, 1877, that a pilgrim bound for the Hills could come to Rapid City in style on the regular coach from Sidney, Nebraska. Rapid City's role as county seat of Pennington County added dignity to the town and doubtless helped bring in its first newspaper, Joseph Gossage's *Black Hills Journal*, which began circulation January 5, 1878. By that time there were about one thousand miners along Rapid Creek, for with the end of Indian hostilities Rapid City's combination of easy access, rich placers, and fertile valley land had made her the "Gate City" of the Hills.[27]

---

26 Tallent, *The Black Hills*, 305.

27 University of South Dakota, South Dakota W.P.A. Writer's Project, "Annals of Early Rapid City, 1878–1887," typescript, Rapid City Public Library, is an invaluable aid to the student of the town.

Meanwhile, several towns such as Harney, Rosebud, and Hayward had sprung up along Battle Creek in the eastern Hills. Gold was found near Hayward, for example, in 1875, when Professor Walter P. Jenney pulled up a rose bush and shook fifty cents worth of dust from its roots. Charles Phillips, Phillip Brown, and Judge Willis settled in the area in the fall of 1876, but Indian attacks soon forced them to desert their promising discoveries.

In November, Charles Hayward, James E. Carpenter, and six Montana miners came to the Battle Creek area and platted the town of Hayward. Two general stores and Hayward's saloon catered to the earthly needs of the miners. Holiday entertainment was provided by stuffing an enormous Christmas tree with a giant powder charge and blowing it to pieces. By 1877 the town had a population of three hundred, three hotels, ten business houses, and twenty saloons. Town lots, 30 by 150 feet, sold for $200. Mines on Iron Creek, Foster Gulch, and Battle Creek all pushed the boom along, while the construction of two huge flumes to work these placers provided employment for those not otherwise engaged.[28]

In 1877 relations between Hayward and Custer were violently disturbed by a quarrel over the location of the Custer County seat. At the decisive meeting of the three-man county board, commissioner Hayward favored his town, while E. G. Ward urged that Custer be designated the county seat. Neither would second the other's motion, and M. D. Thompson, in the chair, was necessarily silent. A brief intermission was called, during which Hayward and Thompson discussed the virtues of Hayward and the rewards its selection might bring to all involved. Thompson then called the meeting to order, and asked Ward to take the chair for a moment. Then, from the floor, Thompson seconded Hayward's motion and called for a vote, and the motion to make the town of Hayward county seat carried unanimously. Ward, as chairman pro tempore, could do nothing but preside over this inspired chicanery. It was Hayward's last bid for prosperity. The county

[28] *Daily Leader* (Cheyenne), January 7, 1877; *Black Hills Herald* (Custer), January 4, 1877; Strahorn, *Handbook*, 234.

seat was moved to Custer in 1879, and in 1881 a well-conducted survey showed that Hayward was not in Custer County at all.[29]

Rockerville, or Captain Jack's Dry Diggins, was discovered in December, 1876, when William Keller panned out a few bits of gold from its waterless placers. Miners worked the gravel with rockers but found the deposits difficult to handle. The gold lay in clay and cement beds and required large quantities of water to wash it free. Hauled in wagons to Spring Creek, the gravel proved rich but hardly profitable. Even so, $150,000 in dust was taken out during 1877 and $250,000 in 1878. The Black Hills Placer Mining Company began building its seventeen-mile flume from Sheridan to Rockerville in 1879, and by 1880 there was ample water at the diggings. The company worked its own dry placers and sold any surplus water to the other miners.

The company took out over $500,000 worth of gold, but the high cost of building and maintaining the flume, coupled with fantastic mismanagement by company officials, made profits impossible. Ambrose Bierce, the local manager at Rockerville, met and mastered innumerable difficulties but could not overcome the interference of his less informed superiors. Some literary critics have imagined that his experience with the flume contributed to the bitterness of his later writings.[30]

The town prospered for a while, and in 1879 had its own newspaper, the *Black Hills Miner*, a lively dance club, a black-faced minstrel troupe, and the usual business establishments.[31] As the flume fell into disrepair and the placers near it were worked out, business fell off and the town stagnated. In recent years it has been rebuilt as a tourist ghost town, but the only piece of the original Rockerville still standing is the mud and stone chimney of Cortland Rush's cabin.

29 Tallent, *The Black Hills*, 396.

30 Paul Fatout, *Ambrose Bierce and the Black Hills*, describes the flume company in detail and quotes many of Bierce's letters; The Black Hills Placer Mining Company, *Prospectus* (n.p., n.d., circa 1879), is a splendid example of the optimistic qualities of early promotional literature.

31 The main street was prophetically named "Ascension Street"; at one end of it is the famous Stratosphere Bowl from which balloon ascensions were made in the 1930's.

In spite of the brevity of their boom, the central Hills played an important part in the gold rush. Their placers on French, Spring, and Rapid creeks brought in the first miners in the fall of 1875, and gave them needed experience in finding and exploiting Black Hills gold deposits. The milder climate of the area offered an opportunity for winter prospecting to the miner who might otherwise have ceased his efforts amid the snowdrifts of Deadwood or Negro Hill. Lastly, by providing an outlet for the unemployed of the more northerly gold fields, the area retained in the Hills those excess miners who so eagerly joined successive stampedes to each new gold discovery.

6

THE RUSH TO THE NORTHERN HILLS

Oh, the dust, the beautiful dust,
I'll squeeze a fortune out of it or bust!
I'll brave Red Cloud and his dusky band,
And pitch my tent in the golden land,
Where with shovel and pick I'll worry the soil,
Until a fortune rewards my toil.
And then I'll waltz home to Mammy and Pappy,
Marry Sarah Jane, sit down and be happy.[1]

The rush to the northern Hills included three main areas: Deadwood along Whitewood Creek in the northern part of the mountains; Negro Hill in the northwest; and far to the south the rich bars of upper Rapid and Castle creeks. Only the placer deposits will be considered here, since discussion of hard-rock mines in these areas belongs to another chapter. The early prospectors, it is true, located quartz claims, but they lacked the experience, machinery, and capital needed to work them and hence at first confined their labors to the placers.

Deadwood Gulch was named for the clutter of charred pines which blocked the explorations of early prospectors. Properly, the name applied to only the valley of Deadwood Creek, but it soon expanded to include the whole area where Deadwood, City, Gold Run, and Strawberry creeks joined the Whitewood. From

[1] *Daily Leader* (Cheyenne), November 2, 1876.

its headwaters to Crook City in the foothills, Whitewood Creek was about ten miles long, while its numerous tributaries provided more than twice that length of potential placers. These canyons were for the most part narrow and winding, with precipitous walls towering three and four hundred feet above the valley floors, natural traps for the gold washed out of the nearby lodes. The sinuosities of the valley caught and held the tumbling nuggets, while the narrow canyon concentrated the gold so it could easily be recovered.[2]

In the latter part of August, 1875, Frank Bryant, John B. Pearson, Thomas Moore, Richard Low, James Pierman, Sam Blodgett, and George Hauser came to Whitewood Gulch. Here they found prospects running from twenty to forty cents to the pan, and built a small log cabin. Bryant and Pearson left for Fort Laramie to bring in reinforcements and supplies. Bryant is generally accepted as the discoverer of gold, but John S. McClintock, who came to the Hills during the rush and was acquainted with most of the miners, disagreed completely. Mr. A. S. Blanchard, Tom Patterson, H. A. Albien, John Verpont, and one other man, says McClintock, came to Deadwood from Custer and found less than a teaspoonful of gold on September 6, 1875. Since there was no one else at work in the gulch, they laid out their claims to include the customary "one for discovery." The next day William Smith, John Kane, and three companions came to Whitewood and discovered gold at the mouth of Spruce Gulch. Smith, a man who considered "a bird in hand the noblest work of God," busied himself staking out three claims "by virtue of discovery" instead of overly exerting himself searching for competitors. It is not surprising that Bryant, Blanchard, and Smith did not see each other; it was not to their advantage to do so; each was anxious to avoid capture by the active Captain Pollock, and each undoubtedly minded his own business.[3]

[2] Deadwood, oddly enough, was on Whitewood Creek, rather than in Deadwood Gulch. It was composed of Montana City, Fountain City, Elizabethtown, Chinatown, Ingleside, Forest Hill, City Creek, South Deadwood, and Cleveland.

[3] *Daily Press and Dakotaian* (Yankton), August 5, 1875, June 6, 1876; Seth Bullock, "An Account of Deadwood and the Northern Black Hills in 1876"

Bryant and Pearson returned to Deadwood Gulch in October, accompanied by a party which included William and Alfred Gay and William Lardner. On November 17 they put up a notice saying that "we, the undersigned, claim three hundred feet below this notice for discovery, and nine hundred feet of three claims above this notice for mining purposes." It is evident that they did not consider either Blanchard's or Smith's claims as having priority. In December the Gay party organized the Lost Mining District and elected Lardner its recorder. This was quickly followed by the Deadwood, Upper Whitewood, and Lower Whitewood districts. Wade Porter and Oscar Clyne, returning to the Hills after having been chased out for a second time by Captain Pollock, found Bryant's trail on Little Spearfish Creek and in December followed it into Deadwood. They in turn were followed by J. J. Williams, W. H. Babcock, Eugene Smith, and others. By New Year's Day, 1876, some fifty miners were at work in Deadwood Gulch, most of them taking out at least $10 a day. One man found a nugget worth $22, and smaller pieces worth from $4 to $6 were common. There was plenty of water, the gold lay close to the surface, and the mines paid well. It was the perfect poor man's diggings.

Deadwood Gulch's value was quickly recognized by the first comers, who promptly moved to assure their rights to most of it. On January 5 it was divided, rim to rim, into forty three-hundred-foot claims, and land not already located was distributed to the miners by lot. By the second week in January every foot of ground in the area was claimed, valuable or not. The Cheyenne *Daily Leader* publicized the new discoveries, and prospectors and suppliers began to pour in as soon as the roads were passable in the spring. Deadwood Gulch, which one immigrant described as "three miles long and fifty feet wide," became a city of cloth. Every man lived in a tent, if he had one, or got a scrap of tenting to cover the brush roof of his wickiup. Merchants displayed thousands of dollars' worth of goods under canvas. In some of the

(ed. by Harry H. Anderson), *South Dakota Historical Collections*, Vol. XXXI (1962), 293–94; McClintock, *Pioneer Days*, 31–41; Rosen, *Pa-Ha-Sa-Pah*, 321.

more elaborate structures "lascivious pictures were profusely displayed," and sounds of unholy revelry might be heard, for mining is rough work and at least some of the prospectors sought the coarsest entertainment. Every other tent was a saloon, its bar an upended barrel, its equipment a dirty glass or two.[4]

Miners, merchants, and entertainers swarmed into Deadwood. Four hundred were in the gulch by February 12, six hundred by March 6. Many consistently washed out five cents to the pan; an industrious miner on Bobtail Gulch took out a steady $5.00 an hour. Heavy spring snows slowed down production, but by June some claims were paying $100 to $2,000 a day. Miners' wages ran from $4.00 to $5.50 for experienced men, but cash jobs were scarce, and living expenses high.

The city of Deadwood, just below the confluence of Deadwood and Whitewood creeks, was laid out on April 26, 1876, by Craven Lee, Isaac Brown, and J. J. Williams. Mr. E. B. Farnum, a merchant, was elected mayor and was often seen seated on a sack of flour or flitch of bacon, dispensing justice and groceries with equal impartiality. Three sawmills produced thirty-two thousand board feet of lumber a day, and the tents quickly gave way to log cabins and false-fronted frame buildings. The General Custer House and the Grand Central Hotel were especially imposing. Mr. J. Vandanicker ran the IXL Restaurant and advertised heavily in the *Black Hills Pioneer*, which began publication on June 8. Soon Deadwood looked like a "heap of lemon boxes propped up on broomsticks," for when the miners came to a house, they kept right on digging, replacing the earth with poles to support the buildings overhead.[5]

Mining became increasingly productive as the weather improved and the best ground opened up. Egan and Company at the forks of Gold Run regularly took out fourteen ounces of gold a day. Claim Number 6 below discovery on Deadwood yielded

[4] Spring, *Cheyenne and Black Hills Stage and Express Routes*, 148; Andreas, *Andreas' Historical Atlas of Dakota*, 110, 122–23; H. N. Maguire, *The Black Hills and American Wonderland* (*The Lakeside Library*, IV, No. 82), 292.

[5] Andreas, *Andreas' Historical Atlas of Dakota*, 122.

$2,300 in a single clean-up; a three-quarter interest later sold for $4,700, after the claim had been worked out. The average placer miner took from $25 to $150 a day, but lucky strikes of $1,500 were common. Gold worth $4,500 was stored in pans around one claim, "like so much old iron," while at another the miners had accumulated three kegs of gold dust and were running out of containers. By mid-June, $500,000 worth of gold awaited shipment to Cheyenne. Claims which had been offered in May at $1,500 readily sold for ten times as much a month later. The Deadwood boom was on.

Although the rich gold strikes received the most publicity, the experiences of tenderfoot Jerry Bryan and prospector John S. McClintock are probably more representative of the luck of the average miner. Bryan and a friend came to Deadwood in the spring of 1876 but could not find jobs until May 12. They then worked fourteen hours a day on a claim in return for half the profits, netting just $5.28 between them. The two men promptly decided to go hungry rather than work so hard for so little. Within a week they were employed on another placer at $4.00 and $5.00 a day, plus one-fourth of the production which they hoped would be worth an additional $8.00. Bryan wrote in his diary "we are liveing high now Tea with Sugar in Slap Jacks and sirup Expect to have Beef soon," which indicates that they had been on a pretty skimpy diet. He and his partner eventually leased a claim of their own, cleaned up a few hundred dollars above expenses, and on August 4 left the Hills for home.[6]

McClintock, on the other hand, was an experienced miner who had been employed on claims Number 17 and Number 18 below discovery in Deadwood Gulch, and thought he knew where the gold lay. When the owners wanted to sink a twenty-by-twenty foot shaft to bedrock as a preliminary to further operations, he took the contract in return for any gold taken out. He cut logs to crib up the shaft, slid them down into the gulch, and commenced digging. Eight feet down he struck an unexpected layer of black sand and gold dust which yielded $60. At twelve feet he

[6] Bryan, *An Illinois Gold Hunter in the Black Hills*, 27–29.

encountered so much water that he had to reduce the shaft to ten-by-twenty in order to keep it pumped out. Reaching bedrock, he panned out another $60, but hoped that the other half of the shaft would be richer. Meanwhile, the owners, anxious to begin their own operations, offered him $200 to abandon the rest of the job; he was happy to take the money. He had cut about one hundred logs and hauled them to the valley, dug out some 270 tons of wet gravel, and run at least some of it through sluices. The whole job was done by hand, in cold, wet weather, under arduous and dangerous conditions, and netted him just $320.[7]

The greatest bonanza of all was the Wheeler Brothers' strike on Claim Number 2 below discovery in Deadwood Gulch. The prudent Wheelers bought the claim for $1,000, having first made sure that there was more gold than that available in plain sight. Once it was opened, they employed from sixteen to thirty men in two shifts and never took out less than $600 a day. They worked the claim for four months, and extracted about $140,000 worth of gold before selling out for $3,000. The new owner took out that much in his first day of operation. The Wheelers hired fifteen heavily armed guards for $200 each, solicited gold shipments from other successful miners, and on September 19 carried nineteen hundred pounds of gold to Cheyenne.[8]

Properties this valuable needed more than the protection of an ordinary mining district. In August, 1876, a miners meeting set up a new provisional government with C. R. Clark, Thomas Short, Henry Feuerstein, Seth Bullock, and J. W. Matkin as city commissioners. Their duties included building a pest house for smallpox victims, supervising a justice of the peace and a city marshal, clearing the streets of obstructions, and acting as fire wardens. This last precaution was essential, for by September two hundred

[7] McClintock, *Pioneer Days*, 99–103.

[8] *Black Hills Pioneer* (Deadwood), September 2, 1876; *Daily Leader* (Cheyenne), September 19, October 26, 1876. Since placer gold varied in purity and in price, from $18 to $21, and even more if cassiterite sand was mixed in with the gold dust, it is not possible to give an accurate value for a given weight of mined gold. The usual estimate for the Wheelers' nineteen hundred pounds is $400,000, but that seems excessive.

frame buildings, dozens of log cabins, and innumerable tents had been crowded into the narrow, windy canyon. Furthermore, though many of the experienced miners left town for a winter vacation, those remaining found seventy-six saloons available in which to disport themselves and were none too careful.

Total gold production in the Hills in 1876 was about $1,500,000. More than seven thousand men came and went during the year, with a peak population of some five thousand, one-half of them around Deadwood. The gold mined would have amounted to a little more than $200 per man if it had been evenly distributed, but it was not. About one-twelfth of the miners were experienced Montana and western prospectors, who customarily ended up working the best claims, either finding them to begin with or buying them from their less perspicacious fellows. Even if he struck it rich, a "pilgrim" usually went home broke, leaving his gold in the hands of suppliers, gamblers, and entertainers generally.[9]

The placer gold rush reached its climax in the spring of 1877. The Indians had been forced to sign away their title to the Hills, and the government had opened the area to settlement. Successful miners returned from winter vacations, bringing with them still more hopeful fortune hunters. Little towns sprouted up wherever there were signs of gold, and the prospectors drifted restlessly from one to the other in hope of a bonanza or employment. Most of the claims had been taken up, and even those prosperous enough to hire labor could not provide jobs for all. Winter cold closed down placer mining in February, and employment remained scarce until April. When the mines seemed likely to reopen, unexpected deep snows in May shut them down again.

The *Engineering and Mining Journal* continually warned the poor man to stay away unless he could borrow enough money to buy a mine, or unless he possessed special skills. There were simply

---

[9] C. L. Fuller, *Pocket Map and Descriptive Outline History Accompanied by a Compendium of Statistics of the Black Hills of Dakota and Wyoming*, 5; Curley, *Guide to the Black Hills*, 80, with the aid of Captain Jack W. Crawford, estimated the population at 5,100 on July 15, 1876.

not enough mines or jobs to go around. The booming population was estimated at 15,250 in May, and was distributed as follows:

Deadwood and Whitewood	5,500
Gayville [Central City]	3,000
Crook City	400
Centennial City	100
Rapid City	250
Bear Butte Gulch	500
Central Hills	2,500
Floating population	3,000.[10]

The summer of 1877 saw a shift from hand-operated placers to hydraulic mining and hard-rock claims. The quieting of Indian title and the establishment of both county and federal courts, as well as the demonstrated value of the mines, made the Hills attractive to investors. As the disappointed pilgrims returned to Yankton or Cheyenne, they generally passed shipments of heavy machinery coming to replace their labor.

It is easy to think of the gold rush as taking place entirely in Deadwood, but that was not the case at all. It was the biggest, richest, and hence the wildest settlement, but there were many others. Central City, up Deadwood Gulch, consisted of Gayville, South Bend, Anchor City, Golden Gate, and Central. In both population and gold production it nearly equaled its more publicized neighbor. The first cabin was built by Alfred Gay in the fall of 1875, and the town grew rapidly thereafter. Mr. L. Parkhurst provided diversification of industry, brewing the famous Gold Nugget Beer that made life in Deadwood happier for all. The town, with a population of about three thousand, was formally organized on January 20, 1877. A Congregational church went up the same year, and the *Black Hills Herald*, edited by J. S. Bartholomew, came in from Custer. By September, Central City had a post office, telegraph office, and the first brick building in the Hills. In a single week fifteen new business buildings were being

[10] *Ibid.*, 130; the names Central City and Gayville were often used as if they were synonymous.

built, including a large hotel, seven or eight stores, as many office buildings, and a new stamp mill.[11]

Crook City, down Whitewood Creek, was the northeastern outpost of the gold rush. Although it was in the foothills and consequently exposed to Indian raids, its inhabitants hoped that gold in the lower reaches of the creek would make up for the dangerous location. It did not, and the town failed, but it put up quite a struggle. The original settlement on the highlands overlooking the valley was too far from the gold deposits and was quickly deserted. Its successor, laid out on March 15, 1876, was first named "Camp Crook" in honor of General Crook, but quickly dignified itself with the name Crook City. Town lots at first were distributed by lottery and eventually sold for as much as $500. Even mining claims, which had less speculative value, did not sell as well. A newspaper, the *Tribune*, edited by H. S. Burke, made a single appearance on June 9, and immediately collapsed. Aside from real estate the main business of the community seems to have been liquor. Indeed, when General Crook's soldiers passed through after their celebrated "Mud March" in the fall of 1876, every other house was a saloon. A correspondent who sampled the whisky said it was more of a menace to the troops than the arrows of the Sioux.

In 1877, Crook City had a population of five hundred and was the temporary county seat of Lawrence County. The town had a sawmill, three hotels, a church, and a public school. Twelve stores did $400,000 worth of business annually. Much of the growth was merely speculative, with houses built more for sale than for occupancy in the hope that Crook City's twin attractions, gold and farm land, would soon provide eager buyers. The anticipated boom did not materialize, for when Captain W. S. Stanton passed through in 1878, he found Crook City only "a small, lifeless village of no importance."[12]

[11] Tallent, *The Black Hills*, 528–35; "Central City," *Sharp Bits*, Vol. XIV (August, 1963); *Daily Leader* (Cheyenne), September 18, 19, 1877.

[12] Tallent, *The Black Hills*, 537–39; Strahorn, *Handbook*, 233; Maguire, *The Black Hills and American Wonderland* (*The Lakeside Library*, IV, No. 88), 304; Captain William S. Stanton, "Explorations and Surveys in the Department of

Sturgis, on Bear Butte Creek at the northeastern edge of the Hills, grew up to profit from a nearby Army camp. To protect the miners, a small post called "Camp Jack Sturgis," in honor of a lieutenant killed at the Little Bighorn, had been established out on the prairie, north of Bear Butte. Soon the post was moved to its present location and renamed "Camp Ruhlen," and later, "Fort Meade." Camp followers saw that a town, protected and supported by the fort, might be a profitable venture. Accordingly, in 1878, Major J. C. Wilcox and others laid out and received title to the town of Sturgis. Those entertainments dear to soldiers were soon established, and the troops came to call the village "Scooptown," from the inhabitants' custom of scooping in all the loose valuables a man might have with him. It was in Sturgis that Poker Alice Tubbs won her fame as a gambler, and later as madame of what was then thought of as a well-run and respectable bordello.[13]

Spearfish, at the northern end of the Hills on the creek of that name, was not built on mining speculations but on farms and sawmills to supply the miners. James Butcher, the first settler, came in during the spring of 1876, built a cabin, stayed a month, and left precipitately when the Indians became troublesome. Shortly afterwards a group of tough Montana men arrived, laid out a town on May 14 and planned a city with streets and avenues from A to Z. They spent $3,000 on an irrigation ditch and several hundred more on a fruitless survey for a direct road to Bismarck. Irrepressible squatters moved in, and the grandiose plans collapsed, for even Montana men could not simultaneously fight both newcomers and Indians.

Hostile raids on Spearfish were a major problem that fall, and a town stockade became the most important community project. Four men built their cabins at the corners of a square block to

---

the Platte," *Annual Report of the Secretary of War for the Year 1878*, Vol. II, Part III, p. 1712.

[13] Andreas, *Andreas' Historical Atlas of Dakota*, 127; *Daily Leader* (Cheyenne), August 15, November 8, 1878; Case, *Lee's Official Guidebook to the Black Hills and Badlands*, 96.

provide bastions and ready storage for arms and provisions. The space between the cabins was fenced with a twelve-foot log palisade, providing ample space for both settlers and livestock. The town soon acquired the usual business establishments, but probably had fewer places of entertainment than most frontier towns. On the Fourth of July, 1878, Judge W. W. Bradley provided it with a nickname:

> We throw open wide the gates of the city and bid you welcome to the land of the wild rose and the home of the golden grain. ...We bid you welcome, yea a hundred times welcome, to Spearfish, "the Queen City of the Hills."

The name stuck, and ever since Spearfish has been noted for its propriety and rectitude.[14]

A far different sort of community sprang up on the northwestern slope of the mountains, near present-day Tinton. The gulches of Iron, Little Spearfish, Potato, Bear, Beaver, and Sand creeks, all draining from the sides of Negro Hill, were rich and easy diggings. Severe winters and lack of water, however, kept the area from booming as fast as Deadwood. Moreover, the gold was scattered over several gulches and did not provide a single focal point about which a rush could center.

As early as November, 1875, prospectors on Negro Hill were washing out five cents to $2.00 to the pan. In December, Frank G. Oliver carried $1,000 worth of dust to Cheyenne from the newly formed Buckeye Mining District. After Christmas, cold weather froze the streams and cut off water to the placers, but up to that time miners had rocked out from $12 to $20 per man. Potato Gulch especially attracted tenderfeet; it sounded as if digging gold there was as easy as digging up potatoes. The name, however, came not from the size of the nuggets but from the experience of four impoverished miners who had made a meal there on one potato. Nuggets in the gulch did run bigger than anywhere

[14] Rosen, *Pa-Ha-Sa-Pah*, 442–46; Tallent, *The Black Hills*, 540–65; Hughes, *Pioneer Years*, 207. A teachers' college and the Black Hills Passion Play are continuing evidence of the virtue of the town.

else in the Hills, but even the largest, which weighed between seven and eight ounces, would have been a pretty small potato.

Negro Gulch was named for half-a-dozen colored miners who prospered mightily therein. Four of them took out $1,700 in a single day, even though they had to haul their gravel several hundred yards to wash it. Another colored group built a small dam to accumulate water for sluicing and washed out $1,500 in half a day. On nearby Beaver Creek water was equally scarce, and efforts to build ditches to bring it to the placers failed when beavers dammed up the waterways. To bring more water to the Iron Creek diggings a tremendous flume, high on the walls of Little Spearfish Canyon, was built at enormous cost. A miscalculation brought it to the crucial hill it had to pass five feet too low, and the project was abandoned.

By the end of May, 1877, there were six miles of placer claims on Sand, Iron, and Potato creeks, and 1,500 miners hard at work on them. Two towns, Forest City and Bernardsville, sprang up to provide local provisioning and entertainment. The gold deposits were shallow, however, and the boom proved evanescent. The local election of 1878 found only 108 voters.[15]

Upper Rapid and Castle creeks also prospered, though the rest of the central Hills did not. Professor Jenney's Camp Tuttle was on Castle Creek near the Wyoming border, and it was here on June 23, 1875, that William Corslett found a few promising "colors." Jenney noted that there was inadequate water, and that the valley did not slope enough to wash away the tailings. He predicted that the deposits would be worthless. The more optimistic miners with him, forced to depart with General Crook, "laid over" their claims until the following spring. In May, 1876, thirty of them returned, dug a two-hundred foot drainage ditch, and with the aid of hand pumps got down to the bedrock. Here they washed out sixty-five cents to the pan, but found the rock full of holes and irregularities which trapped and concealed the gold. These three problems continued to plague the Castle Creek pros-

[15] Negro Hill was so spelled in the contemporary *Black Hills Pioneer*, which is full of references to the area, as are the *Daily Leader* (Cheyenne), *Black Hills*

pectors: an insufficient supply of water, no way to drain it off, and the gold too hard to find at the bottom.

Castleton, two miles up Castle Creek from present-day Mystic, was laid out in July, 1876. The gold here was a rich orange color and the purest in the Hills, but it lay on bedrock twenty-seven feet down. Miners dug a drainage ditch twenty feet deep and nineteen hundred feet long to carry away the water, but the valley was not steep enough to carry away the tailings and the project failed. Two steam pumps, one capable of discharging two thousand gallons a minute, were brought in but could not pump out the water. In September the town had a population of two hundred, most of whom were experienced miners who supported themselves on the side by farming and ranching. By April, 1877, Castleton had several stores, a new hotel, numerous saloons, and fifty cabins. The gold, however, could not be mined at a profit, and the town was gradually abandoned. It revived again as a railroad center in the 1880's, and once more in 1915 when attempts were made to dredge out the placers, but today it is completely deserted.

Mound, or Mountain, City was eight or nine miles up Castle Creek from Castleton. A few prospectors came to it early in the rush, but it did not boom until the spring of 1877 when miners found that the high placers along the rimrock would yield ten cents to the pan. The Mountain City and Gold Creek Mining districts were established but did not live long. The town itself is now beneath Deerfield Lake.

Mystic, originally called Sitting Bull, had a history similar to Castleton: a struggle with water, ditches, pumps, and failure. Farther downstream where Castle joined Rapid Creek, Prospect Camp boomed in 1876, but could not get down to bedrock. Canyon City, a few miles below, was in the same predicament. The problem was finally solved by the Volin Tunnel. Driven through a "gooseneck" of land in a bend of Rapid Creek, the

Herald (Central City), and *Black Hills Weekly Times* (Deadwood). The story of Potato Gulch's name is in McClintock, *Pioneer Days*, 81. Maguire, *The Black Hills and American Wonderland* (*The Lakeside Library*, IV, No. 88), 303, mentions the big nugget, about three and one-half inches long, and quite flat.

tunnel drained the water from a sizable loop of the stream bed and allowed the miners to reach the gold.[16]

Deadwood, the largest and best-known city in the Hills, was the gathering spot for all the disappointed but still optimistic pilgrims. Having come so far and seen so much wealth without getting any of it, these hopefuls were eager to participate in any new rush that came along. The town's seasoned prospectors, too, were accustomed to following up every rumor; each experienced party habitually sent a member to stake out claims in every new gold strike. It is not surprising, then, to find that Deadwood was the point of departure for innumerable stampedes, most of them completely fruitless, and several of them promoted by unscrupulous merchants with mining equipment to sell.

The most important of these minor rushes was the Big Horn stampede. It began in 1876 and was still going strong in 1879 as prospectors continued to look for "Wetmore's lost cabin" and other equally legendary treasures. Montana miners, who perhaps had heard the stories more often, were peculiarly prone to take off for the Big Horns, but their enthusiasm generally proved contagious.

Several parties left for the Big Horns during the summer of 1876. Captain Wilburn with ninety-four men prospected thoroughly on the Powder River and found nothing. Captain Watt, from Rapid Creek, led forty-five more prospectors westward, but his group broke up when it met Indian war parties. It was a poor time to be out on the Wyoming plains, for the Indians were on the warpath and indeed had just finished massacring Custer and his Seventh Cavalry on the Little Bighorn. Many of the Big Horn stampeders were never heard of again, and those who returned had hard words to say about the promoters of the harebrained scheme.

The summer of 1877 found the Indians more peaceful and the

[16] *Daily Press and Dakotaian* (Yankton), June 23, 1875; John F. Finerty, *War-Path and Bivouac: The Big Horn and Yellowstone Expedition*, 327; *Daily Leader* (Cheyenne), October 12, 1876, April 12, May 20, 1877; *Black Hills Pioneer* (Deadwood), February 10, 1877; *Black Hills Miner* (Rockerville), March 9, 1879.

prospectors undaunted. Old prospector Charlie Lyons showed Herman Bischoff, a Deadwood merchant, a sack of dust claiming it had come from the promised bonanza. Bischoff at once resolved to seek his fortune and nailed up a sign on his store saying: "Fifty passengers wanted for the Big Horn Mountains." His party was no more successful than any other. Jack Langrishe, the actor-journalist, summed it all up in the *Black Hills Pioneer*:

> *This is the man of whom we read,*
> *Who left Deadwood on the big stampede;*
> *Now he's returned, all tattered and torn,*
> *From looking for gold on the Big Horn.*

Nevertheless, greenhorns continued to go west whenever a new rumor or a new guide promised them a rich reward.[17]

The rush to False Bottom Creek, a mile or so northwest of Central City, was just as groundless as that to the Big Horns, but a good deal less trouble for all concerned. The creek had been thoroughly prospected down to bedrock and found nearly worthless. Two young fellows in search of entertainment salted one of the deeper prospect holes, then spread the rumor that the supposed bedrock was actually a "false bottom," and that rich deposits lay beneath it. The rush began on June 18, 1876. In a few hours six hundred men were at work on half as many claims, extending from the headwaters clear down to the prairie. The creek again proved worthless, but the miners accepted their disappointment philosophically. Most had joined the stampede, not in the hope of real gain, but from the fear of being left out if there was something to it.[18]

The Polo Creek rush was much the same. Ingenious pranksters told their Deadwood friends "in strictest confidence" that there

---

[17] McClintock, *Pioneer Days*, 190; *Black Hills Pioneer* (Deadwood), September 2, 1876, June 23, 1877; Kuykendall, *Frontier Days*, 183; Herman Bischoff, "Deadwood to the Big Horns, 1877" (trans. by Edna LaMoore Waldo), typescript, Jennewein Western Collection, Dakota Wesleyan University, Mitchell, South Dakota; Tallent, *The Black Hills*, 373–75, quotes Langrishe's poem, in which the accents in "Deadwood" and "Big Horn" have been shifted from the first to the last syllables for the sake of the meter.

[18] *Daily Leader* (Cheyenne), July 29, 1876; Hughes, *Pioneer Years*, 127–28.

was a gold strike on nearby Polo Creek, and urged them to join in without telling anyone else. Of course no one kept the secret; the next day the gulch was alive with miners staking out claims, digging holes, and panning the gravel. Nobody found anything, except for one gullible greenhorn whose friends salted his pan by dropping in a few grains of gold. Instead of sharing his discovery, he tried to buy out his partners and soon offered exorbitant prices for their shares in the claim. It was not until he had made at utter ass of himself by his cupidity that the jokers enlightened him about the source of his "discovery."[19]

The Wolf Mountain stampede in the fall of 1876 was a crueler hoax. Red Clark, the owner of a Deadwood livery stable, found himself with several horses on hand whose keep would be a burden to him during the winter. Clark paid a Swede $50 to spread rumors of a new strike. Other agents, apparently loaded down with gold dust, secretly bought provisions and whispered to each other with pretended concern lest others overhear. No one knew where the Wolf Mountains were—they were simply a vague appendage of the Big Horns—but neither ignorance nor winter could stifle the stampeders' folly. Merchants and miners sold out cheap to get to the mountains ahead of the rush. Some $60,000 worth of mining equipment was sold to the victims of this miserable fraud as miners dashed off on a wild goose chase into the winter snows. For months disillusioned prospectors staggered into frontier towns, frostbitten, exhausted, and impoverished. As was said at the time, "No form of lunacy equals the d——d fool craziness of a crazy prospector!"[20]

Much later and much happier was the Rockerville Hill rush near Rapid City. Some local wiseacres salted a gypsum bed with gold dust. Bart Henderson, a grizzled miner with a sense of humor of his own, saw what was going on and added some large nuggets. The jokers spread the word, and the townsmen rushed to the new "discovery." When Henderson's nuggets were found, even the

[19] *Ibid.*, 129–32.
[20] *Ibid.*, 133–34; McClintock, *Pioneer Days*, 149–57; *Daily Leader* (Cheyenne), November 11, December 12, 16, 17, 1876.

pranksters joined in the scramble to get rich quick. The joke was quickly discovered, and one disappointed wag staked out a claim on a large pine tree and posted this notice: "I hearby claim 300 feet up this tree for climbing purposes. . . . also claim all knobs, limbs, woodpecker holes, etc., for working purposes."[21]

These stampedes demonstrate three points worth noting. First, most of the richer mines that could be worked by the ordinary prospector were discovered and taken up early, leaving most of the rushers at loose ends. Second, they show that although fun was common, fraud and chicanery were also frequent. Lastly, they show that even the experienced miners were incurably gullible and optimistic and the tenderfeet even more so. Even so, a good many of the stampedes did pay. As an old-timer said, "The d——n fools will dig for gold where an old miner would not expect any, and nine times out of ten would strike it rich."[22]

The northern mining boom and the excitement created by the stampedes encouraged both men and money to come to the Hills. First came the prospector and the pilgrim, then the merchant and the entertainer. The speculator and investor quickly followed, bringing with them the heavy equipment needed to work the deep placers and hard-rock lodes. Transporting these men and materials to the Hills was an aspect of the rush that was less dramatic but perhaps as profitable as mining the gold itself.

[21] Tallent, *The Black Hills*, 445–47.
[22] Entry for June 8, 1878, University of South Dakota, W.P.A. Writer's Project, "Annals of Early Rapid City—Mining," typescript, Rapid City, South Dakota, Public Library.

7

THE ROAD TO THE MINES

Who fells the teamster bold and staunch,
With a brace of shoe prints on his paunch?
Who views the corpse with tearful eye,
And heaves a deep, regretful sigh?
The Black Hills canary![1]

This is the story of the trails that led to the Hills, and of the pilgrims, wagon trains, and coaches which passed over them. The trails were hard and hazardous, but bold hearts and eager hands combined to make them passable, for wherever there was a man brave enough to head for the mines, there was generally another who sought to profit from carrying him thither.

It was both easy and cheap for a miner to come to the Hills. The Northern Pacific Railway would carry him first class from Chicago to Bismarck and pay his stage fare to Deadwood for a total of $49.25. The Union Pacific, using Cheyenne as a point of departure, charged the same price, and $10 less if the passenger got off the stage at Custer City. The less affluent could go third class for $28—that consisted of a trip on the emigrant cars, followed by a walk behind a wagon train headed for the Hills. By the spring of 1876 the railroads were doing a rushing business. One pilgrim reported that his train picked up new passengers at every

[1] *Daily Leader* (Cheyenne), August 24, 1877.

station, until five cars were jammed with prospective miners.[2]

It was also easy to come by river boat, generally to Fort Pierre on the Missouri and from there to the Hills on foot or by stage. The steamer *Big Horn* made the Yankton-Fort Pierre trip every week carrying one hundred tons of freight, eight staterooms full of women, and as many miners as could crowd aboard. Another boat, the *Black Hills*, also made a weekly trip, and in 1877 it carried over four million pounds of goods and passengers from Yankton up the river to Fort Pierre.[3]

Once the average pilgrim arrived at the end of public transportation, he continued to the mines on foot. Stage lines were nonexistent early in the rush, and expensive once established. Most prospectors preferred to save their money for the mines. For a few dollars they could throw equipment and supplies onto a passing wagon and accompany experienced freighters to the Hills. Anyone could keep up with the slow-moving oxen, and the rough but experienced company gave protection against the Indians. Nevertheless, a teamster's companionship was a rather mixed blessing. One apprehensive tenderfoot wrote in his diary that he was "on the Road Among horse thieves, Gamblers, & a few honest men. The further I go the more I am impressed I will never live to see my familey in this world again."[4]

Some hardy souls made the trip alone. One prospector named Ford walked all the way from Deadwood to Cheyenne carrying his worldly possessions—ninety cents' worth of soda crackers—on his back. It took him fifteen days, and he arrived in a starving condition. Another loner, blacksmith Ben Fiddler, built a hand-operated tricycle in the Hills and pumped all the way home to Iowa. Men like these were a minority for most preferred company along the way.[5]

---

[2] Curley, *Guide to the Black Hills*, 14; Bryan, *An Illinois Gold Hunter in the Black Hills*, 12–13.

[3] Ralph E. Nichol, "Steamboat Navigation on the Missouri River with Special Reference to Yankton and Vicinity," *South Dakota Historical Collections*, Vol. XXVI (1952), 214.

[4] Spring, *Cheyenne and Black Hills Stage and Express Routes*, 201–202.

[5] *Daily Leader* (Cheyenne), August 27, 1876; McClintock, *Pioneer Days*, 196.

A traveler could run into considerable trouble on the trail. Fuel such as buffalo chips not only was scarce but it stank. Firewood was scarcer, even in settled land. When one group tried to gather some brush from a roadside fence row, "the Ranch man request us very forcibly to By —— leave that fence alone." Most of the pilgrims needed fuel, too, for they traveled in the spring and found the weather wet, cold, and windy. Jerry Bryan wrote in his diary on March 28, 1876: "Our tent was blown down, dishes, Hats, Blankets, and everything that was loose was Scattered. Our blankets was filled with the driving Snow. We sleped with our boots on or they would have been gone." In weather like that it paid to have friends at hand.[6]

The traveler could cross the North Platte on Clarke's bridge north of Sidney, or by the government bridge at Fort Laramie, but there were still deep rivers ahead. The thoughtful teamster generally followed the trails of buffalo and Indians which led to low banks and shallow fords. Even with old roads to guide them, the prudent were careful, knowing that once a wagon sank into the mud, it might stay there permanently. Usually the drivers hitched double teams to the wagons while crossing a river, not so much to give extra power but to make sure that some of the oxen could find a firm footing and keep the wagon rolling. Mud was a problem even on the trail, for the tenacious gumbo of the badlands around the Hills stuck to a man's boots until he left footprints as large as an elephant's. It also got between the spokes of the wheels, rubbed against the sides of the wagon like a brake, and forced the teamsters to stop and clear the wheels every few hundred yards. Experienced drivers carried a long, stout rope and a pulley. Taken ahead to a tree, then looped back through the pulley to a stalled wagon, the rope could double the pull of the team to get the outfit out of the mud and moving again.

At the mouth of Red Canyon, which led from the Cheyenne River northward toward Custer, a poet left the following notice: *"Look to your rifles well./ For this is the canyon of hell!"* At least one guide book advised that scouting parties of four or five well-

[6] Bryan, *An Illinois Gold Hunter in the Black Hills*, 13–15.

armed men ought to patrol each rim of this canyon while the wagons passed along the valley floor. It must have been arduous work for the canyon is several hundred feet deep, and its steep walls are frequently cut by intersecting gulches. When Robert Florman passed through with his wife in late April, 1876, the mounted men of his party had to be restrained at pistol-point from deserting the wagons when they came upon the bodies of several murdered travelers.[7]

Even when he reached the edge of Deadwood Gulch, the traveler's troubles were not over. Here he faced a precipitous declivity down which the wagons must somehow be lowered. Some left their equipment and carried their provisions into the valley on their backs. Others joined the teamsters and skidded the wagons, the wheels tightly secured with chain "rough locks," down the steep slope. Ropes, wrapped around nearby trees, helped brake the descent, while a single team of oxen or horses guided the wagon along the trail. In time the teamsters discovered a less difficult and dangerous route, but the early comers found the path a rough one.[8]

The pilgrim only made the trip once, but the professional freighter made it regularly every thirty or forty days. Generally, he used a heavy wagon drawn by oxen, "bull teams" as they were called, whose slow, steady heaving could move a heavy load. Turned out to pasture on the trail, oxen were ready to go again by daylight when the night herder brought them back to camp. Well trained, they responded to the teamster's call and put their necks beneath the hundred-pound yoke balanced on his shoulder. When tenderfeet yoked the oxen wrong side to, they found their teams totally unmanageable, for the dull-witted brutes would not tolerate even the slightest departure from accustomed routine.

The usual load for a five- or six-yoke team of oxen was between three and four tons, depending on the size and condition of the animals and the state of the road. The wheelers, nearest the wagon, were hitched up first, then the leaders at the head of the team, with pointers and wings later yoked in between. The team-

---

[7] Curley, *Guide to the Black Hills*, 44, 47; Tallent, *The Black Hills*, 165.
[8] Stokes and Driggs, *Deadwood Gold*, 58.

ster, who got from $50 to $75 a month, bread, bacon, and coffee, walked beside his charges armed with a twenty-foot whip attached to a four-foot handle. A broad "popper" at the end of the whip prevented cuts on the animals and made a pistol-like noise which encouraged them even more than actual blows.[9]

The teamster's voice was generally raucous and forceful, as he used a limited but pungent vocabulary. Even these oratorical powers were taxed to the utmost as teams churned across rivers and mud flats or slipped and struggled on the icy streets in Deadwood. Once a Methodist preacher, James Williams, came upon freighter Fred T. Evans in full and glorious eruption, and urged him to be more moderate in his language. Evans replied that getting a bull team to Deadwood was a good bit more difficult than hauling a soul to heaven, and that if Williams would "drive one yoke of oxen one day without cussin' " he would give him $1,000. That, said Evans, was "a straight proposition," and Williams "could either shoot or put up his gun." The preacher did not accept the challenge.[10]

There was some discussion as to whether oxen or mules required the greater objurgatory powers. Oxen were maddening, but mules were downright malevolent, and the "Black Hills canary" seemed to take delight in not only delaying, but maiming his driver. In general, most of the heavy loads were pulled by oxen, but a prime span of mules could haul four thousand pounds of freight at considerable speed as long as they got proper rest and feeding. Mules, though, were expensive. They also tended to get a crippling "mud fever" when the gumbo caked along their bellies and prevented sweating.

Three main shipping points collected freight bound for the Hills. Fort Pierre,[11] on the Missouri, concentrated cargoes from Sioux City, Yankton, and Bismarck and sent them westward in

[9] Brown and Willard, *The Black Hills Trails*, 64–68; Aken, *Pioneers of the Black Hills*, 12.

[10] *Black Hills Pioneer* (Deadwood), January 6, 1877; Estelline Bennett, *Old Deadwood Days*, 100–101.

[11] Both Fort Pierre and Pierre, the capital of South Dakota, are pronounced "Peer" by the natives.

wagons. Sidney, Nebraska, on the Union Pacific, at first shipped freight north through Buffalo Gap to Custer, but traffic soon shifted to a trail east of the Hills which led directly to Rapid City. Cheyenne, Wyoming, shipped via Fort Laramie, thence to the Cheyenne River and up Red Canyon to Custer. This route eventually was abandoned for a safer and easier one leading up the western side of the Hills along Stockade Beaver Creek.

Fred T. Evans, whose oratorical powers have already been mentioned, made the first attempt to haul freight to the new mines. He started out from Sioux City by the sandhills route along the Niobrara on April 26, 1875, but United States troops captured and burned his entire wagon train. Persevering, he united with John Hornick, John H. Clark, and Judge Hubbard to form the Sioux City and Black Hills Transportation Company. They shipped freight by steamer up the river to Yankton, and later to Fort Pierre, where it was forwarded to the Hills by ox team. At its peak the Evans Company employed 1,000 to 1,500 men, 1,500 oxen, 250 mules, and 400 wagons. It continued hauling until 1888 when the railroad to Rapid City put it out of business.

N. L. Witcher and his sons, also of Sioux City, tried to start a freight line to Custer early in 1875, but they, too, were delayed by Army interference. They soon resumed business, and by February, 1877, had made fourteen trips to the Hills via Yankton and Fort Pierre. Witcher used oxen exclusively, but he drove them hard and earned the nickname "the lightning bull freighter" for the speed at which he moved his cargoes.

At Fort Pierre the Sioux City interests soon met with competition from a Minnesota concern, the Northwestern Express, Stage, and Transportation Company. At its peak the Northwestern employed twenty-four "Concord" coaches—ten a week between Pierre and Deadwood—and carried some 5,000 passengers a year. They also hauled sixteen million pounds of freight, employed 500 men, and used 600 mules and 1,600 oxen. Like the Evans Company, the Northwestern Express withdrew from the freighting business when the railroad reached the Hills.[12]

[12] Rosen, *Pa-Ha-Sa-Pah*, 417–18; Eriksson, "Sioux City and the Black Hills Gold

Sidney, too, made shipping a big business. Its leading transportation companies included D. T. McCann, J. M. Woods, Bramble & Miner, and Jewett and Dickinson. These larger concerns competed with numerous "shotgun" freighters who made a trip whenever they could get a load. It is hard to assess the role of the small, independent freighters, but it seems likely that they hauled only a minor part of the total freight brought into the Hills.[13]

Cheyenne did not lag behind the other frontier towns. The enterprising firm of Whipple & Hay advertised on December 9, 1875, that they were about to leave for the diggings and would carry freight to "Custar's Park" for five cents a pound and "passengers" for $10. The goods were doubtless carried in the wagons, but it is pretty certain that the passengers walked alongside. After Christmas the same year the Hicklin Brothers and H. H. Harold left for the Hills with six wagons. A short time later W. A. Dearie and Henry Baltz made the trip to the Spring Creek placers in twelve days and returned to Cheyenne in ten, but they reported that the trip was unduly prolonged in order to save the horses' strength for future journeys. Gilmer, Patrick, and Salisbury, the great stage-line company, were also in the freighting business, and on June 28 they equaled Dearie and Baltz's time to the Hills, hauling in twelve wagonloads of fast freight with forty-eight nimble mules. They, too, excused their time, explaining that they had had to "lay over" some fifty hours at Hat Creek and in Custer.[14]

By 1878, Cheyenne alone had twenty major firms engaged in

Rush, 1874–1877," *Iowa Journal of History and Politics*, Vol. XX (July, 1922), 342–44. The Concord coach was named for the place in which it was made, Concord, New Hampshire.

[13] Mahnken, "The Sidney-Black Hills Trail," *Nebraska History*, Vol. XXX (September, 1949), 203–25, is invaluable regarding Sidney's part in developing the Hills.

[14] *Daily Leader* (Cheyenne), December 9, 27, 1875, January 8, 1876; Spring, *Cheyenne and Black Hills Stage and Express Routes*, 151. Custer was often spelled "Custar," from the notion that George A. Custer's name had been derived from German and had been so spelled.

freighting, with some four hundred wagons capable of carrying 2,000,000 pounds of goods and supplies at a time. Shipments totaling 500,000 pounds were common. Freight rates varied between three and five cents a pound, the higher price applying to fast freight sent via horse or mule-drawn wagons.

Sidney, too, made major shipments, moving between 22,000,000 and 25,000,000 pounds of freight to the Hills in 1878 and 1879. Pratt and Ferris several times contracted to bring in entire eighty-stamp mills for the Homestake Mine at Lead. Such equipment weighed about 400,000 pounds and could be delivered at a cost of $33,000. Once the mines were supplied, the freight business fell off a little only to boom again in the fall of 1879 when the great Deadwood Fire created a renewed demand.[15]

The most widely known shipment to the Hills was Phatty Thomas's famous load of cats. Thomas purchased these in Cheyenne for twenty-five cents each, and loaded them on his wagon in crates. On Spring Creek, near Sheridan, the wagon tipped over, but friendly prospectors helped him recapture most of the cargo. According to one story, he sold the cats by the pound to Deadwood merchants. Others maintain that he disposed of them to the gay ladies of the town at prices depending on the quality of the cat.[16]

Then there is the story, old but good, of the sidewalk loafer who watched a teamster unload twenty barrels of whisky and a sack of flour in front of a Deadwood store. Shaking his head in disbelief, he turned to his companion and inquired, "What in H—— do you suppose they want with all that flour?"[17]

A bull team could follow any trail as long as there was grass and water, but a stage line was a different matter. It needed relay stations for the animals, houses for the employees, and eating

[15] Robert E. Strahorn, *To the Rockies and Beyond*, 17; Mahnken, "The Sidney-Black Hills Trail," *Nebraska History*, Vol. XXX (September, 1949), 224; *Daily Leader* (Cheyenne), April 11, 1877, July 20, 1878.

[16] The story is traditional. My friend Don Parman has suggested that the name "cat house" for a house of prostitution may have arisen from the incident.

[17] Spring, *Cheyenne and Black Hills Stage and Express Routes*, 177. The story, of course, is not original with the Black Hills.

facilities for the passengers, as well as good roads over which the stages could maintain a reasonable speed.

The Gilmer, Salisbury and Patrick stages from Cheyenne at first followed the trail from what is now Edgemont northward to Red Canyon Station, or Camp Collier. It then passed through the Canyon to Spring-on-the-Hill, and continued north to Spring-on-the-Right, Pleasant Valley, and Custer. The route, however, was abandoned in June, 1877, when a new trail leading directly to Deadwood via the Jenney Stockade opened the western edge of the Hills.[18]

From Custer the stage continued north to Hill City, Sheridan, and Camp Crook, and thence across the headwaters of Box Elder, Elk, and Bear Butte creeks to Deadwood. Later the route led northwesterly to Twelve-Mile Station, Gillette's Ranch, Mountain City (Deerfield), then to Reynold's Ranch, Bull Dog Ranch, and thence to the head of Whitewood Creek and on down to Deadwood.

Another feature of trails in the Black Hills was the toll road. These were generally located in valleys where a little work on the road and a considerable amount of enterprise could provide the only usable trail. A toll road was set up in much the same way as a mining district, that is, by means of a miners' gathering at which the participants generally sold out their interests to the promoter of the road. The trail was blazed, a few of the more troublesome stumps uprooted, and the proprietors then sat back to collect tolls from the travelers.

The toll road from Deadwood to Centennial, one of the better ones, was laid out by W. L. Kuykendall, E. B. Farnum, M. V. Boughton, and (Frank?) Towle at a cost of $7,500. The toll for a team and wagon was $1.00 for the round trip, and additional teams twenty-five cents each. Horsemen, who could take to the hills and bypass the toll collectors, passed free. Between Dead-

[18] *Ibid.*, 177, and Hyman Palais, "A Study of the Trails to the Black Hills Gold Fields," *South Dakota Historical Collections*, Vol. XXV (1951), 215–62, are detailed and illustrated with lucid maps. The ruts of the trail can still be followed from Camp Collier to Pleasant Valley, even though the route was abandoned over eighty years ago.

wood and Gayville other toll-road proprietors found themselves continually having to rebuild the road as prospectors in the gulch kept undermining the right of way.[19]

The traveler who came by stage got to the Hills faster, but hardly more comfortably, than the man who walked. The "Concord" coach was an elegant vehicle, but unsteady. Suspended by its rounded bottom on leather straps which allowed it to rock, it caused severe motion sickness among the inexperienced. The diet at the stage stations did little to alleviate an upset stomach, for at least in the early days it consisted of little more than bread dipped in bacon grease. Later, however, the Bismarck stages carried an ice chest for perishable foods and a refrigerated can of milk for children.

No matter what conveniences were introduced, stage stations were neither elevating nor refreshing. Most consisted of a single room, part store, part hotel, with a long bar for thirsty travelers and the idle of the surrounding community. One woman, traveling alone, complained that the loungers and loafers all "looked me over as they would the remains at a well-conducted funeral." So pointed became their attentions that the driver was compelled to arrange for a man to guard his fair passenger whenever she got off the stage. There is no question but that the stage companies did their best to provide a comfortable trip, palatable food, and pleasant surroundings. Sometimes, however, the difficulties were insurmountable.[20]

It was a fool's errand to haul goods to the Hills by stage and pay the long rate for transporting them. Money could buy an outfit in the Hills nearly as cheaply as on the prairie, and thus the stage passenger generally traveled light. He carried, if prosperous, a hand-satchel full of money and, if prudent, a revolver and rifle to protect his belongings. The weapons not only afforded a meas-

---

[19] Maguire, *The Black Hills and American Wonderland* (*The Lakeside Library*, IV, No. 82), 292; *Black Hills Pioneer* (Deadwood), August 5, September 23, 1876; *Daily Leader* (Cheyenne) November 30, 1876.

[20] Matilda H. White Starbuck, "My Trip to the Black Hills," MS, circa 1924, South Dakota Historical Society, Pierre; "The Medora-Deadwood Stage Route," *South Dakota Historical Collections*, Vol. XXV (1951), 383.

ure of security but also were a universal means of entertainment—
so much so that rules for passengers urged that they not shoot
from the coach windows, for the noise bothered the ladies and
tended to stampede the teams.[21]

The trip to the mines in the luxury of a coach was fairly expensive. The thirty-six hour and 211 mile trip from Bismarck
to Deadwood cost $23. Fort Pierre lines, which started 190 miles
from the Hills, charged $20, but of course the passenger had to
reach that forsaken way station on his own. From Cheyenne, the
journey took two days, and cost $30, but for many it was the pre-
ferred route, since it followed the telegraph line and was protected by the troops from both Fort Laramie and the Red Cloud
Agency. Although weather delayed the coaches, it often made
the troops superfluous by protecting them from the hostiles. As
one snow-draped traveler remarked: "Any Injun who would
venture out on such a day [is] a sight bigger fool than most of his
race."[22]

Stage driving was no sinecure. The long hours on the "box"
were cold and lonely, and accommodations meager along the
way. Worn-out horses, exhausted and underfed, often could not
keep the stages rolling fast enough to suit the tastes of the ebullient
jehu. Driver Tom Cooper, for example, complained that his weary
team was constantly overtaken by bull teams, mud turtles, and
men in wheel chairs, and told his employers that if fresh horses
were not provided, he was going to quit, for he "did not care to
drive when a lantern has to be hung on the back of the coach at
night to prevent collisions with all sorts of vehicles."[23]

One driver, who earlier had striven manfully to overcome his
boredom in the barroom of a stage station, fell off the box and so
startled the horses that they ran away. The coach went bounding

[21] A list of advice for stage travelers from the *Herald* (Omaha), October 3,
1877, is reprinted in "Four Wheels, Six Horses, and a Prayer," *Huber News*
(Spring, 1963), 23.
[22] Richardson, "A Trip to the Black Hills," *Scribners*, Vol. XIII (April, 1877),
752.
[23] Kuykendall, *Frontier Days*, 227; stage drivers were called "jehus" after
"Jehu, the son of Nimshi; for he driveth furiously," II Kings 9:20.

and careering wildly for several miles before the team came to a stop and the passengers were able to gain control of the vehicle. The driver later claimed that an agile horse had kicked him on the head and rendered him unconscious, but hardly anyone believed him, and he was summarily discharged.[24]

In general, the stage company did everything it could—from discharging drunken employees to protecting nervous females—to make the trip to the mines pleasant and convenient. There is no record, says McClintock, of loss of life or a serious accident due to any carelessness or oversight. It is difficult to see how single-room stage stations could have been more commodious, or, in the absence of refrigeration, offered more appetizing fare. Whatever the shortcomings, the stage-line employees invariably did their best. One chivalrous driver warmed a baby's milk bottle on his breast when no other means were available. Another, carrying a sick passenger, reached the Missouri River and found the ferry frozen in. Since the ice was not thick enough to support the stage, the driver procured a sled and hauled his grateful patient by hand over to Fort Pierre. A stage trip was rarely a pleasant adventure, but at least the company employees improvised to the best of their abilities.[25]

Like the freighters, the stage lines first began at Sioux City, when on March 10, 1875, James A. Sawyers' Black Hills Transportation Company raised $10,000 to buy horses and equipment. This was quickly followed by Fred Evans' Sioux City and Black Hills Company which, like his freight line, began operations in April but did not do much business until the summer.

The Dakota Central Stage Line commenced business under the management of General C. T. Campbell on January 20, 1876. It soon merged with John B. Dillon's Yankton and Black Hills Stage Company. E. H. Saltiel, also in Yankton, whose guide book doubtless encouraged many to seek the mines, acted as an agent for several boat, rail, and stage lines. John G. Edgar's Missouri River

<hr />

24 Kuykendall, *Frontier Days*, 225–26.

25 McClintock, *Pioneer Days*, 208; Strahorn, *To the Rockies and Beyond*, 17–18, is quite lyrical about the supposed pleasures of the Cheyenne-Deadwood trip.

Stage and Express Line carried travelers on double-deck stages which accommodated from eighteen to twenty passengers. At first it connected with Dillon's coaches at Fort Pierre, but later took pilgrims and fifty pounds of baggage all the way to the Hills for $25.[26]

On the Missouri at Fort Pierre the Yankton stage lines met two serious obstacles: the Northwestern Express and Stage Company and the Indians. General Campbell's efforts collapsed under Indian attack, but the adroit Dillon managed to stave off failure for a few months by making a private treaty with sixteen Sioux chiefs who graciously allowed his six- and eight-passenger spring wagons to proceed across their territory. He, too, eventually failed, and the Northwestern reigned supreme along the route from the river to the Hills.[27]

Sidney likewise joined in the rush to carry miners to the Hills. On April 14, 1875, George W. Homan, Jr., said that he would establish a stage line if local businessmen would build the stations along the route, a proposition to which they happily assented. Homan, however, was overshadowed when the new Marsh and Stephenson firm began triweekly runs in September, 1876, and completely outclassed when it instituted daily service in March, 1877. Clarke's Centennial Express was also active, but devoted itself mainly to carrying the mails and freight. The most important of all was the firm of Gilmer, Salisbury, and Patrick, which got a toehold in Sidney by buying out a sickly outfit called the Western Stage Line.[28]

No matter how the other frontier towns prospered, Cheyenne was fixed in the public mind as the main point of departure for the Hills. Frank Yates and H. E. Brown began signing on passen-

[26] Eriksson, "Sioux City and the Black Hills Gold Rush, 1874–1877," *Iowa Journal of History and Politics*, Vol. XX (July, 1922), 331; *Daily Press and Dakotaian* (Yankton), January 20, February 1, March 1, 2, 22, 24, 25, 1876.

[27] Tallent, *The Black Hills*, 192; Andreas, *Andreas' Historical Atlas of Dakota*, 124.

[28] *Daily Leader* (Cheyenne), April 10, 15, 1875; Mahnken, "The Sidney-Black Hills Trail," *Nebraska History*, Vol. XXX (September, 1949), 214; Deadwood Board of Trade, *The Black Hills of Dakota, 1881*, 11.

gers for Custer in January, 1876, and their first stage left for the diggings on February 3. Brown withdrew from the partnership, however, to join Gilmer, Salisbury, and Patrick in buying out Yates and forming the Cheyenne and Black Hills Stage, Mail, and Express Company. Progress was delayed on February 21, when Brown was shot from ambush by either an irate employee or hostile Indians. Hostiles also ran off the company's stock and burned several stage stations. The depredations, coupled with the death of the capable Brown on February 26, delayed operations until September 25, when the first regular coach rolled into Deadwood.

The trip at first took six and one-half days, but was speeded up as the road improved, the route shortened, and new relay stations built. By February 11, 1877, it took only four and one-half days to reach Deadwood, with stages making triweekly trips. After March 24, 1877, the line ran on a daily schedule. Eventually most of the firm's business came from its Sidney, rather than its Cheyenne, operations, but regardless of the actual point of departure one still went to the Hills "on the Cheyenne Stage." Gilmer, Salisbury, & Company sold out in 1882 to Russell Thorp who continued operations until February 19, 1887. The last regular stage left the Inter-Ocean Hotel on that date for Deadwood and oblivion.[29]

The Deadwood treasure coach is justly famous for the quantities of gold it carried, the valor of its defenders, and the success of its operations. The regular stages were frequently robbed, but the treasure stage only once. "None but fools would carry money, knowing that they were sure to lose it," said an empty-pursed passenger to an irate bandit who held him up. On the other hand, few hesitated to entrust vast sums to the armored, guarded, and invincible treasure coaches on their fortnightly runs.[30]

The express charge for hauling bullion to either Sidney or

[29] The files of the *Daily Leader* (Cheyenne) provide excellent primary source material on Cheyenne stages; Spring, *Cheyenne and Black Hills Stage and Express Routes*, is devoted entirely to the subject.

[30] Thomas G. Ingham, *Digging Gold Among the Rockies*, 227. Bandit depredations on the regular stage routes and failures against the bullion coach are discussed in more detail in chap. x.

Cheyenne for rail shipment was 1 per cent of the value. At first Luke Voorhees, superintendent of the Cheyenne line, simply saw to it that his drivers were well armed. This meager precaution brought through $500,000 in gold during the summer of 1876. The suppression of hostile Indians, however, made life along the trail safer for the bandits and forced on the company a regular system of guarded treasure shipments.

The treasure coach made its trip about twice a month, using a purposely irregular schedule to confuse prospective robbers. Eight mounted guards accompanied the shipment, some in front, some trailing behind, so that no ambush could surprise them all. In the beginning, heavy iron safes were used to contain the gold— one guaranteed by its maker to withstand potential thieves for fifty-six hours. In 1878 these durable containers were augmented by completely armored coaches, inside which the guards could defend themselves with little danger. These coaches, named the "Salamander," "Monitor," and "Old Ironsides," often carried as much as $200,000 at a time, and only once—at Canyon Springs— was one of them robbed successfully.

A major factor in this remarkable immunity was undoubtedly the sheer weight of the gold. A hundred pounds of gold—far more than a man on horseback could conveniently carry—was worth $30,000. If melted into bars, as most of the gold production was, shipments were simply too unwieldly to steal. The familiar movie spectacle of the bandit seizing a fat bag of gold dust and galloping off with it is just plain imagination. The famous $350,000 shipment of 1877, for example, weighed well over one thousand pounds, and to steal it would have required a wagon. Since the use of a wagon meant that a getaway had to be made by roads, such a project was not attractive to the thoughtful bandit. He preferred to make a small but steady living robbing travelers, rather than to attempt to steal an immovable fortune from a well-guarded treasure coach.[31]

[31] *Ibid.*, 219–20; Spring, *Cheyenne and Black Hills Stage and Express Routes*; Stuart N. Lake, *Wyatt Earp: Frontier Marshal*, 158–63, contains a totally fallacious account of Earp's riding shotgun on a "Wells Fargo" shipment; Brown and Wil-

Gold was the most valuable commodity shipped out of the Hills, but the most welcome, and weight for weight, the most expensive item shipped in was mail. A "pony express" of sorts was established in November, 1875, to carry letters at twenty-five cents each from Custer to the Spotted Tail Agency. It did not last long. Private carriers, teamsters, and the like, brought in mail from other towns, usually selling it at ten cents a letter to self-appointed "postmasters" who retailed the letters to the addressees for twenty-five cents each. Long lines of miners waited after every arrival of mail, while half a dozen clerks sorted and distributed the letters. It was an invariable rule that no one might ask for mail in more than one name, so the tenderfoot who thoughtlessly offered to bring back his friends' letters usually spent the whole day in town and returned a sadder and wearier man.

In February, 1876, another pony-express line was established to carry letters from Custer to the Red Cloud Agency for $1.00 each. Later the Seymour and Utter Pony Express-Mail Service carried mail between Deadwood, Fort Laramie, and, eventually, Sidney. The riders traveled at night to avoid the Indians and to keep the horses cool. A skilled rider like "Colorado Charlie" Utter could make the trip to Fort Laramie with two thousand to three thousand letters worth twenty-five cents each in forty-eight hours, which meant a minimum return of $500 to the company. Seymour and Utter sold out to C. T. Clippinger, whose rather erratic service was quickly replaced by the Cheyenne and Black Hills Stage operating out of Cheyenne. H. T. Clarke, the Sidney freighter, also ran a mail line to the Hills. His prepaid envelopes labeled "Clarke's Centennial Express" sold for ten cents each. Even though he soon hired Marsh and Stephenson for $4,000 a year to do the actual hauling, his scheme lost money, and he retired from postal business.

A United States post office was established in Custer on March 14, 1876, with T. H. Harvey, followed by editor J. S. Bartholomew its postmasters. On the same day a post office, with R. O.

lard, *The Black Hills Trails*, is the true story of two men who actually were guards for the treasure coach.

Adams in charge, was set up in Deadwood. Local newspapers regularly listed the names of those who had letters waiting for them, and thus provided historians with the names of many gold rushers who at least started for the Hills.[32]

The telegraph, the most rapid means of communication with "the states," was begun from Fort Laramie in August, 1876. W. H. Hibbard sold scrip, which could be used to pay for telegrams, and solicited $5,000 in cash donations from Deadwood newspapers and businessmen. By October 7 the wires had been strung to Camp Collier at the foot of Red Canyon, and by December 1 they were in Deadwood. A ball at the Grand Central Hotel celebrated the event, and congratulatory messages poured in to the receptive ear of James Halley, the first telegrapher. Within a few months, however, the line broke down due to the transmission of a news item concerning the Russian general Blovitskinourskirosquorobinskinasky. The passage of this ponderous word, the newspapers claimed, ruptured the wires and knocked one lineman, Pat Keeley, off a telegraph pole. Service was quickly restored. By 1879 some 17,500 paid messages went over the wires each year as well as 900,000 words of press dispatches.[33]

With the coming of the telegraph, communications with the Hills were complete. On foot, by ox team, or by stage, the miner could seek out the new bonanza, while regular mails and the prospect of a telegraph line assured him of close contact with home. Only the wronged and brooding Indian remained to bar the way.

[32] *Daily Press and Dakotaian* (Yankton) December 11, 1875; Tallent, *The Black Hills*, 300–301; Hughes, *Pioneer Years*, 111–12.
[33] *Ibid.*, 194; *Black Hills Daily Times* (Deadwood), May 28, 1877, mentions Keeley's supposed accident.

8

THE BLACK HILLS AND THE INDIANS

Did I hear the news from Custer?
Well, I reckon I did, old pard.
It came like a streak o' lightning,
And you bet, it hit me hard.
I ain't no hand to blubber,
And the briny ain't run for years,
But chalk me down for a lubber,
If I didn't shed regular tears.[1]

No side of Black Hills history has been the subject of more sentiment and less understanding than the way in which the area was ultimately wrested from the Sioux. Conscience-stricken chroniclers have portrayed the white man as a monster of callous cupidity; sentiment and ignorance have described the red man as a persecuted saint. Conversely, those who lived on the frontier often considered the Indian a cunning and savage obstacle to the advance of civilization, and the Indian agents who dealt with him marvels of misguided patience, honor, and long-suffering.

The tribes which may be conveniently called the Sioux were only the last of a series of Indian claimants of the Hills. Their title rested upon the provisions of the Treaty of Laramie of 1868 which established a reservation for them on the area between the

---

[1] Crawford, *The Poet Scout*, quoted in Tallent, *The Back Hills*, 222.

Missouri River and the Wyoming border in what is now the western half of South Dakota. This region included the Black Hills, and it is commonly supposed that the intrusion of the miners into it caused the Sioux War of 1876. Although this may indeed have been the precipitating event, the true causes of the conflict were far more subtle.

The occupation of the Black Hills was only one of a series of white moves intended to circumscribe the far-ranging activities of the wild plains tribes. Secretary of the Interior Columbus Delano said in 1873 that he would not "seriously regret the total disappearance of the buffalo," for he regarded the destruction of this staple Indian food as the best means of reducing the savages to a docile and convenient civilization. As the buffalo diminished in number, Indian hunting parties rode ever farther afield. This alone would have made them a nuisance to the settlers, if the acknowledged thievery of Indian agents had not driven the warriors to depredations of their own.[2]

The people of Dakota, although not the only ones to suffer from this scourge, were quick to appeal for help. In 1873 their legislative assembly at Yankton sent a memorial to Congress, urging that steps be taken to prevent "the Black Hills country serving as a retreat for hostile Indians." General Phil Sheridan in his report for 1874 said that for two or three years he had contemplated building a military post in the Hills, "so that holding an interior point in the heart of the Indian country we could threaten the villages and stock of the Indians if they made raids on our settlements." With such a background the Custer expedition of 1874 may be seen as a step toward the military occupation of the Hills. Certainly it was more than a mere exploration.[3]

As the area became prominent in Army thinking, it seems evident that someone in the War Department referred to Lieutenant

[2] E. Douglas Branch, *The Hunting of the Buffalo*, 174–76, clearly shows Delano's attitude; "The Red Cloud Report," *Harper's Weekly*, Vol. XIX (November 6, 1875), 895, mentions the numerous frauds in the Indian Bureau.

[3] Legislative Assembly of Dakota Territory, "Memorial in Reference to the Black Hills Country," 42 Cong., 3 sess., *House Misc. Doc. No. 65; Daily Leader* (Cheyenne), November 10, 1874.

Gouverneur Kemble Warren's "Preliminary Report" of his explorations in 1857. Warren's geographical information on the Hills
was meager, but his military advice was explicit: "The Black Hills
is the great point in their territory at which to strike at all the
Teton Dakota .... They will not, I think, permit the occupation
of the vicinity of these hills without offering a determined resis-
tance." Once goaded into battle, said Warren, "the superiority
of the weapons of civilized warfare would secure a victory to us."
The Army, however, could not at once bring itself to occupy the
Hills in the hope of precipitating a conclusive war with the Sioux.
Fortunately they did not have to, since frontiersmen were only
too happy to do the job.[4]

Western civilian opinion on the subject of occupation was far
ahead of the military. Westerners commonly supposed that the
Hills remained closed to settlement only "in order to gratify the
whim of a few miserable savages," and that this policy of kindness
and forbearance had been a total failure. Bands of "sleek, regu-
larly-fed young Indians of the agencies" roamed the West at will,
plundering settler and traveler alike. It seemed to the frontiersman that one "might as well try to raise a turkey from a snake egg
as to raise a good citizen from a papoose," and that what was
needed was a new policy which granted to white citizens some of
the lands and favors previously wasted on the Indians.[5]

The Sioux themselves were by no means blameless. Tribal organization provided little restriction upon individual raiding and
hunting over a wide area. The latter, at least, was specifically
allowed by the terms of the Laramie Treaty. These two activities,
moreover, were so closely associated in the Indian culture that in
practice they tended to be indistinguishable; what began as a hunt
often ended as a scalping expedition. As conditions on the reservations worsened, the young warriors often evaded the limited

[4] Warren, "Preliminary Report of Explorations in Nebraska and Dakota in
1855-'56-'57," *South Dakota Historical Collections*, Vol. XI (1922), 217–19.

[5] John E. Maxwell, letter, March 20, 1875, quoted in Larsen (ed.), "Black Hills
Gold Rush," *North Dakota Historical Quarterly*, Vol. VI (1932), 305; Maguire,
The Black Hills and American Wonderland (*The Lakeside Library*, IV, No. 82),
286; *Black Hills Pioneer* (Deadwood), June 8, 1876.

authority of weaker chiefs and roamed and robbed at will. Their ferocity abroad was increased by the frustration which they had endured at home.[6]

By the end of 1874 all signs pointed to increasing trouble with the Plains Indians. The efforts of the federal government to reduce them to subservience and self-sufficiency by means of a well-intentioned kindness had come to nothing. Indians who starved in sorrow on the reservations tended increasingly to break away to starve in freedom on the prairies. The Army, wearied by the demands made upon it to "control" the Indians, yearned for a final solution to the problem, and saw in the occupation of the Hills a move which might precipitate a bloody but successful conflict. The frontiersmen, accustomed to living under the threat of savage raiders, had no qualms about fomenting a war to gain a gold rush. At the same time the proud, wronged, and warlike Indian was anxious for another opportunity for revenge.

The Sioux regarded Custer's Black Hills expedition of 1874 as a palpable infringement of their treaty rights. To reduce the possibility of conflict arising out of their resentment, the Department of the Interior sent a commission to secure the relinquishment of the Sioux hunting rights between the Platte River and the northern border of Nebraska. Such a cession, the government hoped, would keep hunting parties well away from the sandhills route from Sioux City to the new mines. The outraged feelings of the Indians, however, prevented acceptance of the proposals, and the baffled and affronted commissioners retreated.[7]

The idea that the Sioux, whose principal subsistence after the buffalo herds had diminished came from government gratuities, had refused to bend to official wishes proved a great irritation to the Commissioner of Indian Affairs. He urged the outright abrogation of those parts of the Laramie Treaty which allowed the Indians to hunt freely in the West, and prophetically remarked

[6] The Plains Indian institution of the "Dog Soldiers," or "Crazy Dogs," police for keeping order on the march and in the hunt, did not extend its authority to hunting or raiding activities beyond the neighborhood of the tribe.

[7] Office of Indian Affairs, *Report of the Commissioner of Indian Affairs, 1874,* pp. 7, 87–90.

that the territory "was of little advantage to the Indian, while the removal of the restrictions [on white entry] would prepare the way for the settlement of our citizens." He further held that "it is a great wrong to the citizens of this territory that its domain should not be settled by a white enterprising population." To implement these suggestions, the Secretary of the Interior hinted that the supplies normally given to the Sioux should be issued or withheld as the Indians' conformity to governmental wishes might suggest.[8]

There is no question that the Army, in spite of the temptation to start a Sioux war in the Hills, at first did its best to drive out the trespassing miners. Their efforts to remove the Gordon party, evict subsequent trespassers, and cordon off the Hills show that the Army both accepted and performed the unwelcome task. Yet it can be argued with some validity that the presence of the troops near the mines was designed as much to overawe the Sioux as to eject the miners. Secretary of War William Belknap repeatedly warned would-be trespassers that the Army would protect the Hills only until a satisfactory agreement to open them was negotiated with the Indians. These instructions were echoed by the generals in command, and although possibly diluted by the time they reached lower military echelons, the activity of Captain Edwin Pollock in removing trespassers is sufficient to show that the orders were carried out.[9]

One reason for Army vigilance during the summer of 1875 was the hope that removing the prospectors would soothe the Sioux and pave the way for negotiations aimed at obtaining the Black Hills. Accordingly, a second Sioux commission, headed by William B. Allison, met with the chiefs on September 20 at the Red Cloud Agency. The commissioners urged three main reasons why the Indians should sell the Hills, or at least the mineral rights to them: First, as the Sioux did not and could not support them-

[8] *Ibid.*, 7, 87–90.
[9] U.S., "Message from the President Transmitting Information in Relation to the Black Hills Country in the Sioux Reservation," 43 Cong., special sess., *Senate Exec. Doc. No. 2*; *Daily Leader* (Cheyenne) March 29, 1875; see also chap. v.

selves, they ought to bend to the demands of the authorities who fed them. Second, the Army could not keep out the miners, and unless the Hills were given up, a conflict between the trespassers and the Indians, and subsequent intervention by the Army, was inevitable. Third, the area, whatever its mineral wealth, was useless to the Indians, and in any event would be handed back to them for a reservation once its gold had been extracted.[10]

Mr. Lo, for all his innocence, was not so easily cozened. The Indians drew the commissioners' attention to the Treaty of Laramie, which not only guaranteed them the Hills but government support as well, and reasonably asked why they should give up the one in order to retain the other. Red Cloud and a dozen lesser chiefs visited the diggings, and upon seeing gold actually being extracted immediately conceived exaggerated notions about the value of the mines. Encouraged by Indian agents, traders, and squawmen in the belief that the Hills were valuable, the chiefs raised their price for the area to $70,000,000. In addition, they urged that some compensation for the gold already removed might be in order, a subject on which the commissioners were understandably diffident. The commission finally offered either a rent of $400,000 a year until the Hills were mined out or a total price of $6,000,000 payable in fifteen annual installments, in return for the mineral rights to the Hills and the right of way for three roads leading to them. The proposal further stated that, if accepted, "a reasonable sum shall be expended in presents to be distributed as is customary among the Indian people."[11]

The conference broke up within ten days without reaching any agreement whatever. The Indians manifested an increasingly hostile attitude toward the commissioners, while the latter were

[10] The best summary of the 1875 negotiations is in Rosen, *Pa-Ha-Sa-Pah*, 341–45; the complete story may be found in Office of Indian Affairs, *Report of the Commissioner of Indian Affairs, 1875*, pp. 6–9, 184–87.

[11] *Ibid.*, 6–9, 184–87. The Indian was jocularly referred to as "Mr. Lo," in reference to Alexander Pope's lines, found in Epistle I of the *Essay on Man:* "*Lo, the poor Indian! whose untutor'd mind/ Sees God in clouds, or hears him in the wind;/ His soul proud Science never taught to stray/ Far as the solar walk or milky way.*"

well pleased to leave the meeting before the outbreak of open war. The report of the commissioners pointed out that the Indian attitude toward selling a part of their reservation would not soften "until they are made to feel the power as well as the magnanimity of the Government." It further observed that "if the Government will interpose its power and authority, they [the Sioux] are not in a condition to resist." Following this failure of negotiations, President Grant ordered the withdrawal of the troops guarding the Black Hills. As we have already seen, this action in effect threw the region open to the miners.[12]

In describing the dealings of the white man with the Indian, it is often customary to attribute all virtue to the latter and every villainy to the former, a habit of mind which does more credit to the conscience than to the judgment of the historians involved. Those who actually dealt with the Indian, fought him on the prairies, or suffered from his thievery held a different point of view. To the frontiersman the Indian was a dangerous savage to be feared when powerful and destroyed when weak. Exaggerated tales of Indian massacres generally had a kernel of truth far removed from the kindly but ill-informed notions entertained in the distant East. Apparently it was quite a chore to love an Indian nearby.

Some of the lurid tales of Indian warfare doubtless resulted from wishful thinking, as in the case of a young man in the barbershop overheard by James E. Smith, one of the early comers to the Hills. This gallant told of a desperate fight to save his wagon train, how he and a handful of men had entrenched and after a long and bloody struggle fought off hordes of hostiles. When the speaker's warlike face at last emerged from the lather, Smith recognized him as a cowardly member of his own party who had hidden in a wagon as long as two friendly Indians remained on the horizon. Similar stories were probably told for the sake of the chills they sent down the hearer's back, and some were doubtless invented outright by prospectors to discourage migration to the

[12] Office of Indian Affairs, *Report of the Commissioner of Indian Affairs, 1875*, p. 194.

mines until the best claims had been worked out. Still other accounts were fabricated, or at least enlarged, by jealous frontier towns which hoped to divert travelers from their rivals' blood-stained trails.[13]

Nevertheless, there was always some degree of truth or probability in the tales of Indian atrocities and battles. Although a party of twenty or thirty well-armed men could travel the plains with impunity, smaller groups were often set upon and massacred. Traveling alone was perhaps the leading reason for trouble with the Indians, and most of the recorded deaths can be attributed to this cause. In only a few cases were war parties large enough to attack a well-organized wagon train, and they were never successful in defeating one. Some groups, as an added precaution, carried a small cannon and credited it with their immunity from attacks. Actually, any party big enough to haul along a cannon was too big for the average war party to tackle. Even when set upon by large bodies of Indians, the travelers could form a corral of their wagons in which to keep their stock and dig a deep pit inside for the women and children, while rifle pits outside the ring of wagons formed the main defense. The Charles W. Pettigrew party was thus besieged for four days near Spearfish, but managed to hold off the Indians with minor loss until aid arrived from Deadwood.[14]

The tribes on the reservation for the most part remained surprisingly docile prior to 1876. Their unpromising crops, planted on sterile soil, had fulfilled every expectation of failure. Their buffalo herds, depleted by white hunters, no longer provided subsistence. The young men, smarting beneath their grievances, strained against the already tenuous authority of their chiefs, while the chiefs themselves soon entertained doubts about the wisdom of continued submission to the whites. At last, during the winter of 1875–76, General Phil Sheridan ordered all Indian hunting parties to return to their reservations or be considered hostile.

[13] James E. Smith, *A Famous Battery and Its Campaigns*, 225–26; Triggs, *History of Cheyenne and Northern Wyoming*, 3.

[14] *Daily Leader* (Cheyenne), May 21, 1876; McClintock, *Pioneer Days*, 148, 199–201; Zack T. Sutley, *The Last Frontier*, 89.

Lack of food at the agencies and the severity of the winter made compliance impossible. Thus, regardless of their desires, the hunters were forced into hostility. With the coming of the grass for their ponies in the spring of 1876, the Sioux, from hunt and reservation alike, took to the warpath in a desperate endeavor to secure in battle what they could no longer retain by submission. Lieutenant Warren's prediction had come true.[15]

United States troops also took the field in the spring of 1876 for the Army was determined to force the rebellious Indians to return to their reservations. The destruction of part of General Alfred Terry's army under Lieutenant-Colonel George A. Custer at the Battle of the Little Bighorn has been so often described that no further comment is necessary except to point out that this victory greatly encouraged the Indians to increase their raids on the Hills. If the warriors had united at this time to attack the miners, there is little doubt that every man would have been killed or driven out.[16]

Custer and his command were wiped out on June 25, 1876, but except for rumors brought by Indian messengers, no official word of the "massacre" reached Deadwood until July 20. The *Black Hills Pioneer* issued a special edition, and Captain Jack Crawford wrote a lugubrious poem, a part of which is reproduced at the beginning of this chapter, in sorrowful commemoration. Already alerted by increasing Indian raids, the Black Hillers now began to look to their defenses.[17]

Within the Hills quickly formed militia units provided armed protection for the larger towns. Custer's Minute Men under Captain Jack Crawford were imitated in Deadwood. Three com-

[15] Office of Indian Affairs, *Report of the Commissioner of Indian Affairs, 1876,* 11–23.

[16] General Custer, to give him his brevet rank, has always been closely identified with the Hills. His expedition in 1874 publicized them, his death on the Little Bighorn is generally attributed to their invasion, and the remnants of his Seventh Cavalry Regiment for years were stationed at Fort Meade, near Sturgis.

[17] Stokes and Driggs, *Deadwood Gold*, 70, says that an Indian runner brought news of the battle to Deadwood on June 27, which indicates incredible agility. The extra issue of the *Black Hills Pioneer* has been totally lost, and no copies of it are known to exist.

panies totaling 325 men were formed there, in addition to cavalry units in Gayville, Spearfish, and Crook City. Rapid City likewise organized for its own protection, and as late as the fall of 1878 petitioned the United States marshal of the territory for fifty stand of rifles and ammunition. Since the Army at that time used the single-shot Springfield, it would seem that almost any weapon the settlers might have had would have been preferable for defense against hostile Indians armed with Spencer and Winchester repeating rifles.[18]

The powerful forces of private enterprise were also called upon to war against the Sioux, and as in uneasy Colonial times, rewards were offered for the heads of Indians. A miners meeting in Deadwood offered a bounty of $50 per head, the assembled citizens donating the money at once. Later the amount was raised to $300. An Indian-hunter known as Texas Jack displayed a head in various bars, and was said to have been rewarded by the local board of health, "on the theory that killing Indians was conducive to the health of the community." By July, 1877, the menace had declined to the point where the bounty could be reduced to $25. The wide variety of sums and the differing dates ascribed to them are sufficient to cast doubt upon the authenticity of the stories. Nevertheless, there was at the time a widespread belief that rewards were offered, and had been paid, for Indian heads.[19]

Precautions taken in the Hills did little to prevent Indian trouble on the trails. Even the Gordon party had run into a little trouble

[18] *Black Hills Pioneer* (Deadwood), July 22, 1876; *Daily Leader* (Cheyenne), July 27, August 1, 1877; University of South Dakota, W.P.A. Writer's Project, MS, "Annals of Early Rapid City, 1878–87—Indians," 5, 15, Rapid City Public Library.

[19] Bullock, "An Account of Deadwood and the Northern Hills in 1876" (ed. by Harry H. Anderson), *South Dakota Historical Collections*, Vol. XXXI (1962), 312, 328–29; Smith, *A Famous Battery and Its Campaigns*, 222; Brown and Willard, *The Black Hills Trails*, 222–25; Hughes, *Pioneer Years*, 184; "Brief Chronology of Early Deadwood," *Black Hills Engineer*, Vol. XVIII (January, 1930), 35. The only well-substantiated case of a reward being paid is that involving a Mexican, who cut off the head of an Indian killed near Crook City, carried it to Deadwood, and was rewarded with gold and liquor in the various bars, a story which is repeated by the above-mentioned authorities with some degree of unanimity.

when young David Aken wandered away from his companions and was twice captured and twice released through the assistance of an affectionate squaw. The Indians did not long remain so merciful. John S. McClintock, who came to the Hills in 1876, later compiled a list of violent deaths in the early days which mentions some sixty persons known to have been killed by Indians. Two scouts, Jesse Brown and A. M. Willard, describe other killings which McClintock omitted and bring the total to about one hundred. Richard B. Hughes, a reporter for the *Black Hills Pioneer*, believed that there were not more such deaths only because the influential chiefs did all they could to restrain the younger warriors. "Under the circumstances," says Hughes, "the Indians having all the right on their side, and the white invaders not even a shadow of right—it is a source of wonder not that so many Black-Hillers were killed as that the number was not infinitely greater."[20]

To list in detail those killed in or near the Hills would weary the reader without honoring the dead. Nevertheless, a few instances, drawn from various localities, may show the scope of the problem and explain to some degree the animosity of the miner for the Indian. For example, George V. Ayres, who came to Custer in the spring of 1876, listed in his diary twelve Indian attacks near that town from April 24 to May 20, including thirteen men killed. The attacks continued into 1877 and could not be stopped until the Indians themselves abandoned their raiding habits.[21]

At Rapid City, on the eastern edge of the mountains, the attacks fell even more heavily. From the middle of March, 1876 to the end of April, ten men, out of an already slender population, were killed on the roads around the town. Their bodies were generally subjected to "horrible and unmentionable mutilations," an Indian habit which markedly increased the anger of the survivors. In August, following the numerous Indian uprisings encouraged by the massacre at the Little Bighorn, four more men, Thomas E.

---

[20] Aken, *Pioneers of the Black Hills*, 55–56, 62, in spite of this flight of imagination, appears to be reliable in the rest of his account; Hughes, *Pioneer Years*, 26.
[21] Brown and Willard, *Black Hills Trails*, 84.

Pendleton, O. Patterson, George W. Jones, and John Erquahart, were killed a few miles up Rapid Creek. The miners soon concentrated near the protection of the Rapid City blockhouse, but even so the population dwindled to less than a score of hardy pioneers. Here, too, the raids continued into 1877, and livestock stealing continued into the next year.[22]

Deadwood was to some degree protected by the cordon of settlement around Crook City, Centennial, and Spearfish. The town's most famous Indian victim was the Reverend Henry Weston Smith, whose sad death August 20, 1876, was considered the nadir of Indian ruthlessness and ferocity. Smith, a quiet, kindly man, had first come to Custer, then moved northward with the rush to Deadwood, where he supported himself by carpentry work and occasional sermons. When murdered, he was on his way to preach in Crook City. Although warned of lurking Indians along the trail, he persevered in his intention to bring his message to the neighboring miners. Ambushed, he fell at once, but his body was undisturbed, a mercy generally attributed to the respect in which the Indians reputedly held godly men.[23]

Several other deaths in the northern Hills caught the public mind and typify the problems which the settlers encountered. Jimmy Irion (or Iron), a scout employed by haymakers on False Bottom Creek, made the mistake of using the same hill day after day as a lookout. One day the Indians got there first. Their bullets hit a shell in his cartridge belt, and when found, his body was described as "horribly mutilated" by the explosion. Charley Nolin, a pony express rider anxious to reach Deadwood with the mail, left the protection of a group of freighters and rode on ahead. He was ambushed along Deadman Creek, and his body was dis-

22 Brennan, "Some Early History of the Black Hills of South Dakota," MS, n.d., Shelf 2, Tier 6, South Dakota Historical Society, Pierre; Hughes, *Pioneer Years*, 174; A. C. Townsend, letter to I. C. Develling, 431 Main Street, Springfield, Mass., from Rapid City, September 1, 1876, typescript, Black Hills File Cabinet, Drawer 3, Rapid City Public Library.

23 McClintock, *Pioneer Days*, 123, supposes that Smith was killed, not by Indians, but by malicious white men. His undelivered sermon, found on the body, is given in outline in *ibid.*, 124–27.

covered by the trail of scattered mail about it. The Wagner family, which had started alone for the East, was attacked near Crook City, and all members of the party were murdered and their bodies brutally abused.[24]

Buffalo Gap, where the Sidney trail led into the Hills from the south, was the scene of many Indian attacks. Here several parties often noticed the same bodies, and their garbled reports multiplied single deaths into a dozen. The most noted fight at Buffalo Gap was that of eight well-armed buffalo hunters who defended their five wagons with grim determination before literally taking to the hills. Passers-by, seeing the burned wagons, surmised that a large party had been destroyed, and spread the word of yet another Indian massacre. Actually, the Indians, rather than the hunters, were the losers on this particular occasion.[25]

The most famous of all Indian atrocities was the massacre of the Metz party in Red Canyon. Metz, a baker who had made a good living in Custer, sold his business for $3,000 when the miners moved north, and departed for Cheyenne with a small party which included his wife, a teamster named Simpson, and a colored maid. Accompanying them were W. J. "California Bill" Felton and his two friends, Beergessir and Gresham. Felton and his comrades got about three-quarters of a mile ahead of the rest of the party and were attacked by Indians. Cutting loose his wagon, Felton flung his dying companions on the backs of two horses, mounted a third, and dashed down the valley to the safety of a nearby stage station. The Indians, meanwhile, proceeded up the canyon where they met and killed the rest of the Metz party and left their bodies a horrible example for passing travelers to find.[26]

The Indians, however, may not have been alone. There is no doubt that they attacked Felton, for he survived his five wounds and testifed to that effect. On the other hand, it was commonly held by the local people that the bandit "Persimmons Bill" had

[24] *Ibid.*, 86; *Daily Leader* (Cheyenne), September 27, 1876; Brown and Willard, *Black Hills Trails*, 98–99.

[25] *Daily Leader* (Cheyenne), April 27, 1876; Hughes, *Pioneer Years*, 62–63.

[26] *Daily Leader* (Cheyenne), April 21, 22, 23, 26, June 21, 1876, April 7, 1878, provides the most authentic account.

co-operated with the Indians. Jesse Brown, who helped move the mutilated bodies, says that he found the spot where the attackers had hidden while waiting for the Metz party, and that boot and shoe marks, as well as knee prints of cloth breeches, showed clearly in the mud. There is no question that white bandits often worked with the Indians, encouraged them in various depredations, and later shared in the loot.[27]

The many massacres in Red Canyon brought demands for military protection of this vital route from Custer to Cheyenne. These demands were answered on May 8, 1876, when Company K of the Second Cavalry and Company F of the Ninth Infantry were sent to the mouth of the canyon to build a small military post. Named Camp Collier, this fort was about seventy-five feet square, with projecting bastions at its southeastern and northwestern corners. The troops decorated their tents with evergreen boughs and made themselves at home, while the Red Canyon Stage Station and Harlow's Eating House soon provided refreshment for trooper and traveler alike. While the infantry guarded the post, a cavalry unit scoured the countryside for hostiles or accompanied threatened wagon trains northward to Custer.[28]

Crook regrouped his forces following the Custer disaster, and on August 5 set out toward the Yellowstone River in hope of intercepting both Sitting Bull and Crazy Horse. Sitting Bull and his warriors headed for Canada, while Crazy Horse seemed bent on destroying the miners in the Black Hills. On August 26 Crook's troops, exhausted by a rapid chase after the latter, began their famous "mud and horsemeat" march to the Black Hills. Crook reached the headwaters of the Heart River on September 5, then crossed the Cannon Ball, Grand, and Moreau. On September 7, he sent Captain Mills and 150 troopers from the Third Cavalry ahead in an attempt to obtain supplies. This advance guard ran

[27] McClintock, *Pioneer Days*, 59; Brown and Willard, *Black Hills Trails*, 75.

[28] *Daily Leader* (Cheyenne), May 8, June 2, July 4, 9, August 6, 1876, May 5, 1877; *Black Hills Pioneer* (Deadwood), August 12, 1876. The post was also known as Camp Collins. The outline of the stockade can still be seen across the road from the Jim Bell ranch, two or three miles north of Edgemont.

into American Horse and a small body of warriors and defeated them in a brisk but minor action. The arrival of Crazy Horse with the bulk of his men threatened Mills with extermination, but Crook came to his rescue in time to fight off the attack in the Battle of Slim Buttes.[29]

Having diverted Crazy Horse from the Hills, Crook and his men resumed their desperate and starving march toward Deadwood. On September 13 they camped on the Whitewood, near Crook City, where they received supplies from the welcoming miners. The General and his staff later were royally received in Deadwood, especially after Mayor E. B. Farnum had discreetly directed them to the public bathhouse and a neighboring clothing store. A ball was held in their honor at the Grand Central Hotel, and the meeting afterward adjourned to Jack Langrishe's theater where the General shook hands with all who wished to greet him. He also received a petition asking him to establish a fort in the northern Hills, a blessing which the citizens believed would be "a great measure of safety and protection to the people here now, as well as affording the means of a more rapid exploration and development of other portions of this interesting country."[30]

Crook advised the miners to form their own militia and not wait for government assistance. His troops, however, remained in the Hills for about two months and gave a marked degree of protection to the miners. In addition, Camp Sturgis was built near Bear Butte. Here, two troops of cavalry and two companies of infantry under Major Henry Lazelle provided a secure bastion of defense for the northern Hills.

It is now necessary to turn from war to peace, and to look for a moment on the negotiations which ultimately gained the Black Hills for the miners. Obviously, as long as the mines remained a part of the Sioux reservation, there would be continued clashes

[29] Finerty, *War-Path and Bivouac*, 303–12, is a firsthand account of the campaign.
[30] Tallent, *The Black Hills*, 233; *Daily Leader* (Cheyenne), September 28, 1876, says that Crook's soldiers, too, were well entertained, the Deadwood restaurants taking turns treating them.

between the trespassers and the rightful owners. As in practice it had proved impossible to keep the miners out, the only alternative to continued fighting was to remove the Indians.

Furthermore, the Hills were seen as a key to returning prosperity for the nation, which had already suffered for three years from the effects of the Panic of 1873. Monied interests were anxious to invest in the new mines, but hesitated to do so as long as these remained a part of the Indians' treaty lands. The outlet for investment, the jobs which it might generate, and the flow of gold which it might produce were all potent arguments for removing the mines from the Sioux reservation.[31]

The Indians, too, had good cause to negotiate. It was obviously impossible for them to hold on to the Hills, and prudence dictated that they get what price they could. They also needed to secure governmental assurance of the supplies upon which they had come to depend, and to arrange for some way in which they could in time adjust themselves to the white man's society. These considerations, coupled with a judicious government selection of the chiefs who were to attend the parley, made agreement inevitable.

The negotiators met at the Red Cloud Agency in September, 1876. The government commissioners had been instructed to seek the relinquishment of all but the permanent reservations established by the Treaty of 1868, and especially the cession of all Indian claims west of the 103rd meridian. The latter extended some ten miles east of Rapid City and included all of the Black Hills. The commissioners also wished to obtain the right of way for roads across the remaining reservations, an agreement on the part of the Indians to receive their supplies on the Missouri River— well away from the mines—and the establishment of a system of Indian schools. In return, the commissioners were authorized to offer assurance that the supplies already promised under the Treaty of Laramie would not be discontinued.[32]

---

31 *Black Hills Pioneer* (Deadwood), December 2, 1876.

32 *The Report and Journal of Proceedings of the Commission Appointed to Obtain Certain Concessions from the Sioux Indians* was omitted from the ap-

Even the hand-picked chiefs could not stomach this barefaced robbery without protest. Said one, "I hear that you have come to move us . . . since the Great Father promised that we should never be moved we have been moved five times . . . I think you had better put the Indians on wheels and you can run them about wherever you wish."[33]

Chief Red Dog advised a degree of deliberation in the negotiations: "I do not wish you to be in haste about it; it is only six years since we came to live on this stream . . . and nothing that has been promised us has been done." Running Bear sneeringly asked the commissioners to take up a collection for him out of their own pockets: "You are not particularly modest in asking for the things you want, and I see no reason why I should not ask for the things I want." Standing Elk, however, stated the case in bald simplicity when he said: "Whenever we don't agree to anything that is said in council they give us the same reply—'You won't get any food.' "[34]

Another chief, Fool Dog, sadly remarked: "I am an Indian and am looked on by the whites as a foolish man, but it must be because I follow the advice of the white man." Coming forward with reluctance, Two Strike told the commissioners: "The reason we are afraid to touch the pen and are silent before you is because we have been deceived so many times before." Nevertheless, he signed the treaty—they all signed the treaty— there was nothing else for them to do.[35]

Even the commissioners, who were honest men burdened with a distasteful task, were moved by the Indian protests:

> The recital of the wrongs which their people had suffered at the hands of the whites, the arraignment of the government for gross acts of injustice and fraud, the descriptions of treaties made only to be broken, the doubt and distrusts of present professions of

propriate reports of the Commissioner of Indian Affairs, and appears only as 44 Cong., 2 sess., *Senate Exec. Doc. No. 9.*

[33] *Ibid.*, 8.

[34] *Ibid.*, 34, 42, 73.

[35] *Ibid.*, 43, 52.

friendship and good-will were portrayed in colors so vivid and language so terse, that admiration and surprise would have kept us silent had not shame and humiliation done so.[36]

Nevertheless, the treaty was concluded on October 27, 1876, and ratified by the Senate on February 27 the following year. At last the Black Hills were legally open to the white invaders.

[36] *Ibid.*, 8.

9

LIFE IN A GOLD RUSH TOWN

Put away his pick and shovel,
He will never prospect more;
Death has sluiced him from his trouble,
Panned him on the other shore.[1]

The tale of the men who came to the Hills, of the way they lived, and of the amusements with which they whiled away their idle hours is a fascinating one. Obviously, it is easier to read their story now than it was to live it then, but, all things considered, it was a rewarding experience.

The first-comers were men, for few women and no "ladies" joined the rush to the early placer mines. Even Mrs. R. B. Fay, who arrived on the first coach to Deadwood, was referred to as "the first lady passenger," a compliment which seems rather thoughtless inasmuch as there already was a well-patronized millinery shop in town. Nor were there many children in the Hills in comparison to the total population, judging by the small number attending the various schools.[2]

Photographs taken during the gold rush show bearded miners in profusion, and the first impression is that the rushers were older men. A closer look, however, reveals youthful eyes behind the

[1] Miner's epitaph, *Black Hills Daily Times* (Deadwood), July 18, 1877.
[2] Tallent, *The Black Hills*, 376; Curley, *Guide to the Black Hills*, estimated that not more than 150 women were in Deadwood in 1877.

whiskers, and well it might: the median age in Deadwood was thirty, five years less than that of the adult population in the United States at the time. The following table, derived from the roster of the Society of Black Hills Pioneers, tells the story:

POPULATION OF THE BLACK HILLS, 1875

Age	Per cent
Under 20	10
Between 21 and 30	43
Between 31 and 40	35
Between 41 and 50	10
Over 50	2
	——
Total	100*

* *Constitution and By-Laws of the Society of Black Hills Pioneers Together with a Roll of Members*, gives a roster of members who came to the Hills prior to 1877. The figures doubtless make the rushers seem younger, for some of the oldest must have died by the time the roster was published in 1891.

Most of these men came from the East; nearly two-fifths were born in New York, Pennsylvania, Ohio, Illinois, and Kentucky. Another two-fifths were born in foreign countries, a proportion which far exceeded even that of the West as a whole where only 25 per cent of the population in 1870 was foreign-born. Of course, many who came to the Hills had originally joined gold rushes to California, Nevada, Colorado, and Montana, but then turned eastward when the new Dakota mines were discovered. Two other groups were prominent in the rush: the Chinese and the Negroes. The former came to Deadwood in sufficient numbers to form their own Chinatown in the heart of the city, from which incense wafted over the whole gulch. The latter, although less cohesive, staged at least one large picnic, on August 2, 1879, in honor of the freedom earlier achieved by their race in Santo Domingo.

This heterogeneous aggregation soon developed a unifying spirit of co-operation and mutual responsibility. A few prospectors were secretive and suspicious, keeping all knowledge of new discoveries to themselves. Most, however, shared good news and anything else they had, even with total strangers. The campfire was free to everyone, for the miners understood that in a new land hospitality was a virtue upon which all might one day need to call. In addition, strangers brought news and made good company for isolated miners tired of faithful friends and faces. At any rate, the generous hospitality of the miner was proverbial. To be on hand at mealtime assured an invitation, and to arrive in camp at dusk always meant that there would be a place to sleep in the tent or cabin.

POPULATION OF THE BLACK HILLS BY PLACE OF BIRTH

	per cent		per cent
New York	14	British Isles	18
Pennsylvania	8	Germany-Prussia	13
Ohio	7	Canada	5
Illinois	6	All other foreign	6
Kentucky	4		—
	—	Total, foreign born	42
Total, 5 states	39	Total U.S.	58
All other states	19		—
	—	Total	100*
Total, U.S. born	58		

* *Constitution and By-Laws of the Society of Black Hills Pioneers Together with a Roll of Members.*

The miners' friendliness is generally said to have been equaled by their honesty, but the latter virtue was represented more by tradition than by the actual conditions. Nevertheless, custom dictated that a miner's claim, his tools, and his gold were inviolable, as safe when he went to town as if he had remained to watch them. Furthermore, most of the miners were well armed and did not hesitate to shoot in defense of their property. In the early days of the rush personal law enforcement probably prevented many petty crimes. Unfortunately, as the rush progressed, the prospectors were joined by camp followers who would pick up anything not solidly attached to bedrock. "Not even a bucket, brush, broom, strap, halter, or, in fact, any small article," grumbled the *Black Hills Pioneer*, was safe outside after dark. One woman complained that a thief had removed three joints of pipe from her stove and would have taken the stove, too, if it had not been too hot to handle. These petty crimes increased as the early community spirit of the placers gave way to the more business-like attitude of the hard-rock miners. Nevertheless, a tradition of "frontier honesty" persisted until the railroads came in the 1880's, even though the prudent did not rely upon it very heavily.[3]

Isolated male groups doing essentially the same work tend to develop their own slang and their own catchwords, remarks which by continued use are accepted as meaningful in the most unexpected contexts. Such a phrase was "Whoa, Emma!" It was vague enough to be available for general use and yet capable of inflections suited to every need. The uninitiated may have supposed it to be somehow connected with the "Emma Mine" swindle, and thus both topical and appropriate during a mining boom. Actually it seems to have been derived from the lines *"O day, the fairest one that ever rose,/ Period and end of anxious Emma's woes,"* by the seventeenth-century English poet Matthew Prior.

Another common phrase of Deadwood Gulch was the cry "Oh, Joe!" which would start after supper at the head of the valley and work its way from tent to tent. It gathered volume as additional voices swelled the chorus, until it echoed away in the rocks and rubble beyond the farthest camp. The call was said to have originated in the piteous cries of a drunken prospector who fell into a hole one evening and spent the night fruitlessly bellowing for assistance.

To lugubrious calls for "Joe" was often added the plaintive, penetrating lone-wolf howl of Smokey Jones. His was a sound calculated to raise the hackles, chill the blood, and undo the resolution of even the bravest miner. It was dearly loved by all. Jones one day made his pile in the mines and departed for the East. Several months later he came back again, a shaved and polished stranger who passed unrecognized amongst his dearest friends until one night at the Gem Theater where he joined in the ap-

[3] Strahorn, *Handbook*, 237–38; *Black Hills Pioneer* (Deadwood), September 23, 1876.

plause by giving his old, familiar howl. Great was the miners' rejoicing—Smokey Jones was back again!

An aspect of Western talk which strangers found amusing was the indiscriminate bestowal of military and judicial titles. Among 1,500 names in the Pierre directory, for example, there were 800 colonels, approximately 200 majors and judges, and a liberal sprinkling of captains. "Professor," however, seems to have been reserved for school and music teachers and men who "played piano" in theaters and bars.

When introduced to one of these titled luminaries, the proper salutation was always "Howdy." If the new acquaintance proved a good fellow, one said he was "a white man, yes *sir*," with heavy emphasis on the final word. If he possessed learning, he was said to be a "sharp," as in "rock sharp" for an assayer or a geologist, or "gospel sharp" for a minister. When death dissolved a friendship, the departed was said to have "gone up the flume." An epitaph like the one at the beginning of this chapter might be rudely hand-carved on a headboard, and pious hopes expressed that everything would "pan out all right" for him in "the big diggings up the crick."[4]

Room and board offered a staple topic for conversation or doggerel:

> *The beefsteak is of leather,*
> *And the pies are made of tin;*
> *The bread you could not cut it with a sword.*
> *The butter wears side-whiskers,*
> *The coffee's very thin,*
> *In the little, one-horse hash-house where I board.*

The best quality board cost as much as $14 a week, but thrifty miners "batching" in a mess of five or six could eat for half that

---

[4] Edmund Mandat-Grancey, (trans. by William Conn), *Cowboys and Colonels*, 21, 130; Hughes, *Pioneer Years*, 68, 104; *Daily Leader* (Cheyenne), September 12, 1878, mentions "Whoa, Emma"—a remark analogous to World War II's, "That's what she said!"; "Facts About the Black Hills," unidentified newspaper clipping, Deadwood Public Library, mentions the way the miners talked in further detail.

amount if they could stand their own cooking. Flour cost about $10 for one hundred pounds (although it once soared to $60 during a winter shortage), bacon approximately twenty-five cents a pound, butter, forty cents, eggs, thirty-five cents or more per dozen, depending upon supply. Two- and three-room cabins rented for $25 to $40 a month—but many men built their own of logs, brush, and canvas. An astonishing decorative feature was the brightly printed calico that the miners used for wallpaper. It fitted nicely over the rough logs and gave the cabins a cheerful look. George Stokes sold thousands of yards of it from his clothing store in Deadwood and astonished his wholesaler, who wondered how so few women could use so much cloth.[5]

The first hotel in Deadwood was Charles H. Wagner's Grand Central. Here a traveler could get a rude bunk or space on the floor for his blankets at $1.00 a night. Wagner's board, fortunately, was much better than his beds for he had secured the services of "Aunt Lou" Marshbanks, a highly talented colored woman, and his table was justly famous. As the hotels improved, prices rose from $2.00 to $4.00 a day. Ordinary dining rooms and restaurants issued tickets good for a week's fare for about $10. Such places also acted as hotels, for the "meal tickets" often included the dubious privilege of sleeping on the floor of the establishment.

The comfort of a warm meal and a dry bed were especially appreciated during the gold rush, for the weather then was colder and wetter than at present. November, 1876, saw a heavy snow, and the editor of the Cheyenne *Daily Leader* mentioned that he was able to heat his office by burning the manuscripts he received from local poets about the "snow, beautiful snow." In October, 1877, Deadwood had a two-foot snowfall. The following spring a memorable five-day storm left seven feet of "the beautiful," as it was called, on the ground. Many roofs collapsed, and not surprisingly, for a platform scale used to weigh hay wagons registered 3,165 pounds of snow. When winds came up at the end of the

[5] Rosen, *Pa-Ha-Sa-Pah*, 381; Curley, *Guide to the Black Hills*, 80, 130; McClintock, *Pioneer Days*, 72; *Black Hills Herald* (Custer), December 27, 1876, gives a long local price list.

storm, the snow was whipped into twenty-foot drifts, which later melted and resulted in severe flooding. The next month a second flood, caused by four days of steady rain, washed out placer workings, ruined roads, and filled up mines. A week later the weather turned cold again, and nearby Rapid City was blanketed with still another three feet of snow. Often these storms were followed by a chinook, a warm, southerly wind which could raise sub-zero temperatures fifty degrees in an hour or two and turn the ice to slush and mud.[6]

Deadwood mud, moreover, was not ordinary mud, but "of a rich quality, its adhesive properties rare, its depth unfathomable, its color indefineable, its extent illimitable, and its usefulness unknown." Six and eight mules to the wagon could scarcely navigate through this Stygian liquid, which daubed the animals to their ears and completely disguised their color. Pedestrians waded through the tenacious muck and bellowed long, generous, liberal curses at the teamsters who had splashed them, the roadside buildings which blocked the drainage, and the fate which had brought them all to Deadwood. The streets continued in liquid condition most of the year for winter snows gave way to spring and summer rains. The local habit of throwing garbage into the street and the contributions made by passing livestock did little to make the slime more attractive.[7]

The stinking mud and general lack of sanitation attracted swarms of flies. These, however, were common everywhere and were usually ignored. Lice, on the other hand, received more attention, for miners considered their presence a disgrace. One bullwhacker said that he had been plagued continuously by these pests for six years and still had not got used to them. Most of the

[6] *Daily Leader* (Cheyenne), November 22, 1876, mentions the excess of poetry, based on James W. Watson's "Beautiful Snow! It can do nothing wrong . . ."; Jack Langrishe, of the *Black Hills Pioneer*, wrote a parody, "Stove, beautiful stove . . . beats the h—— out of beautiful snow." The author has seen a chinook raise the temperature from —30°F. to 40°F. from 6:00 A.M. to 10:00 A.M. Precipitation recorded during the rush seems to have been approximately ten inches per year more than at present.

[7] *Black Hills Pioneer* (Deadwood), March 24, 1877; Curley, *Guide to the Black Hills*, 129.

men were more fastidious and boiled their clothes, applied "blue ointment" (*Unguentum Hydrargyri*), and tried to keep their shanties clean. One of the main exceptions to frontier hospitality was the hostility shown the lousy visitor, though usually his condition did not become apparent until the damage had been done.[8]

The miner who found himself afflicted with lice or, indeed, almost any disease could resort to the Deadwood Bath House. This establishment advertised "hot baths, cold baths, dry vapor, sulphur, alcohol, and shower baths," and in smaller type discreetly mentioned "private disease, *sure cure or no pay*." One wonders what heroic treatments made possible such a guarantee.

If the bathhouse failed, the sufferer could always turn to Swayne's Tar and Sarsaparilla Pills, which were offered as a patent cure for "headache, constipated bowels, inward piles, costiveness, fevers, torpid liver, yellowness of skin and eyes, indigestion, dyspepsia, and all derangements of the internal viscera," a comprehensive catalog of the ills then prevalent. The advertisement for this panacea made clear that "unlike many other purgatives they [the pills] do not irritate the stomach and bowels," but keep "the system in . . . healthy condition by arrousing the torpid liver to healthy action in expelling by the bowels and kidneys the matter that poisons the foundations of life." A thorough dose of Swayne's Pills must have been quite an experience.[9]

Weakened by hard work, poor food, and patent medicines, the miners fell easy victims to the smallpox which broke out during the summer of 1876. By August new cases were reported every day. The women of Deadwood organized a committee to care for the destitute sick and ably solicited donations for this good cause. The city government built a smallpox hospital, or pest house, in which to quarantine the patients. Fortunately the disease was in a mild form, and the epidemic was over before its presence could discourage immigration to the Hills.[10]

[8] Spring, *Cheyenne and Black Hills Stage and Express Routes*, 178; Hughes, *Pioneer Years*, 224–25.

[9] *Black Hills Pioneer* (Deadwood), December 16, 1876; *Daily Leader* (Cheyenne), March 27, 1878.

[10] *Black Hills Pioneer* (Deadwood), August 12, 16, 23, 26, 1876.

Having discussed the way in which men lived, let us now look at the way they earned their living. Not all were fortunate enough to find a paying mine; most had to work for others or go into business for themselves. Wages for skilled miners varied from $4.00 to $7.00 a day, and since only half a dozen men could work efficiently at the average placer operation, the owners generally preferred to pay high wages and get the best men available. Inexperienced miners, when they could get work at all, received from $1.00 to $3.00 a day and board. Jobs were scarce and probably not more than one-third of the men in Deadwood were permanently employed.

The unemployed pilgrim could find a number of things to do. Often his friends supported him in idleness, for an extra hand was always useful, if only to go along with each new stampede to stake out claims for his busier companions. Hunting, too, was a pleasant avocation which supplied food for one's friends and often an income, for the successful usually sold their game to restaurants or to other miners. In a last extremity a man could always beg like "Swill Barrel Jimmy," who affected a shabby frock coat and a clean paper collar, but was supported by the generosity of Main Street restaurants which gave him leftovers and tablescraps. An enterprising man could go into business on his own, like the "Bottle Fiend" whose shack was surrounded by tubs and barrels of empty bottles which he offered for sale.[11]

Whatever the transaction, gold dust was the medium of exchange. It could be converted to greenbacks only at a discount. Gold dust commanded a higher price than bills of exchange, for it was assumed to be worth $20 an ounce, when actually the price of even refined gold was considerably less. Local merchants of course compensated for the artificially high price of gold dust by charging correspondingly high prices for their goods. Lastly,

[11] *Engineering and Mining Journal*, Vol. XXIII (April 21, 1877), 251–52; *ibid.*, XXIII (June 16, 1877), 414; *ibid.*, XXIII (February 17, 1877), 108; Strahorn, *Handbook*, 227; Bennett, *Old Deadwood Days*, 7. Pictures of the home of the "bottle fiend" often appear labeled as saloons, etc. Actually, he seems to have collected bottles as a hobby, selling only when he had to.

making a purchase with "dust" was a good way to impress visitors with the wealth and gold production of the Hills.

Gold scales and a "blower," or shallow tin pan in which sand and trash could be blown out of the dust, were essential business equipment. The scale was only used for major transactions, because a practiced clerk or bartender could pick up an accurate fifty cents' worth of gold dust between his thumb and forefinger. Some of the dust generally spilled, so the thoughtful put a small square of carpeting under the scales and blower to catch it. After a good day's business this "side money" might amount to as much as a ten dollar addition to a bartender's salary.[12]

The gold, once collected and taken to the bank, was shipped to New York where it sold for $17.50 per ounce, less 1½ per cent for stage- and rail-transportation charges. In the summer of 1877 the Deadwood merchants agreed among themselves to reduce the price of gold dust from $20 to $18 an ounce, but the uproar made by the miners forced a return to the old rate. By the summer of 1879, however, a more business-like arrangement was accepted, with gold valued according to its source: Deadwood dust brought $17.10 per ounce, and the purer product from Rapid and Castle creeks brought $18.25.

The first bank in Deadwood, managed by J. M. Wood, dealt mainly in gold, exchanging it for greenbacks at a discount of 10 per cent, or storing it in a safe at a charge of 1 per cent a month. One tenderfoot arrived in camp with his money tied up in Wells Fargo certificates—the predecessors of modern traveler's checks—and changed them at the bank for gold dust for a 5 per cent charge. Leaving the Hills a week later and wanting his assets in more portable form, he had to buy back the same certificates at another discount.

Transactions like these quickly brought in competing bankers and correspondingly lowered charges. There was still profit enough for all, for banking business often exceeded $100,000 a day. The price paid for gold was based on the New York market,

---

[12] Finerty, *War-Path and Bivouac*, 324; Hughes, *Pioneer Years*, 110; Young, *Hard Knocks*, 197–98.

less a profit of $2 an ounce when the gold was "coined" and credited to the bank's account. As hard-rock mills increased in number, dust gradually gave way to gold bars about 1 by 2½ by 8 inches in size and worth approximately $3,000 each. Jovial bankers often told small children that they could have one if they could lift it off the table, but the sloping sides of the bars made this feat impossible.[13]

When the town board of Deadwood took a business census in September, 1876, the list revealed twenty-seven saloons, twenty-one groceries, fourteen gambling houses, and eleven haberdasheries, out of a total of 166 establishments. Also, there were five peanut-roasters and one soda-water plant. Surprisingly, butter was big business. One retailer sold eighteen tons of it in three months. Eggs, too, were a promising speculation. The Gardner brothers brought in several thousand from Yankton during the winter of 1876. They were individually wrapped in paper and then packed in barrels of oats. The barrels were stacked in wagons, and the interstices between them filled with more oats to protect the cargo from breakage and freezing. The Gardners' wagon train consisted of thirty wagons, twelve of which carried lumber and the rest eggs, flour, pork, and butter. Cigars also came in by the wagonload, but the *Pioneer* deplored the growing sale of deleterious and effeminate cigarettes which were then just becoming popular.

Charles Sasse and Jacob Shoudy started a butcher shop early in the spring of 1876 when they bought a few crippled oxen that could not make the trip back to the states. They quickly built up a thriving meat and ranching business. Trade was brisk in horses, too. The villainous Charley "Red" Clark, who helped promote a stampede to the Wolf Mountains in 1876 in order to sell his excess stock, ran one stable. Wes Travis ran another. The latter advertised his merchandise by riding up and down the streets on a

[13] "Days of '76 and Later," *Black Hills Engineer*, Vol. XVIII (January, 1930), 23; Bullock, "An Account of Deadwood and the Northern Black Hills in 1876" (ed. by Harry H. Anderson), *South Dakota Historical Collections*, Vol. XXXI (1962), 316; Robert E. Driscoll, *Seventy Years of Banking in the Black Hills*, 52–53.

bucking, pitching bronco, ending up at his own corral, where he often sold his gentler animals to customers attracted by the performance.

"Corners" on various commodities were a common way to lose friends and make money. Jim Wardner, a notorious speculator, bought up all the grain in town during the summer of 1879 and hoped to make a killing during the winter. His warehouse, unfortunately, burned to the ground during the great Deadwood Fire. He recouped his losses by speculating in fresh eggs which he bought in Iowa for $4.50 a case and sold in Deadwood for $15. "Coal Oil Johnny" Spencer cornered the kerosene market and tripled the price to $3.75 a gallon. His customers complained, but paid. Perhaps it was this sort of commercial practice, as well as the prospect of mining litigation, that attracted over fifty lawyers to Deadwood. Even so, there was not enough business for all of them, and many had to find other jobs. One lawyer, for example, dealt faro at the Melodeon, and another worked the windlass on a nearby mining claim.[14]

Once the gold rusher had established himself in his mine, job, or business, he began to look around for entertainment. Depending on how hard he searched, he could find almost anything he wanted, from the coarsest saloons and bawdy houses to libraries and literary societies.

The most popular institution of entertainment, sociability, and refreshment was the saloon. It was, of course, totally illegal, for until 1877 the Hills were part of an Indian reservation where liquor technically was outlawed. One malefactor, Fritz Drogmund, was actually convicted and punished for having sold it. His example, however, did not deter other bartenders, who were ever willing to risk fines in order to provide the miners with cooling and sustaining beverages. It was a great relief to all when in

[14] Tallent, *The Black Hills*, 376; Charles Collins, *Collins' History and Directory of the Black Hills*; Bob Lee and Dick Williams, *Last Grass Frontier: The South Dakota Stock Growers Heritage*, 47; Jim Wardner, *Jim Wardner of Wardner, Idaho*, 42–44; Sutley, *The Last Frontier*, 118–19; Bullock, "An Account of Deadwood and the Northern Black Hills" (ed. by Harry H. Anderson), *South Dakota Historical Collections*, Vol. XXXI (1962), 310–11.

June, 1876, the U.S. commissioner in charge of enforcing the law decided that it was all right to bring liquor onto the reservation, just as long as none of it was sold to the Indians.[15]

The first saloon in Deadwood was run by Ike Brown, who also owned the adjoining grocery store. Across both buildings he put a sign "Zion's Cooperative Mercantile Institution," indicating that he adhered, at least in part, to Mormon principles. Other saloons quickly followed, until by July, 1877, there were seventy-five in town. Their managers, if not already corrupt, rapidly became so, and practiced every skullduggery they could devise for the rapid separation of the miner and his money. The drunk who ordered "drinks for the house" without the dust to pay for them found himself in the street, unless he could persuade the bartender to accept a watch, overcoat, or other valuables instead of money. Instances of such transactions were fairly frequent; ill-disposed persons have even claimed that some of the bartenders accepted goods worth more than the bill and even encouraged their customers in their riotous extravagance.

Coexisting with the saloon was the gambling house. Most of the professional gamblers put on a good, raucous show, like the white-haired old fellow who urged "Come on up, boys, and put your money down—everybody beats the old man—the girls all beat the old man—the boys all beat the old man—everybody beats the old man—forty years a gambler—the old fool—everybody beats the old man—put your money down, boys, and beat the old man." He was not as big a fool as he pretended for he usually ended up with all the money.[16]

Women, too, acted as dealers at many of the gaming tables, "and more resembled incarnate fiends than did their vulture-like male associates." Most of the miners preferred to play with men, for "the women were generally old and unscrupulous hands whose female subtlety made them paramount in all the devices of cheating and theft." Most of the gambling games were said to be

[15] *Daily Press and Dakotaian* (Yankton), April 21, 1876; *Black Hills Pioneer*, (Deadwood) June 8, 1876.
[16] Sutley, *The Last Frontier*, 130.

honest, but from the popularity of faro, a game at which the dealer has practically no percentage if honestly played, it seems unlikely.[17]

The man who did not spend his money on liquor or lose it gambling often managed to spend it on loose women. Dance halls, known as "hurdy-gurdy houses," soon sprang up to provide this opportunity. The first dance hall opened on May 1, 1876, with only the proprietor's wife and daughter to entertain its customers, but it soon added six more women of more questionable virtue. Within the month two more dance halls were available, and these were quickly joined by variety theaters wherein a customer might be entertained by the woman of his choice in the clandestine privacy of a curtained box.

The most notorious of the dance-hall proprietors was Al Swearingen, owner of the Gem Theater. He first established himself in Custer, but then moved with the miners to the riper fields of Deadwood Gulch. Swearingen made frequent trips to the East to recruit young women for his business, promising them respectable employment as "waiter girls" or actresses, only to force them into an abandoned life of shame when they reached Deadwood. An ordinary night's business at the Gem amounted to $5,000, and on occasion reached twice that figure, yet Swearingen died broke, killed in Denver while trying to hitch a ride on a freight train. The Gem, however, "continued to the end in maintaining its notorious record as a defiler of youth, a destroyer of homes, and a veritable abomination."[18]

To keep order in places like the Gem, the Deadwood *Daily Times* proposed a monthly "fine or license fee" which would not only replenish the city treasury, but would have "a most salutary effect in driving women of the street out of town or into the house of a responsible madame." These establishments were generally in the news. In one, for example, a woman named "Tricksie" was beaten by her lover. She snatched up a pistol and shot him, the bullet passing through his head behind the eyes. Fortunately, there

[17] Finerty, *War-Path and Bivouac*, 319–23.
[18] McClintock, *Pioneer Days*, 65–71; Bennett, *Old Deadwood Days*, 118–19.

154

were no brains, at least in that section of his skull, and he recovered in a few weeks.[19]

Another Deadwood girl had a specially embroidered dress, ornamented with the brands and initials of her admirers. Some of the initials caressed her shoulders and ample bosom, some occupied only outlying portions of this novel garment, while others were so placed as to be frequently sat upon. As her affection for each lover dictated where she placed his mark, a man could tell at a glance just what she thought of his attentions.[20]

Many of these gay ladies were well known in town. Judge Granville Bennett gravely tipped his hat as he passed them, saying, from the eminence of his magisterial dignity, "I can afford to." Mrs. Bennett did her best to reform some of the less willing victims of a life of sin, and in this noble work she was assisted by a few kindhearted madames. Some successes were obtained, for as one madame said, "some girls just don't make good prostitutes." Other citizens pretended to ignore this seamy side of Deadwood's social life as beneath their notice.

The poor girls who remained in the business did not last long. Within two or three years drink, drugs, crime, and disease removed them from their supposedly glamorous life. Many deaths reported in the newspaper as pneumonia or fever were actually due to laudanum or a lover's bullet. Only a few of the facts, however, seeped through to plague the conscience of the town. The deaths of Emma Worth, from an overdose of morphine, or of Katie Smith, madame of the Hidden Treasure Number Two, from the same cause, made only a ripple on the surface of Deadwood's so-called high society.[21]

The forces of morality gradually prevailed. "Colorado Charley" Utter was brought before the district court in 1879 on a charge of keeping a "nuisance" in Lead City. One witness, disposed to describe in detail the cancan dance which one of Utter's

[19] *Black Hills Daily Times* (Deadwood), April 28, 1878, quoted in Harold E. Briggs, *Frontiers of the Northwest*, 86; McClintock, *Pioneer Days*, 70.

[20] Spring, *Cheyenne and Black Hills Stage and Express Routes*, 307.

[21] Bennett, *Old Deadwood Days*; *Black Hills Pioneer* (Deadwood), February 10, May 19, 1877.

girls performed, was quickly silenced by the judge. It did not matter, said his honor, just how high the poor girl kicked—the main point was that Utter's house permitted gambling, drinking, boisterous talk, and men and women "herding together like animals." Without further qualification he declared it a nuisance which ought to be closed.

Years later the good people of South Dakota prohibited the sale of spirituous liquors in their state, and the once-thriving dens of immorality faded one by one. Young Carl Leedy, meeting the proprietress of one of Rapid City's leading houses asked her if she planned to reopen her establishment. "Kid," she replied succinctly, "you can't run a sporting house on creek water!"[22]

The theater, except when debased by the addition of bars, gambling, and wild women, as in the Gem and other "variety" houses, provided more cultivated entertainment. The leading actor in the Hills was Jack Langrishe, who came to Deadwood with his troupe in July, 1876. He quickly built a theater, roofed it with slats and canvas, and opened it for business. Seats consisted of stakes driven into the ground and topped with pieces of board. Admission to the first performance, Brownson Howard's *Banker's Daughter*, cost $1.50. A violent thunderstorm poured water through the makeshift roof and drenched players and audience alike, but did not stop the show. Whenever business was slack, Langrishe wrote for the *Pioneer* or panned gold from his own placer claim. He stayed in town through many vicissitudes until September 2, 1879. While in Deadwood he and his competitors presented a total of 168 plays, one-half of which were drama, the rest comedies and a few light operas.[23]

Not even the melodrama of the 1870's could equal the dramatic impact of one performance at the Melodeon. "Handsome Banjo Dick" Brown and his partner, Fanny Garrettson, were in the

[22] *Black Hills Weekly Times* (Deadwood), June 21, 1879; Leedy, *Golden Days in the Black Hills*, 74–75.

[23] Henriette Naeseth, "Drama in Early Deadwood, 1876–1879," *American Literature*, Vol. X (November, 1938), 289–312, and Lawrence Carl Stine, "A History of Theater and Theatrical Activities in Deadwood, South Dakota, 1876–90," MS, State University of Iowa, 1962, are excellent on the drama in Deadwood.

midst of their act when a dim figure staggered to the footlights, muttered incoherently, and hurled an ax upon the stage. Brown coolly drew his pistol and shot the attacker dead. He was found to be Ed Shaunessey of Laramie, Miss Garrettson's discarded lover, who had come to Deadwood with the hope of regaining her affections. Miss Garrettson, or, as she then styled herself, Mrs. Brown, wrote to the papers to stifle a malicious rumor that she had once been Shaunessey's wife. This, she said, was totally untrue, for though she had lived with him for three years, they had never married, and so there was nothing immoral about her having run away with Mr. Brown.[24]

Historians have frequently used a reputed 130-day run of the *Mikado* in Deadwood as evidence of culture on the mining frontier. Since the Gem could seat five hundred customers, such a phenomenal performance assumes that every person in the Hills attended between three and four times. Actually, the *Mikado* was not written until 1885, and the whole story is based on a brief description in Estelline Bennett's *Old Deadwood Days*. The Gem really did put on a series of Gilbert and Sullivan burlesques in 1887, but the costumes, or lack thereof, were apparently the main attraction.[25]

Sundays were the miners' shopping days. As many as three thousand ragged, unwashed, and boisterous men and women crowded into Deadwood's narrow, muddy main street, eager for excitement. All stores remained open (the saloons never closed), and only a curb-side preacher or two and a few onlookers served to remind passers-by of the true nature of the day.

Other than Sundays, the first great celebration in the Hills with the Fourth of July, 1876. The miners wanted to have a holiday for their own enjoyment, and in addition wished to show their numbers, patriotism, and prosperity in order that the federal government might extend recognition and protection from the hos-

[24] Hughes, *Pioneer Days*, 114–17; *Daily Leader* (Cheyenne), November 21, December 16, 1876.

[25] Bennett, *Old Deadwood Days*, 107; Gem Theater *Program*, February 24, 1887, Adams Memorial Museum, Deadwood. Miss Bennett gives the correct date, but those who quote her generally omit it.

157

tile Indians. Beginning at midnight, July 3, the miners patriotically fired one hundred cannon salutes. A tall liberty pole gaily flaunted an assortment of flags made from garments of "mystical sublimity," donated by the ladies of the city. Judge W. L. Kuykendall presided over the oratorical effusions, which included the reading of the Declaration of Independence by General A. R. Z. Dawson, the federal revenue collector, and the presentation of a petition asking Congress for help and protection. Montana City and Elizabethtown, down the gulch, had their own celebrations. The day was concluded with a Grand Ball at the Grand Central Hotel.[26]

The local newspaper was one of the most effective means of spreading culture and decorum on the mining frontier. Most of the early papers were founded in the hope that publication of mining-claim notices would provide a steady income, for federal law required such publication. The miners, however, blithely ignored this technicality and worked their mines with no legal assistance other than the approval of their neighbors. The papers had also hoped that the publication of notices for corporations, towns, and counties would keep them going, but this business, too, either failed to materialize or was dissipated among competitors without profiting anyone in particular.

A weekly edition of the Cheyenne *Daily Leader* was the first paper issued specifically for the Hills. It began printing news from the mines on May 1, 1876, under startling headlines such as: "Nuggets of News from the Ledges and Gulches," or "Golden Breezes Wafted Southward from the Treasure Vaults."[27]

At least four efforts were made to start a paper in Custer. Around March 1, 1876, two "blacksmiths" (heavy-handed, in-

[26] Tallent, *The Black Hills*, 356–59.

[27] McMurtrie, *Early Printing in Wyoming and the Black Hills*, 51–74, although compiled entirely from evidence in the Cheyenne papers, is the best survey of early Hills publications. The papers mentioned are, for the most part, available on microfilm at the South Dakota Historical Society, Pierre. The first forty issues of the Deadwood *Black Hills Pioneer*, long supposed to have been lost, are available at the Library of the South Dakota School of Mines and Technology, Rapid City.

competent printers) left Cheyenne to go into the business, but were evidently unsuccessful. A week later printers W. A. Laughlin and A. W. Merrick arrived in Custer, but decided to go on to Deadwood when Captain C. V. Gardner offered to finance the move. James Thorn brought a press from Nebraska City, Nebraska, only to abandon his editorial efforts at Cheyenne. The Custer *Herald*, edited by J. S. Bartholomew, began publication in October, but, as previously mentioned, eventually moved northward to Central City. Lastly, the Custer *Chronicle*, which continues to the present, was begun early in 1880.

In Deadwood, the *Black Hills Pioneer*, which was first issued on June 8, 1876, soon ran into difficulties. A shortage of newsprint forced it to print some issues on wrapping paper and various shades of handbill stock. A competitor, the *Black Hills Daily Times*, edited by W. P. Newhard and Porter Warner, appeared April 7, 1877. In 1897 it merged with the *Pioneer*, forming the paper which still serves the community. Charles Collins, the Sioux City editor who had done so much to publicize the Hills, came to Deadwood and on June 2, 1877, started the *Black Hills Champion*. In the fall the Deadwood *Miner* appeared briefly, followed in the spring of 1878 by Captain Gardner's *Mining and Real Estate Journal*.

Neighboring towns, too, had their journals. The *Black Hills Tribune*, published in Crook City by X. S. Burke, appeared once, June 9, 1876, but was never heard from again. In Carbonate Camp, a new silver town northwest of Deadwood, the Carbonate *Reporter* had boomed and collapsed by the end of 1881. Bartholomew's Central City *Herald* was joined by the *Register* in 1878, and in 1879 by the Reverend B. Fay Mills' Central *Christian*, which the Deadwood *Times* described as "editorially well gotten up, but typographically . . . awful." In Lead the *Sunday Register*, Lead City *Telegraph*, and *Western Enterprise* competed with each other for the meager news of that rather sober city.

Outlying communities also had their papers. In Rapid City, Joseph Gossage began the *Black Hills Journal*, which today serves the whole of South Dakota west of the Missouri. Mr. W. D.

Knight published at least two editions of the Rockerville *Black Hills Miner*, apparently using a press bought from the defunct Crook City *Tribune*. At Rochford the *Black Hills Central*, and later the Rochford *Miner*, consisted mainly of "boiler plate" (preset advertisements) and "patent insides" (preprinted paper with one side left to be filled with local news and editorials). To these were added the poetry of H. N. Maguire and T. F. Walsh, as well as excerpts from the former's books on the Black Hills.

The most civilizing influence of all was the church. Preacher Henry Weston Smith delivered his first sermon in the Hills at Custer on May 7, 1876, and then moved on to Deadwood with the rush. He usually spoke out of doors, standing on a packing box with his hat at his feet to receive contributions. One day "Calamity Jane" Cannary took the hat and passed it through the crowd bellowing, "You sinners, dig down in your pokes now; this old fellow looks as though he were broke and I want to collect about two hundred dollars for him." She did, too. When Smith was killed on his way to preach at Crook City, Jane summed up the public reaction pretty well: "Ain't it too bad the Indians killed the only man that came into the Hills to tell us how to live. And we sure need the telling."[28]

The Congregational Church, represented by the Reverend L. P. Norcross, came early to Deadwood and held services wherever it could—in a butcher shop, in the dining room of the Centennial Hotel, or in a carpenter shop. It ultimately built a church in January, 1877. Father Lonergan, the Catholic priest, also used a carpenter shop when he celebrated the first Mass in May, 1877. The Episcopalians borrowed Jack Langrishe's theater for their services.

One Sunday, Billy Nuthall, proprietor of the Melodeon, allowed the Reverend W. L. Rumney to hold services in his bar. Gambling equipment was pushed to one side, while Rumney, an ex-Confederate officer, preached from the vaudeville stage. When the sermon was over, "Nutshell Bill," a well-known gambler, spoke up saying, "Now boys, the old man has been telling you

[28] Young, *Hard Knocks*, 209; Bennett, *Old Deadwood Days*, 217–18.

how to save your souls; come this way and I'll show you how to win some money."[29]

Unfortunately, Deadwood was not populated solely by men who thirsted for religion. Some even did their best to still further enliven the already boisterous entertainment available in the local bars and gambling houses. Others, impoverished and corrupted by drink and dissipation, turned to a life of crime and became the badmen, murderers, and road agents who did so much to make life in the Hills a varied and exciting experience.

[29] McClintock, *Pioneer Days*, 146–47.

10

BADMEN OF THE HILLS

Here lie the bodies of Allen, Curry, and Hall.
Like other horse thieves they had their rise, decline, and fall;
On yon pine tree they hung till dead,
And here they found a lonely bed.
Then be a little cautious how you gobble horses up,
For every horse you pick up here adds sorrow to your cup;
We're bound to stop this business, or hang you to a man,
For we've hemp and hands enough in town to swing the
whole damn clan.[1]

The number of men who died violent deaths during the gold rush was not as large as might be expected—about one-half a man per year per thousand—but each murder and lynching received as much publicity as if it had been a dozen. Many of the victims were associated with the more depraved classes: bartenders, gamblers, gay ladies, and their customers. Others were the victims of bandits and thugs, killed in the course of robberies. Still others were the highwaymen themselves, who preyed on honest citizens but eventually bit off more than they could chew. One way or another, most of the graves of men who had come to a violent end could have been marked like one between Laramie and Rawlins, "Killed by a son-of-a-bitch."[2]

[1] Spring, *Cheyenne and Black Hills Stage and Express Routes*, 209.
[2] *Daily Leader* (Cheyenne), January 12, 1876.

To list in detail all the murders in the Hills from 1874 to 1879 would tax the patience, if not the credulity, of the reader. Only the more notorious killings, therefore, are discussed as examples of the Black Hills' gold-rush era.

The earliest recorded killing, an accidental one, occurred in March, 1876. Tom Milligan and his partner Alex Shaw were both drunkenly shooting at a target, during which the latter was hit. A Custer mob was inclined toward lynching Milligan, but since he was a Freemason, local brothers protected him. He was ultimately punished by a $25 fine for having discharged a firearm within the city limits.[3]

The first recorded duel in the Hills took place in Crook City in July, 1876, between two unsavory characters, Tom Moore and Jim Shannon. Shannon demanded a $50 loan from Moore and assaulted him when he refused. Both went to get their weapons and then returned to the street in front of the bar where they had quarreled. They fired simultaneously, and Shannon was killed. A jury of twelve miners, presided over by Dr. R. D. Jennings, quickly returned a verdict of justifiable homicide, for Shannon was known to have frequently engaged in shooting and was reputed to have stabbed two soldiers to death in Bismarck.[4]

The murder of Jack Hinch of Gayville on July 9, 1876, shows frontier life and justice at its worst. Bill Trainor, Hinch's partner, was happily playing cards with John R. Carty and Jeremiah McCarty when Hinch became suspicious of the game and urged his friend to quit. This angered Carty and McCarty, who later went to Hinch's lodgings, broke into the room in which he slept, and attacked him. McCarty fired two pistol shots, and Carty finished the job by stabbing Hinch several times with a large knife.

The murderers fled to Fort Laramie, where they were arrested. Deputy Sheriff Jack Davis brought Carty back to Gayville hidden in the bottom of a wagon for fear of mob violence. Presenting Carty to a miners court for trial, Davis said:

Boys, I've brought this man from Fort Laramie to the Hills,

[3] *Daily Press and Dakotaian* (Yankton), March 24, 1876.
[4] *Black Hills Pioneer* (Deadwood), July 22, 1876.

163

through a country swarming with hostile Indians, to be tried for his life. When I arrested him I gave him the choice of being brought back here to be tried by miner's jury or to go to Yankton to be tried in the regular courts. He decided to come here and here we are. I promised him that you would give him a fair trial, and a fair trial he must have. If you give him this and find him guilty, hang him, and I'll help you pull the rope. But until you do this, the man who touches a hair of his head will do so over my dead body.[5]

Bill Trainor tried to stir up the mob to omit the trial and hang Carty at once, but a peace-loving bystander, Johnny Flaherty, beat him over the head with the barrel of a Smith & Wesson revolver until he subsided. The miners decided that Carty was guilty only of assault and battery, and he was punished by being run out of town. McCarty, who had chosen to go to Yankton for a regular trial, languished there in jail for a year or so and was then released for lack of witnesses to appear against him.

The most famous killing in the Hills was the murder of James Butler "Wild Bill" Hickok by Jack McCall. Wild Bill was a gambler, part-time gunman, and full-time liar who worked all three professions. Soon after the Civil War, *Harper's Monthly* published a diverting but highly exaggerated account of Bill's valorous deeds, which included a single-handed combat with ten of the ruffianly "M'Kandlass gang." Bill lived on the publicity ever after. His feats with a pistol were famous, partly because he was a good shot, and partly because he cheated, perforating targets at close range, and then later betting that he could hit them from a great distance. He had a supply of the usual frontier stories about gold and Indian fights, which he told to tenderfeet in exchange for drinks. At the time of his death he was an unimpressive gambler who had come to Deadwood after being run out of Cheyenne as a vagrant.[6]

[5] Hughes, *Pioneer Years*, 157; *Black Hills Pioneer* (Deadwood), July 15, 1876.
[6] The most recent book on Hickok is Joseph G. Rosa, *They Called Him Wild Bill: The Life and Adventures of James Butler Hickok*; G.W.N. (George Ward Nichols), "Wild Bill," *Harper's Monthly*, Vol. XXXIV (February, 1867), 284, tells of the M'Kandlass (which is variously spelled in other accounts) battle.

Whatever his shortcomings, Wild Bill's fame was larger than life. He was widely hailed as "the prince of pistoleers," a title which made him the target of every would-be badman in the West. When he arrived in Deadwood, he evidently believed that fate was closing in on him, for his eyesight was failing, and he confided to his friend, "Colorado Charley" Utter, "I have a hunch that I am in my last camp and will never leave this gulch alive." His last letter to his wife, written the day before he died, also struck a mournful note, saying that "if such should be we never meet again, while firing my last shot, I will gently breathe the name of my wife—Agnes—and with [best?] wishes even for my enemies I will make the plunge and try to swim to the other shore."[7]

The next day, August 2, 1876, Bill was playing cards with Carl Mann, Charles Rich, and Captain William R. Massie in Nuttal & Mann's Saloon Number Ten. Contrary to his usual custom he sat with his back to the rear door, for Rich stubbornly refused to give up the seat by the wall. McCall entered by the rear door, walked to within three feet of Wild Bill, and shot him through the back of the head. The bullet passed out through Bill's right cheek, crossed the table, and lodged in Captain Massie's wrist. McCall snapped his pistol several times at the other players, but it misfired. He then ran out into the street where he was quickly captured. Local tradition has it that Wild Bill had both guns out and cocked before he slumped over the table, but Bud Goode, of Sturgis, whose father helped move the body, says that this is an exaggeration—he only had his hands on his guns. Others, equally reliable, say he never moved at all. On the table before him lay the cards which became famous as the "deadman's hand," black aces and eights, and the Jack of Diamonds.[8]

---

[7] Rosa, *They Called Him Wild Bill*, 213; Frank J. Wilstach, *Wild Bill Hickok: The Prince of Pistoleers*, 281; Young, *Hard Knocks*, 218–23, mentions Hickok's blindness.

[8] The controversy which rages around the death of Wild Bill is extremely murky—all the uninitiated can do is accept the sources which seem most reliable. Even Ramon Adams, *Burrs Under the Saddle: A Second Look at Books and Histories of the West*, has provided some new, but erroneous, details. A contemp-

McCall, who was also known as Bill Sutherland, was a medium-sized, swarthy, sullen, and unprepossessing chap, with scanty whiskers and a reputation to match. Immediately after being captured, he was tried before a miners court convened in the Gem Theater. His defense was that "Wild Bill killed my brother in Abilene, and swore he would kill me if ever I should cross his path. Here in Deadwood I found myself in the same town with him, and knew I must either kill him or leave." On the other hand, Judge William Littlebury Kuykendall, who presided over the trial, comments in his memoirs that McCall offered no motive at all, other than a love of notoriety and a glass of whisky taken in the saloon across the street. The jury, after an hour and one-half of deliberation, returned a verdict of "not guilty."[9]

McCall's motives have remained obscure. The criminal class in Deadwood, fearful that Wild Bill might be employed as town marshal, may have hired McCall to murder him. The *Black Hills Pioneer* published a story, later retracted, that gambler Johnny Varnes had bribed McCall to do the job. A few writers, some claiming to be eyewitnesses, say that Wild Bill and McCall had quarreled over a game of poker in which McCall had not been able to pay what he owed. The most probable explanation, however, is that McCall, a cheap and unknown failure, was stone drunk and hoped to redeem his beardless manhood by killing the biggest gunman of them all.

Acquitted in Deadwood, McCall went to Fort Laramie, where he continued to brag about his exploit. Since the miners court which had freed him had no legal standing, he was again arrested, taken to Yankton, and tried before Territorial Chief Justice C. P. Shannon. His story about Wild Bill having killed his brother was shown to be a complete fabrication, and he was convicted. His

orary account may be found in the *Black Hills Pioneer* (Deadwood), August 5, 1876.

[9] Hughes, *Pioneer Years*, 163; Kuykendall, *Frontier Days*, 185. The jury consisted of Charles Whitehead, foreman, J. J. Bump, J. H. Thompson, J. F. Cooper, K. F. Towle, L. A. Judd, L. D. BooKaw, S. S. Hopkins, Alex Travis, J. E. Thompson, Ed. Burke, and John Mann. A Frank Towle was later killed while robbing a stage—if it was the same man, his presence might explain the jury's odd verdict.

only defense was that he was drunk at the time and could not remember what happened. He was confined in a cell with Mc-Carty, the Hinch murderer, and hanged on March 1, 1877.

Wild Bill was buried in Deadwood, under a headboard saying "J. B. (Wild Bill) Hickock, aged 48 years; murdered by Jack McCall, August 2, 1875." Captain Jack Crawford, the poet scout, later wrote:

> *Under the sod in the land of gold*
> *We have laid the fearless Bill;*
> *We called him Wild, yet a little child,*
> *Could bend his iron will,*
> *With generous heart he freely gave*
> *To the poorly clad, unshod—*
> *Think of it pards—of his noble traits—*
> *When you cover him with the sod.*

The body was eventually moved to Mount Moriah Cemetery, where it has since become a tourist shrine. When Calamity Jane died, years later, she was buried in the adjoining grave. An old timer sadly shook his head, saying: "It's a good thing Bill is dead—he'd never have stood for this!"[10]

Indeed Bill would not have stood for it, for although closely associated with Calamity Jane in the public mind, he was of a thoughtful and fastidious nature and had little to do with that notorious bawd. She was born Marthy Cannary on May 1, 1852, in Princeton, Missouri. Already a well-known harlot, she accompanied the soldiers of Professor Walter P. Jenney's 1875 expedition to the Black Hills. Many stories are told about how she got her name, but the most likely is that her paramours were generally visited by some venereal "calamity."

Following the Jenney expedition, Jane was in and out of the Hills several times. In the spring of 1876 she came to Deadwood with "Colorado Charley" Utter, his brother, and Wild Bill, but

[10] *Daily Leader* (Cheyenne), September 26, 1876, printed the first epitaph, but later a more flowery version was provided by Colorado Charley Utter; Crawford, *The Poet Scout*, 68; Case, *Lee's Official Guidebook to the Black Hills and Badlands*, 88.

that is the closest connection that ever existed between the two. At that time eyewitnesses said she was "built like a busted bale of hay," and was "about the roughest looking human being" the miners had ever seen. She habitually dressed in men's buckskin clothing, wore two guns, and was generally drunk when she had the money. Friends in Custer called her "the best scout in the camp," but the word probably denotes good-fellowship rather than any real ability at tracking or fighting Indians.

During the Deadwood smallpox epidemic Calamity Jane nursed the sick in the local pest house and even went so far as to steal money to buy them food and medicines. Even so, the editor of the *Daily Champion* could not bring himself to praise her, and wrote that:

> As far as real merit is concerned, she is a fraud and a dead give-away. A hundred waiter girls or mop squeezers in this gulch are her superior in everything .... Her form and features are not only indifferent but repulsive. It makes me tired to see so much written about such a woman.

She drifted away from the Hills after the gold rush, but came back again in her later years to beg support from old acquaintances. A typical source of her income was the sale of patent "bachelor buttons." Approaching a prospective customer with a pair of scissors, she would adroitly snip off the most essential button from his trousers, and then blandly sell him one with which to replace it. She died at Terry on August 1, 1903. Judge Kuykendall, when he heard that a monument was to be built in her memory, snorted that "charity dictates that the veil of oblivion should be drawn over the character of that woman."[11]

Whatever the reason for the death of Wild Bill, there is no doubt that gambling led to many homicides. Harry Varnes, for example, got into an argument with N. Hartgrove, a local black-

---

[11] There is even more controversy about Calamity Jane than there is about Wild Bill. The most authoritative account is J. Leonard Jennewein, *Calamity Jane of the Western Trails*; her own biography, often reproduced in facsimile, is worthless; the *Daily Champion* (Deadwood) quotation is from Briggs, *Frontiers of the Northwest*, 81; Kuykendall, *Frontier Days*, 191, is very critical of her.

smith, over a game of cards. Varnes picked up a chair, and Hartgrove drew his gun, but bystanders temporarily quelled the fight.
Later the two again fell into a heated discussion with the result
that Hartgrove shot Varnes, wounding him mortally. He then
surrendered to the Deadwood marshal, Con Stapleton. The marshal, not having a jail in which to put him, released Hartgrove on
his own recognizance, and he was never seen again.[12]

Another fatal quarrel over "accounts" took place in Cyrus Iba's
restaurant. James Ferrell and a man named Cook came to blows,
and when Iba did his best to eject one of them, both drew their
guns and fired simultaneously. Ferrell died three days later. Cook
was tried before Mayor Farnum's "court," but was judged to
have shot in self-defense and was released.[13]

Bandits, too, caused their share of deaths. On March 25, 1877,
a gang composed of Sam Bass, Joel Collins, Jim Berry, Frank
Towle, and Robert "Little Reddy" McKimie tried to stop the in-
coming stage at the mouth of Gold Run, near Deadwood. They
hoped to seize a shipment of $15,000 in currency destined for
Stebbins, Wood and Company's bank. The stage driver, Johnny
Slaughter, refused to stop and urged the team forward. McKimie's
shotgun blast killed Slaughter instantly, leaving twelve buckshot
in an almost perfect circle around his heart. McKimie afterward
swore that it was a mistake—the horses had brushed by him and
jarred his arm. If such were the case, it was pretty good shooting
for an accident. When the stage got to town, Slaughter's blood-
stained vest was nailed to the station door as an encouragement
for local citizens to form a vigilance committee. McKimie and
his gang escaped, but ultimately most of them were captured or
shot down while committing other crimes.[14]

Disputes over land—usually mining claims—were another common source of fatalities. Samuel F. "Turkey Sam" May and John
Blair shot Dan Obradovitch, mortally wounded Steve Corsich,

[12] *Black Hills Pioneer* (Deadwood), February 3, 1877.

[13] *Ibid.*, November 28, 1876.

[14] Most books on Sam Bass mention the Slaughter killing; Wayne Gard, *Sam
Bass*, 61–73; J. W. Bridwell, *The Life and Adventures of Robert McKimie*, 1–8,
describes the life of this outlaw, whose name is variously spelled.

and nicked N. Millich (or Millage) for attempting to build a cabin on disputed ground. From the evidence at the trial it seems that May and Blair had prepared themselves for the fight by studious application in a local bar. The jury, which evidently frowned on drunken murders, convicted both of manslaughter in the first degree. Since it took eight hours to reach the decision, a few of the jurymen may have thought that killing a foreigner was not a serious crime.[15]

The famous Tuttle murder in 1877 was also the result of a dispute over property—in this case an underground trespass. Cephas Tuttle, one of the owners of the Aurora Mine, was highly incensed when Henry Keets, who owned an adjoining property, obtained the right to dig a tunnel from his shaft under the Aurora. When the tunnelers broke through into Tuttle's main shaft and began burrowing their way through his most valuable ore, he protested violently but without effect. He accused Keets's men of trespassing, but they laughed at him. Later they smirked innocently at Tuttle's charge that they were stealing his richest ore, and kept right on digging.

At last Tuttle threatened to blow up the whole mine with Keets and all the others in it, by dropping a case of dynamite down the shaft. The miners withdrew a little, and some of them came up to the surface. As Tuttle lit the fuse to the dynamite, a well-placed bullet from Keets's men snuffed it out. He succeeded the second time and hurled the explosive down the shaft. By this time all but one of the men had got out of the tunnel by another exit, and the explosion only deafened the remaining miner. Tuttle went down into the mine laughing and chuckling to survey the damage. When he came out again, Keets's men shot him dead. No one was ever convicted of the crime, but several likely candidates for that honor were put forward by Tuttle's friends and survivors.[16]

Two Central City miners, John S. Bryant and A. William Adams, killed each other in a similar dispute. Adams posted a

---

15 *Black Hills Daily Times* (Deadwood), April 24, 26, 1877; Obradovitch's name is often given as "Bradovitch" or other variants.

16 McClintock, *Pioneer Days*, 192–93.

claim to a mill site on a placer mine, Number 13 above discovery on Deadwood Creek, which Bryant already owned. When the two met, Adams pulled out a concealed revolver, shot Bryant through the body, then turned and fled. The wounded Bryant drew his own gun and fired. His first shot missed, but the second knocked Adams down. Bryant then staggered up to his opponent, placed his pistol to Adams's head, and shot him through the brain. He then collapsed over the body of his fallen foe and died a few hours later.[17]

Attempted robbery resulted in many other killings, of which the death of Bob "Texas Frank" Castello is typical. Henry Myers of Deadwood had accumulated $16,000 worth of gold during the summer of 1877 and left the Hills accompanied by four friends and his son "Kid." Camped at Pleasant Valley, twelve miles below Custer, they were joined by three affable men who cooked on the communal campfire and made themselves generally agreeable. Concerned about his father's gold, Kid Myers remained suspicious and stayed away from the fire. It was just as well, for after supper one of the visitors, Bob Castello, snatched up a gun and ordered Myers and his friends to throw up their hands. About this time young Myers stepped from behind a wagon with a shotgun and fired at Castello. The latter turned and ran, only to be shot down and killed. The other two bandits escaped. Castello, it turned out, was already a fugitive from justice, having killed his own father in Bismarck.[18]

Jealousy brought about the murder of young Charles Forbes by Bill Gay, one of the founders of Gayville. Mrs. Gay was an exceptionally attractive young woman whom Gay had chosen from among the professional ladies of the town. He was naturally somewhat dubious about the constancy of her affections and kept an annoyingly close eye on her conduct. Forbes, a rather stupid young man in his late teens, sent Mrs. Gay a note, via Sam "Nigger General" Fields who specialized in such work, asking her to "meet me this evening, my darling, by moonlight at 8:00 o'clock, at the corner of the big barn." Mrs. Gay, who had no affection

[17] *Daily Leader* (Cheyenne), October 5, 1877.
[18] *Ibid.*, October 7, 1877, May 28, 1879.

whatever for Forbes, took the opportunity to demonstrate how faithful she was and immediately showed her husband the letter. Gay at once cornered "General" Fields, found out who had sent the note, and then found Forbes and killed him. Tried and convicted, Gay spent three years in prison. On his return to Gayville he was met at the station by a brass band. He later committed another murder in Montana and was promptly hanged.[19]

On August 20, 1878, Mrs. John Collison, a Deadwood school teacher, was discovered in her bed with her head beaten in. In the subsequent trial it was revealed that Martin Couk, her lover, had murdered her to keep her from telling Mark V. Boughton about his plan to kill Boughton and elope with his wife. Mrs. Collison naturally objected to this project, both because of the crime proposed and because she wanted to hold onto Couk herself. Mrs. Boughton and "General" Fields were also implicated. Couk was sentenced to hang but later pardoned because the evidence against him seemed, on review, to have been less than conclusive. Released from prison, he returned to Deadwood where he spent considerable time and money hunting for the alleged murderer. Years later in New Mexico he was convicted of another murder, and before he was hanged, he confessed that he really had killed Mrs. Collison.[20]

Often attempted murders were foiled by some freak accident. Frank McGovern, for instance, came into Manning's saloon, paid for a drink with gold dust, then bellowed at bartender Billy Madden, "Put half an ounce of dust back in that bag or I'll . . . ." Billy paused, reached under the bar for a six-gun, and shot McGovern in the face. The bullet struck a little above the middle of his forehead, skidded upwards along the scalp under the skin, and came out at the top of McGovern's head. The victim was badly scarred, but lived to tell the story.[21]

James E. May, a lover of Mollie Mickey, quarreled with the

19 McClintock, *Pioneer Days*, 170–74.

20 *Daily Leader* (Cheyenne), August 21, 25, September 13, November 14, December 1, 4, 1878, January 29, 1879; Brown and Willard, *The Black Hills Trails*, 365–66.

21 Stokes and Driggs, *Deadwood Gold*, 86–87.

172

frail lady, punched her on the nose, and then shot her with his revolver. The whalebone in her corset saved her. May fired again, hitting her right thumb. Fortunately, another lover, stagecoach messenger Jesse Brown, arrived in time to prevent further bloodshed.[22]

Sometimes quirks of fate worked the other way, as in the Blanchard-Hedges fight. Robert Hedges, a thoroughly unsavory character, went to pick raspberries on "Old Man" Blanchard's property, muttering as he went that he was "going to shoot somebody," a threat he had often made good before. When Blanchard appeared, Hedges fired at him from ambush. The old man at once took cover, and when Hedges stepped out to get a better shot, Blanchard killed him with a revolver at a distance of seven hundred feet. Nobody regretted Hedge's death, and all complimented Blanchard on his exceptional marksmanship.[23]

Approximately thirty men were murdered in the Black Hills during the gold-rush period from 1875 to 1879. Other deaths, unnoticed murders and lynchings, which are separately considered, increase this total to an average of about forty violent deaths per year per 100,000 population, which is approximately eight times that of the United States today. This figure does not seem excessive, considering the number of badmen available.

Lesser crimes than murder were so common that only the most striking found their way into the news. There is no question that as the mining excitement increased, dangerous and lawless men came to the Hills. They tended to congregate in Deadwood because most of the money and most of their comrades already were there. This left the rest of the Hills pretty quiet but turned Deadwood into a sink of iniquity.

A few examples of petty crimes will suffice. Richard B. Hughes, for instance, had a huge pile of cordwood laid by in Deadwood, which he intended to sell during the winter. When he went to get it, he found that someone else had saved him the trouble of hauling it to market. Mr. O. C. Peck, of Gayville, was robbed of

[22] *Daily Leader* (Cheyenne), April 20, May 7, 1878.
[23] *Black Hills Weekly Times* (Deadwood), July 19, 1879.

$500, but the thief was apprehended and run out of town. Robbers broke into Dick Berry's cabin in Deadwood and stole a one-hundred-pound sack of flour. Fortunately the sack leaked, and the trail led to the robber's hideout and to the recovery of much other stolen property. A chap named California Jack was arrested for passing counterfeit $50 bills—that was swindling on a grand scale. A six-man gang operated up and down Deadwood Gulch in 1877 robbing miners cabins, storehouses, and sluice boxes. Sheriff Seth Bullock and a posse arrested three of the men, but the others fled toward Crook City where they were overtaken and one seriously wounded in a gun fight. Crimes of this nature were so common that they received only passing notice, and many of them went unrecorded.

The *Black Hills Pioneer* complained that burglars in Deadwood were a regular plague. Mr. Rosengarden heard a thief in his chicken house, fired at random, and mortally wounded Frank Miller, who was busily stealing four chickens. Public opinion held that accidental death was a little too severe a penalty for such a petty crime, so Rosengarden was held under $1,500 bond until he was released by a grand jury.

By the end of the rush in 1879, petty thievery was all too common. Tools were taken from mining claims, sluice boxes were robbed of nuggets and amalgam, and odds and ends were picked up with a casual abandon that seemed quite out of step with touted frontier honesty. Perhaps the old attitude of mutual cooperation had faded out and been replaced by an ungenerous spirit of selfish immorality. Even so, many doors remained unlocked, and many miners continued to be trusting clear up to the arrival of the railroad in the late 1880's.

More thrilling and notable than petty thefts were the stagecoach robberies. As soon as roving bands of hostile Indians were driven back onto their reservations in the fall of 1876, it became possible for outlaws to live in safety along the roads and trails, eagerly awaiting opportunities to fall upon the travelers.

By 1877 stage robbing was a booming business. The same gang that killed Johnny Slaughter attempted three other holdups, but did not gain much loot. "Dunc" Blackburn, John Wall, and their companions also stopped a good many stages, usually with indifferent profit. Once, when three road agents tried to rob a coach, the passengers even jumped out and fought them off. Toward the end of June the stage was held up near the Cheyenne River, and the passengers were robbed of $1,400. Fortunately, the treasure chests, riveted to the framework of the coach, proved to be both impregnable and immovable, and the bandits got nothing out of them. During July the robbers stopped the Sidney coach near Battle Creek and took what few valuables the three passengers possessed. On July 21, two bandits stopped two more coaches again near the Cheyenne, but the travelers were not carrying anything of value. A day or two later, six bandits repeated the performance at the same place, but got just $20. In October, Blackburn and Wall held up the Sidney coach near Buffalo Gap and robbed its only passenger of $7. Indeed, stage robbing was not always a profitable business.[24]

The next year, 1878, saw the peak of stagecoach robberies. In July eight highwaymen attacked the coach at Whoop-Up Canyon, near modern Newcastle. The six passengers fought back, and in the ensuing battle three of them were wounded, but the robbers were driven off. On July 23 the coach carrying Reverend J. W. Picket was held up two miles north of Lightning Creek. The preacher was not molested, but the United States mails were robbed. Three days later a messenger who accompanied the coach—E. S. Smith—fought off six road agents by firing some twenty shots at them. Smith was not so lucky on September 10 when the bandit "Lengthy" Johnson and his gang stopped the Cheyenne-bound coach at Lance Creek. During the holdup the Deadwood coach arrived on the scene with Smith. The latter tried to put up a fight, but the outlaws used captured passengers as shields and forced him to surrender.[25]

[24] *Black Hills Pioneer* (Deadwood), July 14, 21, 1877; *Daily Leader* (Cheyenne), June 3, 27, 29, July 25, October 4, 1877.

[25] *Daily Leader* (Cheyenne), July 3, 26, 27, August 23, September 14, 20, 1878; Spring, *Cheyenne and Black Hills Stage and Express Routes.*

Although the bandits often opened the so-called "treasure chests" which accompanied the passenger coaches, they only once successfully robbed well-guarded bullion shipments from the mines. Even this brilliant coup, which took place at the Canyon Springs Stage Station on September 27, 1878, did not result in any great profit since most of the treasure ultimately was recovered. This treasure coach, carrying a shipment supposedly worth $250,-000, was driven by Gene Barnett and guarded by three messengers, Gail Hill, Bill Smith, and Scott Davis. The only passenger, Hugh Campbell, a telegrapher, was carried as a special favor to the telegraph company. The bandit gang, led by Charles Carey and composed of Frank McBride, Thomas Jefferson "Duck" Goodale, Al Speer, and Big Nose George, descended on the Canyon Springs Station about half an hour before the stage was due. They tied up "Stuttering Dick" Wright, the stock tender, and prepared a hot reception for the treasure coach.

The robbers' first volley wounded Bill Smith and killed Campbell. Gail Hill, although badly injured, managed to crawl to cover and shoot down one of the bandits before collapsing. Scott Davis hid behind a stout pine tree and kept up a hot fire on the bandits in the stage station. Carey grabbed the driver Gene Barnett and, using him as a shield, advanced toward Scott's position. Unwilling to risk wounding his friend, Scott abandoned the fight and ran for help.

Once the guards were disposed of, the bandits pried open the safe with a crowbar, loaded $27,000 worth of gold on a wagon with their wounded comrade Frank McBride, left the corpse of Big Nose George where it fell, and took off. A posse of messengers composed of Boone May, John Brown, Jesse Brown, and William Taylor was soon on their trail.[26]

The messengers picked up additional members as the chase progressed and very nearly caught up with the robbers east of Rapid City. The hunted men, however, slipped away in the darkness

---

[26] *Ibid.*, 270–73. The amount stolen is disputed, but the stage company offered a reward for only $27,000. The robbery is often called the "Cold Springs" holdup, from the nearby ranch by that name.

but left behind a gold bar worth $11,000, which later was picked up by Dr. N. C. Whitfield. No further trace of the treasure came to light until "Duck" Goodale allowed his father, a prominent banker in Atlantic, Iowa, to display his share of the loot in a bank window, supposedly the money he had received from the sale of a Black Hills mine. Goodale was quickly arrested, but on the way back to the Hills for trial he escaped from his guard, William Ward, by jumping out of the washroom window of a moving train. He was never heard from again. Al Speer was arrested in Ogallala, Nebraska, with messenger Gail Hill's gun and some jewelry from the treasure chest in his possession. A man named Gouch, who was supposed to have been connected with the bandits, though not present at the holdup, was arrested at Fort Thompson, South Dakota, and led peace officers to some retort gold hidden near Pino Springs. Eventually, nearly all of the treasure was recovered, one bandit killed, another badly injured, and two arrested. It should have taught the criminals a lesson.[27]

Although it was difficult to rob a treasure coach successfully, the passenger coaches enjoyed no such immunity. Frequent holdups were accepted as one of the hazards of traveling in the Hills. No sensible person thought of carrying much money on the stage unless it could be ingeniously concealed in his baggage or secreted somewhere in his clothing. The bandits quickly became aware of these attempts at concealment and would inspect not only pockets and purses but the hair, shoes, and "any bulges or bumps not accounted for by the average human anatomy in their search for valuables." One gay lady from Deadwood twisted her folding money into her back hair, where it escaped detection in spite of an enthusiastic search. Another good woman, anxious to save her watch, pleaded "Please, Mr. Robber! good Mr. Robber! dear Mr. Robber! don't take my watch." The highwayman, unable to withstand this guileless appeal, returned her trinkets. Still another pas-

[27] University of South Dakota, W.P.A. Writer's Project, typescript, "Annals of Early Rapid City, 1878–87—Crime," 9, says that Whitfield's find weighed 650 ounces, and was worth between $10,000 and $12,000. Goodale's name, often given as "Doug," was actually Thomas Jefferson; "Duck" was a boyhood nickname. Speer's arrest is mentioned in the *Daily Leader* (Cheyenne), November 2, 1878.

senger, who was doubtless a professional humorist, complained when the bandits ordered "hands up!" that "this is a high-handed piece of business," a bit of wit which so convulsed the outlaws that they let him keep his watch.[28]

Horse thieves likewise were a nuisance in the Hills. To steal a man's horse and leave him on foot in Indian country was considered the utmost depth of depravity. "Persimmons Bill," who reputedly murdered stage superintendent "Stuttering" Brown, commanded a ring of white and Indian thieves which centered its operations around present-day Edgemont. In October, 1876, two men, probably from this gang, stole twenty horses near Custer, but were tracked down and killed by a detachment of soldiers from Camp Collier. On the Fourth of July, 1877, Charles Howard was so filled with patriotic (or other) spirit that he hired a horse at a livery stable but failed to return it. A posse tracked him down and hanged him. The same year "Dunc" Blackburn and his gang added horse stealing to their other crimes, emerging unscathed from a battle with the redoubtable "Long John" Brennan outside of Rapid City. A similar gang, led by James Heffran and Tony Pastor, broke up early in 1878 when the two were captured and made to show where they had hidden the stolen stock. In November, "Lengthy" Johnson, "the terror of Spearfish Valley," was captured and sent to jail, which made owners of good horse flesh "feel much easier in their minds."[29]

Slowly but inexorably roughhewn law and a semblance of order came to the community. Horse thieves and bandits were gradually caught by posses and vigilantes, and generally received a "suspended sentence" on the spot. The most notable of these frequent lynchings was the sad death of Louis "Red" Curry, A. J. "Doc" Allen, and James "Kid" Hall (or Mansfield) on June 24, 1877. The first two men were hardened criminals who had picked up a few horses near Crook City and then headed south. On their way

[28] Tallent, *The Black Hills*, 386, 389–90; *Daily Leader* (Cheyenne), January 12, 1878.

[29] *Ibid.*, April 21, October 15, 1876, July 4, 1877, February 13, May 2, June 29, August 27, November 30, 1878.

178

to Rapid City they met young Hall and allowed him to ride one of their new acquisitions.

While camped beside the trail, the three were captured by a posse of irate Rapid Citians, taken into town, and imprisoned in a log cabin pending trial. Hall cursed and swore at his captors in a most abandoned and uncivil manner, which undoubtedly prejudiced acceptance of his claim that he had had nothing to do with stealing the horses. Late that evening a group of masked men broke into the log-cabin prison, carried the three to a hill south of town (afterward known as Hangman's Hill), and there hanged them. When Hall's innocence later became apparent, the lynchers were sorry, but it did not do much good. For years afterward Rapid Citians were known as "stranglers."[30]

The next big "necktie party" was held in honor of George W. Keating and O. B. "Beans" Davis, two Deadwood butchers who appeared to have an almost inexhaustible supply of beef. One day a rancher from Spearfish Valley came into their shop, examined a hide or two, and then gazed at the two butchers with marked suspicion. One look was enough, and the partners departed in haste, for, as the *Enterprise* piously remarked, "The wicked flee where no man pursueth." Shortly afterward the bodies of Keating and Davis were found suspended from a tree about five miles north of Spearfish. Local opinion held very strongly that they "did not get up there of their own selves."[31]

Rough and ready justice steadily continued to rid the Hills of their less desirable citizens. A rascal known only as "One-eyed Ed" was hanged in Red Canyon by cowboys who resented his having killed a friend of theirs named Porter. Dick Burnett was caught stealing horses in the same area and met with a similar fate. These lynchings were probably spur-of-the-moment affairs. Less easily excused was the premeditated killing of Archie McLaughlin

[30] G. B. Mansfield (comp.), "Scrap Book of Black Hills Early Days," 34, Leedy Collection, Society of Minnelusa Pioneers, Rapid City; Brown and Willard, *Black Hills Trails*, 292–96. The poem at the beginning of this chapter was reputedly put up over the graves of Allen, Curry, and Hall.

[31] McClintock, *Pioneer Days*, 181; University of South Dakota, W.P.A. Writer's Project, typescript, "Annals of Early Rapid City, 1878–87—Crime," 7.

and William Mansfield. These well-known thieves attracted suspicion when they tried to sell $31,000 worth of stolen gold bullion for $11,000. After having been arrested, they were sent toward Deadwood guarded by Jesse Brown and Boone May. Vigilantes stopped the stage about a mile north of Fort Laramie and promptly hanged the two outlaws from a convenient tree—apparently without the least interference from the accompanying peace officers.[32]

Cornelius "Lame Johnny" Donahue met with a similar fate. A graduate of Girard College in Philadelphia, he had been injured in a boyhood accident and had acquired a recognizable limp. He came to the Hills an honest man, took to horse stealing and stage robbery, and was eventually captured. On the way to Rapid City in the custody of Sheriff "Whispering" Smith, vigilantes stopped the stage near Hermosa, removed Johnny, and hanged him. He had, in addition to his limp, a noticeably large mouth, in honor of which John B. Furey posted a sign over his grave: *Stranger, pass gently o'er this sod:/ If he opens his mouth, you're gone, by God!*[33]

Lee "Curley" Grimes died in much the same way. He was arrested about fifty miles north of Deadwood and was taken during a blizzard toward Fort Meade in the custody of Boone May and W. H. Llewellyn. He asked to have the handcuffs removed in order to warm his hands, and immediately plunged his horse into the deep snow in an effort to get away. The officers fired, killing him "while trying to escape," a story about which those who knew Boone May were justifiably skeptical. Both May and Llewellyn were tried for murder, but neither was convicted.

May's character is further illustrated by the case of Frank Towle. A gang of bandits held up the Cheyenne coach near Hat Creek, Wyoming, and sent Towle, one of the robbers, down the road to watch for any messengers who might be following at a distance. The messengers, May and John Zimmerman, heard Towle coming, hid in the bushes, and shot him dead as soon as he

[32] *Daily Leader* (Cheyenne), October 22, 1878.

[33] Ellis Taylor Peirce, "Odd Characters and Incidents in the Black Hills During the '70's," MS, Box 6-3, South Dakota Historical Society, Pierre; University of South Dakota, W.P.A. Writer's Project, typescript, "Annals of Early Rapid City, 1878-87—Crime," 13; Brown and Willard, *Black Hills Trails*, 298-301.

View of Terraville, South Dakota, during late 1870's. Note the stamp mills and flume in the valley.

Courtesy South Dakota State Historical Society

Overland stagecoaches brought the more affluent gold-rushers to the Black Hills from Cheyenne, Wyoming, or Sidney, Nebraska. Each of these coaches was capable of carrying twelve to fifteen passengers.

Courtesy Carper-Tscharner Photo Collection

The Hart and Keliher freight train hauling heavy mining equipment, probably near present-day Rapid City, South Dakota. Most freight was brought into the Hills by oxen before the coming of the railroads.

Courtesy Carper-Tscharner Photo Collection

Railroad track being laid north of Custer, South Dakota, in 1890. With the arrival of the railroad, stage lines and freight companies soon went out of business.

Courtesy Carper-Tscharner Photo Collection

By 1885 the Homestake Mine was the largest producer in the Hills. The railroad (top left and center) brought in cordwood which was delivered to the mill's hoist and boiler rooms via the open cut down the face of the hill (center). Not the pile of tailings (center foreground).

Courtesy Homestake Mining Company

"Clean up" day at the Homestake's Deadwood Terra Gold Stamp Mill in 1888.

John Brennan's American House at Seventh and Main streets in Rapid City, South Dakota.

An early-day school house in the Black Hills.

Courtesy Carper-Tscharner Photo Collection

got within range. May later took Towle's head to Cheyenne in a sack in order to claim an expected reward, but he never managed to collect it.[34]

Honest and regular government took a while to get established. In the Dakota territorial election of 1874, for example, Moses K. Armstrong claimed to have received 2,876 votes from "Custer Gulch" in support of his candidacy as delegate to Congress. His opponent, Jefferson P. Kidder, sourly pointed out that this was a good many votes to come from a place then known to be totally uninhabited.[35]

As already described in Chapter IV, local governments, mining districts, and miners courts handled the early judicial business in the Hills. In Deadwood, Mayor E. B. Farnum's court was a popular place to settle ordinary disputes, and since no court of appeals was available, its decisions had the added advantage of finality. An unused mine tunnel in the side of the gulch served as the city jail, and town marshal Con Stapleton kept peace in minor cases and a discreet silence in the rest.

As soon as the federal government acquired title to the Black Hills from the Sioux, it established a federal district court, with Granville G. Bennett its presiding judge. The first court session was held in Sheridan. Everyone involved—judge, lawyers, witnesses, and accused—slept on the dirt floor of the log courthouse. When they woke up after the first night, they found that the prisoner at the bar had escaped by digging his way out under the logs. The court soon moved to Deadwood, where Judge James Barnes in time replaced the respected Bennett. When Barnes' first term convened, there were six murderers awaiting trial, which gives some idea of conditions in the town.

Even with the proper legal trappings the Deadwood courts still

---

[34] Spring, *Cheyenne and Black Hills Stage and Express Routes*, 300–301; Brown and Willard, *Black Hills Trails*, 252–54. There is little doubt that Boone May was one of the rougher characters in the law-enforcement business, for several other killings are reliably attributed to him.

[35] Bullock, "An Account of Deadwood and the Northern Black Hills in 1876" (ed. by Harry H. Anderson), *South Dakota Historical Collections*, Vol. XXXI (1962), 361.

were far from reliable. One coroner's jury, for example, was called upon to determine the cause of death in the case of a man found with his throat cut, twenty-seven bullet holes at various places, and his skull beaten to a pulp. It took them five hours to decide "whether the death was caused by violence or a visitation of Divine Providence."[36]

The town marshal, and later the sheriff, was the principal law-enforcement officer in the frontier community. He needed all the courage he could muster. One day, for example, a marshal—probably Con Stapleton—was peacefully playing poker in a bar when a ruffian, T. Tom Smith, walked in with drawn gun, glowered on the assembled company, and announced that he did not want anybody to get excited, but he "aimed to kill some one" before he departed. The marshal watched for an opportunity and threw himself on Smith in a desperate effort to disarm him. Smith fired. The bullet passed through the marshal's hat, then through his collar and his coat tails, and went across the room where it hit another man squarely on the forehead. There the bullet split in two, the halves sliding under the victim's skin until they came to rest, one at each temple. Smith was subdued and sent to Yankton for rest and meditation at government expense. The wounded man recovered.[37]

Guile, as well as courage, was required in an effective law officer. When miners in the Aurora Mine became disgruntled over their pay, they moved into the tunnel, set up a stove under an air-shaft, and told the management that they would stay put until their demands were met. Cavalry and a cannon from Fort Meade were summoned to the scene and threats and arguments bellowed into the mine, all to no avail. It looked as if bloodshed would be necessary—a thing that Judge Bennett strictly opposed—when Sheriff Seth Bullock appeared with a small package and a wide grin. Climbing up the side of the mountain to the air shaft,

[36] Bennett, *Old Deadwood Days*, 37–38; *Daily Leader* (Cheyenne), June 6, September 4, 1878.

[37] *Ibid.*, January 20, 1877.

he dumped a quantity of asafetida down upon the recalcitrant miners. The strike broke up without further discussion.[38]

The gradual evolution from lawlessness to order came in response to the changing needs of the mining community. As the placer miner and his trusted "pards" were replaced by hired labor, community spirit dwindled, and with its passing came a need for more formal law enforcement. Furthermore, the hired miners came to the Hills, not to dig gold for themselves in the streambeds, but to work for others deep in the hard-rock mines. It made a difference in the way they looked at things.

[38] Bennett, *Old Deadwood Days*, 51–53.

11

THE HARD-ROCK MINES

The gold is thar, 'most everywhar,
And they dig it out with a big iron bar.[1]

There is no question that hard-rock mining was a distinct and separate branch of the art, attracting men of different inclinations, abilities, and resources than did the "poor man's placers" at the beginning of the rush. In those carefree early days all a miner needed for success was a few tools and luck enough to dig in the right gravel bank. Even men who worked for wages hoped that they might one day stumble on a pocket full of nuggets which would make them rich. The hard-rock mines were different. It took a long time to dig down to paying ore, investigate its possibilities, and then build a mill to extract the gold. The hard-rock man needed outside capital to get started, and he hired miners whose sole interest in the job was the wage that they were paid.

It is difficult to determine when hard-rock mining began in earnest. Many claims were staked early in the rush but remained undeveloped until the placers had been worked out and capital and mining machinery had been brought in. Even in 1875, miners fresh from the Hills bragged about quartz ledges running for

[1] *Daily Press and Dakotaian* (Yankton), December 29, 1875, quoting John Williams who had just returned from the Hills.

miles, in which the rock was said to contain one-eighth to one-half pure gold. As the hard-rock mines became productive, these glowing estimates dimmed considerably; they were probably due to an overly judicious sampling of the ore. No matter what their value, these early claims were at first neglected, though Moses "California Joe" Milner located a quartz claim in Palmer Gulch as early as Christmas, 1875, and shortly thereafter John B. Pearson and Frank Bryant staked out hard-rock claims in what later became Central City.[2]

Although not worked actively until the placers had played out, hard-rock prospecting could go on merrily during the winter when the placers were frozen solid. By the time the gravels had been exhausted, a solid backlog of quartz claims had been discovered and was awaiting development. In the fall of 1876 there were 147 hard-rock claims around Deadwood, 70 near Custer, and nearly as many in the Bear Butte and Sand Creek areas. Once Indian title to the Hills was extinguished, investors dared to risk capital in developing the new mines, and the placers, already producing diminishing returns, gave way to a hard-rock rush. These new rushers did not carry a pick and pan but hard cash or the prospect of easy credit, for they tended to be men of means and experience. By the end of 1877 hard-rock mines produced $1,500,-000 a year compared with $1,000,000 worth of placer gold, and disappointed pilgrims who had left the Hills began to return, encouraged by the prospect of new bonanzas and employment.[3]

Gold and silver were by far the most important Black Hills products during the rush, but other minerals also showed promise. James Brewer, for example, discovered coal within thirty-five miles of Deadwood, just over the Wyoming border west of Spearfish. There the Blossburg Coal District for years produced fuel

---

[2] Brennan, "Some Early History of the Black Hills of South Dakota," MS, n.d., Shelf 2, Tier 6, South Dakota Historical Society, Pierre, 11; Tallent, *The Black Hills*, 528.

[3] *Black Hills Pioneer* (Deadwood), October 7, 1876; "Dakota," D. Appleton, *The American Annual Cyclopedia and Register of Important Events of the Year 1877*, p. 246.

for the mines. Other coal deposits near Sturgis and Rapid City were thought to offer possibilities of further development, but soon proved difficult to mine profitably.[4]

Mica, mined around Custer, has been produced steadily in the Hills since 1879 when George Clark discovered the McMaken mine. This flexible, transparent mineral was at that time used for stove windows, and later for insulating electrical equipment and for automobile curtains. By 1881, McMaken was shipping out 2,500 pounds of mica a month. Oil, too, seemed promising when small deposits were found near the Jenney Stockade. Mr. L. J. Harlow went into the oil business and sold crude petroleum for lubrication in Deadwood at a dollar a gallon. Salt, needed for the chlorination of refractory ores, was discovered in springs north of Newcastle and evaporators were soon brought in to extract it. For years each stop that the leaking salt wagons made on their way to Deadwood provided a salt lick for the deer in the vicinity. A mercury mine at Victoria, eight miles west of Rapid City, also raised hopes that this essential mining material might be locally produced, but nothing ever came of it. Uranium oxides, then valuable solely as dyes, were found near Rochford but not mined until seventy years later.[5]

It was the gold ores, however, that most attracted the miners' attention. Prowling the hills, the prospector looked for "outcroppings" of white or iron-stained quartz among the more mundane rocks. When he found a likely sample, he ground it up in an iron mortar and then panned the resulting powder for gold. This simple test was accurate if the ore found was "free-milling," and held the gold in a mechanical combination. "Refractory" ore, in which the gold was contained in the rock in a quasi-chemical bond, required the more esoteric analysis of the professional assayer. This learned individual took the sample of ore selected by the

[4] Ingham, *Digging Gold Among the Rockies*, 228.

[5] Deadwood Board of Trade, *The Black Hills of Dakota, 1881*, p. 23; *Daily Leader* (Cheyenne), March 6, 1878; Brown and Willard, *The Black Hills Trails*, 431–32; University of South Dakota, South Dakota W.P.A. Writer's Project, "Annals of Early Rapid City, 1878–87—Mining Camps," MS, Rapid City Public Library, 5; *Ibid.*, "—Mining," 8, 23.

prospector and ground it to a fine powder, sifting and mixing it to obtain a uniform distribution of its mineral contents. He then measured out a sample weighing exactly 2.9 grams, which he mixed with lead and a flux and heated until the lead had absorbed all the gold and silver. The remaining rock floated to the top of the molten metal to be skimmed off as slag. The assayer then put the remaining "button" of lead, gold, and silver in a "cupel," or little cup of bone ash, and heated it to a high temperature, driving off the lead and leaving only the precious metals. This small button was weighed, then the silver in it was dissolved off with nitric acid, and the remaining gold tested for purity and fineness, and weighed again. For every milligram of gold in the sample, there would be one ounce of gold in a ton of ore. Of course everything depended on the honesty and skill of the assayer and on the representative nature of the sample tested. The absence of one or both of these requisites generally explains the fantastically high assay values placed on many of the early mines.[6]

Like the placer miners, the hard-rock men were not above salting their mines to make them appear more valuable than they really were. Some filed up gold coins and scattered the filings on the ore. One thoughtless chap even chopped up coins with an ax, but prospective customers got to wondering about nuggets already marked "U.S." and lost faith in him. Often a salter would fire a shotgun loaded with gold dust into his mine tunnel and then let a prospective buyer select his own ore. Others introduced extra gold while the ore was being milled—a test run of a ton or two being one of the favorite trials—often dropping nuggets onto the amalgamation tables or into the grinding mills. Once a drunk staggered up to a pile of ore awaiting a test run. He hiccuped, staggered, and fell, breaking his whisky bottle over the rock. The bottle proved to have been filled with gold chloride. Other sellers bought or stole valuable ore, dumped it into their mine, and then blandly assured prospective buyers that "it's just

---

[6] Rosen, *Pa-Ha-Sa-Pah*, 364-72; *Daily Leader* (Cheyenne), March 10, 1876, tells of the Colorado assayer, given bits of a stone jug, who judged that it ran $17.82 to the ton.

like the stuff they're taking out over at the Father De Smet." It often was, exactly.

Once a prospector had assured himself that his mine was worth something, he located a mineral claim on it, which ran 1,500 feet along where he assumed his vein of ore might be and 150 feet on either side of it. This gave him the right not to the ground but to the vein itself, which he could follow even onto another's property. When two men, on opposite sides of a hill, located opposing ends of the same vein, there was bound to be trouble when they met in the middle. Furthermore, it was customary to suppose that a claimant owned all the land beneath his claim, subject only to the right of another to follow a distinct and separate vein across the property. Discussion about just what constituted a separate vein had a marked tendency to become acrimonious.[7]

To these sources of disagreement was added any conflict which might appear between district mining laws, territorial mining law, and federal statute, each of which tended to differ from the others. Perhaps this is why Deadwood had fifty lawyers by the time the hard-rock mines began serious operations. Added to this confusion was the troublesome notion that since the Hills were Indian land until February, 1877, claims located prior to that time might be totally invalid. This controversy, at least, was decided by Judge Granville G. Bennett on May 7, 1877, and later confirmed by the territorial Supreme Court in the celebrated Hidden Treasure case. The decision held that the miners, as trespassers on the Indian reservation, could not claim to have title before the cession of the land to the United States. Nevertheless, said Judge Bennett, the trespasser with the earliest title had the prior and better claim.[8]

---

[7] The United States government further complicated the matter by the introduction in 1872 of the "apex law" which provided that the miner could follow his vein indefinitely *only* if he had originally located his claim at the apex of the lode, i.e., where it came to the surface of the ground; Rodman Paul, *California Gold*, 210–39, has an excellent discussion of mining-law problems.

[8] The various laws can be compared in the *Black Hills Pioneer* (Deadwood), July 15, November 25, 1876, and "Mining Laws of the Ida Gray Quartz District," March 24, 1877; *Daily Leader* (Cheyenne), June 8, 1877, reported Judge Bennett's decision.

The art of taking the ore out of the ground in the cheapest and safest way is the subject of limitless books on mining engineering, and can be dealt with only briefly here. The most important point to bear in mind is that the miners wished to lift the ore as little as possible. By proper management it could almost be made to fall out of the mine into the mills. Often this effect could be achieved, at least to a degree, by tunneling into the bottom of an ore body. The ore was then mined from underneath by a process known as "shrinkage stoping," and put into trams which ran by gravity out of the tunnel to the mill. When the ore could not be reached by a tunnel, a shaft was sunk to below the level of the proposed mining area and drifts driven under the ore. The only difference was the added expense of hauling the ore cars up the shaft.

The mining was done by teams who were paid by the "drifting" or "sinking" they accomplished, or by the amount of ore which they removed. The miners used steel drills driven into the rock with sledges, one man holding the drill and turning it while the other drove it. They dipped the resulting dust out of the hole with a long "miner's spoon," and of course used longer and longer drills as the holes grew deeper. A good team could sink a hole nearly two inches a minute, but of course could not keep up that pace for long, or go so fast if drifting horizontally. When deep enough the holes were charged with black powder or "giant powder," as dynamite was then called, and fired with short fuses. The thoughtful miner carefully cut his fuses so that even though lighted one after the other they would all go off together and thus increase the effect of the blast. He then cut a piece of fuse shorter than the rest and used it as a "spitter" from which to light the others. In this way, as long as the fuse in his hand was burning, he knew that none of the others was about to go off. It was when, by some miscalculation, he could not get all the fuses lighted from his spitter that he became nervous. Unless all the charges were fired, he faced the possibility of drilling into one later on, but to remain too long when some fuses were already lighted was an easy way of becoming a statistic.

The miners usually paid for their own powder and fuse and so tended to be economical with both. As a result of using too little powder the rock generally came out in large chunks and had to be "block-holed," or drilled again and broken up into smaller pieces with further charges. The chunks were then "mucked" or loaded into ore cars which ran on small rails leading out of the mine.

As the work progressed, the roof of the mine had to be held up with stulls—heavy pieces of timber set vertically—and caps, which were equally large timbers laid across them. As the mines grew deeper these pieces were generally cut on the surface, carefully dovetailed to fit into each other, and then sent down into the mine to be put up as the miners moved forward. Often the miners left pillars of ore, which served the same purpose, but eventually had to be removed.

Mining, then as now, was a dangerous business, but in those days the negligence of the miners and the unconcern of the mining companies made it even more hazardous. The miners, paid in proportion to the work accomplished, tended to neglect precautions. Timbers were left out, and roofs fell in when a post or two would have held them up. Miners returned to the working face too soon after blasts and were choked by the fumes and dust, or were caught by the delayed explosion of carelessly packed charges. Powder, handled by the light of flickering candles, often went off when it should not have, although this was much less of a problem when dynamite came into common use.

Falls were a constant danger. Men fell into the shafts from the top, or walked into them from tunnels, or wandered into "winzes" leading downward from unfamiliar drifts. Buckets of ore broke loose and smashed miners engaged in sinking shafts below. Sometimes the hoist engineer was careless and pulled a "cage" full of men clear up to the top of the headframe. Jammed against the timbers, the "rope" (actually wire cable) would break, and the miners drop to the bottom again. Fourteen-inch timbers were always hard to handle, and they smashed fingers and toes regularly. Often miners forgot to bar down overhead rock after a blast, and it came loose when least desired. In the mills, too, unguarded machinery could catch the unwary hand or flapping coat tail, and very few survived a serious argument with a ten-ton flywheel. The companies provided no compensation whatever for accidents, but the miners themselves usually contributed a dollar a month toward maintaining a hospital for the injured.

One day a political orator in Lead was holding forth in great style. He concluded his speech with the stirring appeal: "If'n every word I'm a-saying ain't the gospel truth, may this here earth open up and swallow me." It did. A grizzled miner nudged his partner as they were fishing him out of the cave-in and murmured, " 'Pears to me, Pard, that that young feller waren't very reliable." Such collapses were all too common. Houses shifted and creaked as the ground shook and settled beneath them. Once the ground under two Homestake shops fell away into abandoned mine workings, leaving a pit sixty feet deep. In time the whole city of Lead had to be moved to a new location as mines beneath gnawed away the rock. The problem was not solved until the Homestake mine developed a way of filling up the cavities created by pumping the sand "tailings" from the mills back into its excavations.[9]

Once the ore was mined, the next step was to remove the gold from it. This could be done at a custom mill which would process anybody's ore for a fixed fee, but most miners preferred to build a mill of their own. Their mill could produce gold, finance further exploratory drifting, and the resulting additional ore finance yet a larger mill. This became a sort of "operation bootstrap" in which a small investment could snowball into a much larger return. Generally, the money to build the mill was obtained through the sale of stock. Some promoters sold shares so successfully that they never felt it necessary to get around to producing gold at all. Others did their best, but ran into difficulties and had to call for more money, which the stockholders were usually unwilling to supply. This sort of operation gave the Hills a bad name in investment circles, but it was some years before the supply of suckers was entirely exhausted.

[9] Ingham, *Digging Gold Among the Rockies*, is an interesting account of contemporary mining and milling methods.

When the ore arrived at the mill, it was dumped onto a "grizzly," a grid of iron bars designed to keep pieces too big for the crushers from getting into the works. Large lumps were set aside and broken up with sledges, while the smaller bits were allowed to fall into a hopper for storage. The ore was then ground to a coarse powder in a Blake or jaw-type crusher and fed into the stamp mills. These stamps, arranged in "batteries" of five, weighed about eight hundred pounds each and could grind from one and one-half to two tons of ore a day, depending on the degree of fineness desired, and the hardness of the rock. The stamps worked up and down in a water-filled iron trough called a mortar where they ground the ore to flour-like fineness. Often mercury was added to the mortar to catch some of the gold and form an amalgam, but some mine operators thought this wasteful since the mercury tended to get under the stamps and lose its efficiency.

When the ore had been sufficiently ground, it passed through a fine screen in the side of the mortar and flowed over mercury-coated copper tables. The mercury caught the gold which had not been formed into amalgam in the mortars, while the residue, called "tailings," flowed off the tables and was drained away. Every week or so trusted employees scraped the amalgam off the tables and from beneath the stamps and boiled off the mercury in a retort, saving it for use again, while the gold "sponge," or "retort," remained behind. The process had the advantage of showing when any gold was being stolen, for the owners expected to get back about as much mercury as they had put in. Even so, a sensible superintendent usually hired an armed guard to keep an eye on the stamps and tables.

The stamp mill and mercury process worked fairly well on the free-milling ore found near the surface, but were a failure on the deep refractory ores. These required intricate roasting, chlorination, smelting, and cyanidation processes to free or dissolve the gold from its close union with the rock. Roasting, at a carefully controlled temperature, sometimes softened refractory ore so it could be milled in the regular way. Chlorination, which was generally preceded by roasting, required treating the ore with chlorine obtained by the reaction of heated salt and sulphuric acid and then precipitating the gold from the resulting gold chloride in a variety of ways. Smelting, which attempted to melt the metal out of the rock, was not much used except with ores containing large amounts of silver. The cyanide process, introduced in the 1890's, dissolved the gold from the ore with potassium or sodium cyanide, and made possible the utilization of many gold deposits previously considered totally unprofitable. The great Wasp Number Two at Flatiron, south of Lead, for example, milled ore worth $1.60 a ton at a profit, using cyanidation and moving the ore through its mill entirely by gravity flow.

As previously mentioned, the southern Hills towns boomed a second time with the coming of the hard-rock enthusiasm. Custer was soon surrounded by a ring of villages—Tenderfoot, Junction City, Kiddville, Atlantic City, and Williamsburg—each with its mine and its hopes, none of which were destined for fruition. Hill City, too, boomed briefly as Tigerville, Newton Fork, and Queen Bee grew up around the new mines.

New towns also grew up with the hard-rock boom. Rochford, where gold ledges had been found by Michael D. Rochford, Richard B. Hughes, and others, prospered during the summer of 1878 and by the end of the year had a population of over one thousand. Many of its mines seemed promising—Golden Rock, Queen of Venice, Ophir, Maid of Athens—but only the Stand By flourished, and even it operated sporadically. Nearly one dozen little towns sprang up around Rochford: Alta, Diamond City, Florence, Grand View, Gregory, Montezuma, Ochre City, Myersville, and Lookout. They, too, faded away as their mines proved unprofitable. Today Rochford makes its living almost entirely from a nearby Forest Service establishment.[10]

Silver mining caused a rush to Galena, on Bear Butte Creek southeast of Deadwood. Prospectors had found galena, a lead ore containing considerable quantities of silver, as early as March, 1876, but the town did not materialize until the following year.

[10] Hughes, *Pioneer Years*, describes Hughes' activities in Rochford; Tallent, *The Black Hills*, is also useful for descriptions of the early towns.

By January, 1877, it had four hundred miners, seventy-five houses, and six months later three smelters were busily melting ore and extracting silver. The greatest impetus to development came from Colonel J. H. Davy, who in 1878 gained control of the Florence mine, built a huge mill, and began large-scale operations. Some of his ore yielded 1,341 ounces of silver to the ton. It also contained traces of gold, and large amounts of lead, which of course was useless until it could be economically shipped to market by rail. Davy eventually followed his vein of ore under the adjoining Richmond mine, and the ensuing litigation ruined both of the contestants. Other towns in the area—Virginia City, Gibraltar, Strawberry Gulch, and Bear Butte—met essentially the same fate or collapsed when silver prices declined to a point where the ores could no longer be worked at a profit.

Carbonate, northwest of Deadwood, was another silver town. It came into existence when miners discovered that the limestone, or "carbonate," ores of the area contained appreciable amounts of silver which recently invented methods were able to extract. The Iron Hill mine alone produced over $1,000,000 during more than fifty years of intermittent operation. A decline in the price of silver and a disastrous diphtheria epidemic, which was said to have been brought on by the smelter fumes, ultimately ruined the town, though occasional efforts to reopen the mines continued to the 1930's. Nearby, Bald Mountain and Trojan boomed briefly during the gold rush, but did not become important gold producers until the invention of the cyanide process made possible the efficient processing of their highly refractory ores.[11]

Deadwood, however, was the center of the hard-rock mining area, just as it had been the center of the placers. With its neighboring towns, Gayville, Central City, and Lead, it formed the heart of the mining area and served the most notable and productive mines. Many of these were contained within the famous mineral "belt," extending from Lead to Central City. This rich

[11] Fielder, "Carbonate Camp," *South Dakota Historical Collections*, Vol. XXVIII (1956), 99–178, is a detailed account of this silver town. The Bald Mountain mine operated steadily until the 1950's.

strip contained an enormous but discontinuous vein of ore—sometimes 40 to 150 feet wide and several miles long. Indeed, optimistic prospectors looked for its continuation at Maitland, north of Central City, and as far south as Custer. They imagined, with some justification, that the best mines in the Hills were all located upon a single north-south line of ore.

One of the best-known Central City mines was the Hidden Treasure, which adjoined the ill-fated Aurora. In October, 1876, the Black Hills Gold Mining Company bought a three-quarter interest in it for $25,000. By the spring of 1877 it was yielding $24 to the ton, running its ore through Pearson's custom mill. The company, trying to economize, installed a ball mill of its own, only to find that expenses went up and production diminished. Soon litigation with the Aurora slowed down production, and the mine eventually closed. Its long contest with the Aurora, however, kept it in the public eye and helped publicize the Hills.

Another famous mine was the Father De Smet, named in honor of the missionary who was believed to have found gold while preaching to the Indians. Gus Bowie, a mining engineer educated in Germany, took charge of operations at a salary of $1,500 a month, plus living expenses. His first step was to assure the well-being of his subordinates by hiring "Aunt Lou" Marshbanks away from the Wagner Hotel to cook for the executive table. He planned his operations for the future, building slowly and well in order to insure not only immediate but continued economical production. By 1879, he had eighty stamps in operation and three more mills on order. The mine yielded about $60,000 a month, processing ore worth $12 a ton, which in itself is a testimony to the efficiency of Bowie's management.[12]

By January, 1878, some seven hundred stamps were grinding ore in the Deadwood area, with three hundred more under construction. Annual gold production came to about $2,000,000. The next year, 1879, it increased to nearly $300,000 a month. Mine prices soared. The Golden Terry with the Ophir sold for $50,000

[12] Stokes and Driggs, *Deadwood Gold*, 122–24, gives an excellent account of the De Smet and its great water fight with the Homestake.

on February 3, 1877. A year later the Father De Smet and its adjoining properties brought $400,000. Hundreds of lesser mines sold at prices between $4,000 and $25,000. By 1878, California capitalists had probably invested over $1,000,000 in Black Hills mineral properties, bringing nearly as large a boom as the original discoveries of gold.[13]

It was the Homestake at Lead that topped them all. The mine was discovered by Fred and Moses Manuel, Alex Engh, and Henry Harney in the spring of 1876. At first it seemed no more important than the other mines in the Washington (as Lead was then known) area, but soon six excavations along five hundred feet of its ore body showed its vast potentialities. Mr. H. B. Young, a Deadwood merchant, helped to finance exploratory shafts in return for one-fifteenth of the mine. A ten-stamp mill demonstrated that the ore was rich, and the mine was soon recognized as one of the most promising on the "belt."

In July, George Hearst and J. B. Haggin sent a mining engineer, L. D. Kellogg, to look over Black Hills mineral properties. He bought the Manuels' share in the Homestake for $50,000, bought out Harney and Engh for $45,000, and then found that Young's interest was still outstanding. Young, who was a pretty shrewd chap, finally sold his hundred feet of the mine for $10,000 plus the privilege of working the ore for twenty days, which netted him another $8,000.

Hearst at once began to pour money into developing the Homestake. He shipped in an eighty-stamp mill, via Cuthbertson and Young's freight line, that cost over $30,000 in transportation charges alone. The mill went into operation on January 1, 1878, but full production did not begin until July, when the mine produced $40,000 worth of bullion. By the end of 1879 the yield had doubled. From 1878 to 1962 bullion production totaled $715,000,-000. The mine, which is still in operation, now pays a profit of

13 "Dakota," D. Appleton, *The American Annual Cyclopedia and Register of Important Events of the Year 1877*, pp. 245–46, estimates the number of stamps will be from 550 to 650 on January 1, 1878; Strahorn, *To the Rockies and Beyond*, makes a higher estimate; *ibid.*, 24, mentions a representative selection of mine sales prices.

about $4,000,000 a year, although one-half of this is derived from uranium operations in Utah and New Mexico.[14]

In its early days the Homestake was not noted for good public relations. In the course of expansion the company came into conflict with a nearby claim-owner, Alexander Frankenburg, who was shot and killed by four Homestake employees. Tried and acquitted by a jury which was obviously bribed, the murderers were released. The judge, G. C. Moody, snorted afterward that he would "sooner have a jury of Pagan Indians." The climax of the Homestake's legal troubles came in the big fight with the Father De Smet over water rights. Each of the mines had, more or less by accident, secured the rights to water that was essential to the operations of the other. They fought a long legal battle, involving numerous trials and city elections, and eventually the Homestake emerged victorious. Its operations today are a model of efficiency and good employee relations.

The gold rush ended on September 26, 1879, when most of the business district of Deadwood burned to the ground. There had been plenty of warning that this might happen. From the earliest days the town fathers had urged the need for fire-fighting equipment, sound chimneys, and alert fire wardens. Every fire that started served as a warning that the whole town was in danger, for it was built almost entirely of wood and located in a deep and windy valley. Little was done, however, and when a fire broke out in Mrs. Ellsner's Star Bakery on the evening of September 25 only a few men responded to calls for assistance. The fire soon spread to Jensen and Bliss's hardware store. When the flames reached eight kegs of gunpowder the store blew up, scattering burning embers all over town. An area one-half mile long and one-quarter of a mile wide was completely destroyed. Brick

[14] Lead is pronounced "Leed," Manuel, "Manwell." A complete history of the Homestake is of course not possible in a small space; moreover, the company avers that its early records, shipped to the Hearst office in San Francisco, were destroyed in the fire of 1906. Deadwood Board of Trade, *Black Hills of Dakota, 1881*, 15–20, is a good contemporary account of the mine's early days; Moses Manuel, "Forty-Eight Years in the West," dictated to Mary Sheriff, Helena, Montana, 1903, MS, Homestake Library, Lead, is fragmentary.

buildings, whose owners had supposed to be fireproof, were shaken by the numerous explosions, and the fire entered through the gaps. Some three hundred buildings burned, with a loss estimated at $2,000,000 to $3,000,000. The business district of Deadwood was completely gutted, and 40 per cent of its population was rendered homeless.

The inhabitants, no longer casual placer miners but solid men of business, began to rebuild at once. Merchants whose goods had escaped the fire continued in business with no increase in prices. Neighboring towns sent assistance and supplies. Workmen tore down unused buildings in Gayville and South Bend to provide materials with which to rebuild Deadwood. Sawmills worked around the clock. General Sturgis at Fort Meade sent troops to prevent looting and claim jumping, and the Deadwood city commissioners—with the same goal in mind—at once ordered that all surviving saloons be closed. The daily papers, printed in Lead, did not miss a single issue and did much to unite and encourage community spirit. Makeshift hotels cared for the homeless, although not always for nothing: one posted a sign "meles fivty cens" which indicated at least some desire to profit from the disaster. In six months the town, rebuilt largely of brick, was better than before the fire. By now the gold rush was over, for the miners had come to stay.[15]

[15] Most books on the Hills contain some information on the Deadwood fire; the best contemporary accounts are found in the local papers and in the *Daily Leader* (Cheyenne), September 27, 28, 1879.

12

THE HAPPIEST GOLD RUSH

I am sitting by the camp fire now,
On wild Dakota's Hills,
And memories of long ago
Steal o'er me like the rills
Adown yon canyon deep and dark,
Steal through the leafy glades,
A glimpse, a murmur here and there,
Then vanish in the shades.[1]

When Deadwood was rebuilt after the fire of 1879, the gold rush was over. The adventurous vigor of the early prospectors had given way to the more calculating self-interest of the promoter, speculator, and mining engineer. The carefree spirit which moved a prospector to write in 1876, "out of a job and no claim and a few hundred dollars ahead . . . so ho for the States," was replaced by a less cheerful but more business-like attitude. It is time, therefore, to look back over the history of the rush from 1874 to 1879 and to draw together the varied strands of its story into a somewhat unified conclusion.[2]

To begin with, it is evident that the gold rush began, not merely because gold was discovered in the Hills, but in response to a

[1] Henry Weston Smith, found on his body after he was killed by Indians, quoted in Brown and Willard, *The Black Hills Trails*, 400.
[2] Bryan, *An Illinois Gold Hunter in the Black Hills*, 33.

variety of interacting forces. Gold had been known in the Hills since 1803, but until 1874, when it was given suitable publicity by General Custer's expedition, its presence had not excited much response. Moreover, the news of Custer's discoveries fell upon ears already made receptive by the financial and agricultural depression of 1873. It was also greeted with enthusiasm by western miners, who had long thirsted for a new bonanza in which to try their luck. Frontier towns, which had boomed with the arrival of the railroads and declined as the construction gangs departed, saw in the mines an opportunity to regain their old prosperity. They, too, did their best to publicize and promote the Black Hills gold fields. Lastly, the United States Army, faced with the problem of controlling the increasingly troublesome Sioux, saw in the opening of the Hills a move which would precipitate an Indian war and settle forever the problem of controlling this quarrelsome tribe.

The rush began in the spring of 1875 and by summer five or six hundred miners had invaded the Hills. At first they concentrated their mining efforts in the central area around Harney Peak, where Custer had made his gold discoveries. Here the miners learned to identify and work the Black Hills placers and began to formulate the laws and customs which prevailed throughout the rush. The federal government, however, was sensitive about its treaty obligations to the Indians and at first used the Army to guard the Hills and eject trespassing miners, while the Department of the Interior bargained for the disputed territory. When negotiations broke down due to excessive Indian demands for compensation, the soldiers were withdrawn and the rush was allowed to proceed without hindrance.

This new permissiveness on the part of the government came just in time, for the profitable placers of the northern Hills were discovered in the fall of 1875. By the spring of 1876 thousands of miners had flocked into Deadwood Gulch and begun the mining operations which made the Black Hills famous. Gradually the placers "played out," and the miners turned their attention to the hard-rock ores. The end of the Sioux War in the fall of 1876 and the ratification of a treaty for the Hills in February, 1877, gave the miners clear title to the land and attracted the capital which had previously feared to enter the disputed territory. The Hills continued to be wild and lawless, but once mining became a business rather than an adventure, the gold rush was over.

It is difficult to make an accurate estimate of Black Hills gold production during the early years of the rush. Gold circulated freely as currency, was carried out of the Hills by the miners themselves, and only part of the amount produced passed through commercial channels to be recorded. The South Dakota School of Mines has offered the following figures:

Year	Amount
1876	$1,200,000
1877	2,000,000
1878	2,250,000
1879	2,500,000
1880	3,305,843

The suspiciously rounded figures prior to 1880 suggest that no reliable data were available before that year. Contemporary estimates were nearly twice as large.[3]

Population figures before 1880 were also open to question. The Census of 1880 counted 16,486 persons in Lawrence, Pennington, and Custer counties, with town populations as follows:

Town	Population	Town	Population
Anchor City	291	Minneapolis	35
Central City	1,008	Myersville	103
Crook City	100	Pennington	51
Custer	271	Rapid City	292
Deadwood	3,777	Rochford	315
Diamond City	30	Rockerville	321
Elizabethtown	316	Sheridan	142
Galena	59	South Bend	209
Gayville	130	Spearfish	170
Hayward	38	Sturgis	60
Lead	1,437	Terraville	775

[3] "Gold Production of the Black Hills," *Black Hills Engineer*, Vol. XVIII (January, 1930), 77; Rosen, *Pa-Ha-Sa-Pah*, 348–49, gives the following: 1878,

The balance of the population was of course scattered among individual mines, ranches, and unidentified hamlets. A fair guess would be that from 1874 to 1880 more than thirty thousand men passed through the Hills. Of all the towns, Deadwood (which included Elizabethtown, Gayville, and South Bend) was the largest and the wildest: In 1881 its Board of Trade happily bragged that it had "the prettiest women, the bravest men, the laziest dogs, the meekest hackmen, the homeliest newspaper reporters, and the toniest bar-tenders in the world."[4]

Although the Hills have continued to produce gold to the present, and indeed even enjoyed a considerable mining boom during the depression of the 1930's, other industries have long since supplanted gold mining. The largest business in the Hills is probably ranching. As early as 1879, 150,000 cattle grazed in and around the Hills as the disappointed miners turned to less spectacular but steadier employment. Farming, too, played its part in keeping the miners in the Hills for the climate and soil lend themselves to the production of hay, oats, and potatoes. Lumbering, based on ample supplies of pine, has been another steady source of income, at first supplying the mines with timbers and fuel, and later producing for shipment out of the area. Since the visit of President Calvin Coolidge in 1927 the tourist trade has grown steadily until today it is one of the major industries.

The traditions of gold-rush times still linger in the Hills. After a storm small boys still shuffle through muddy streets, hoping to find a nugget washed down from some yet undiscovered mine. Land buyers argue over "mineral rights" when the time comes to sign a deed. The Homestake, now mellowed with age, pays its steady dividends, but it is the only gold mine still in operation. The highways, it is true, are lined with cheap tourist attractions, but the side roads are much as they used to be, and at the end of them

---

$3,500,000; 1879, $4,500,000; 1880, $6,000,000, which more nearly approach the figures commonly accepted at the time.

[4] U.S., Tenth Census, Vol. I, 52–53, 115–16; H. N. Maguire's figures, in the *Black Hills Central* (Rochford), March 30, 1879, are surprisingly close to the next year's official ones; Deadwood Board of Trade, *The Black Hills of Dakota, 1881*, p. 6.

heaps of tailings, gaping holes, and crumbling mills mark early mining efforts and bring to mind the days gone by. None of the old-timers are still alive, but their sons and daughters still remember the tales they told about the wild old days, when adventure stood by a man's elbow, fortune lay at the tip of his shovel, and it was good to be alive.

Mining Laws of the Cheyenne Mining District, Bear Rock, near Custer, Black Hills, D.T. Adopted June 11, 1875

This district commences at the Stockade and extends to the head waters of French Creek and from Summit to summit.

A Quartz Claim shall not exceed fifteen hundred feet in length or one hundred and fifty feet on each side of Crevice.

A placer claim consists of three hundred feet up or down the Gulch, and extends from base to base.

Any Miner leaving there Claims for fifteen days without a representation, and that to consist of a days labor with a shovel and pick, at any one time shall forfeit them.

The Mining Season will close on the fifteenth of November and remain closed until the 1st day of May of each year.

No flume or Sluices shall empty on another Miners Claim without his permission.

Every Miner shall have the right to dig a drain ditch or Tail row through another Miners Claim—

Five days will be given to prospect any one claim in. Claims not recorded in that time will be considered vacant ground.

Claims taken up in Company after being duly recorded can be represented by one or more of the Company, but they must be recorded by the individual owning them.

The Recorders fee for recording Claims, properly Measuring them, furnishing a Certificate and numbering the Claims, will be two dollars for each Claim.

The Recorders duties will be to keep a correct list of all the claims, keep the records of the district, issue notices of the Meetings, Measure the Claims when requested to do so, open the Meetings and preside with the president over all Meetings. And also keep a Correct plat of the Gulch to give information to those seeking Claims in our district.

Every Miner is entitled to a Claim in every Gulch and along every Creek in this District.

The water shall be returned to the Bed of the Creek, or on the surface, at or before reaching the end of every Miner or Miners Claims, no water rights shall be taken or recorded. Along this Creek, the water will be free to all. No Tailings shall be dumped on another Miners Claim, without his consent.

The Claims will be numbered, Commencing at the Bear Rock Claim, numbering up and down the Gulch from that Claim, numbers running each way from there. None of these laws can be changed without a two-third vote and no one will be allowed to vote at a Miners Meeting, excepting those holding Claims in this District and those Claims Recorded.

The Recorder will post up Notices of a Meeting at least five days before the Meeting in four Conspicuous places.

A Stake must be erected at the end of each Claim of four by six inches in thickness two and one half feet in the ground, four foot out of the ground with a face and the number and owner of the Claim written in plain letters and figures, thereon, on or before the 10th day of August '75.

These Mining Laws, Made on June 11th 1875, where [*sic*] signed by the following miners.

W. Harrison	W. Tillotson
D. Alston	J. Caviness
J. McCrary	J. Strater
Jr. Umphrey	C. Phillips
G. Donahue	W. Porter
J. Crosby	E. Haggarty
H. Bishope	Alvah Trask
W. Trainor	

June 27th these Laws, where [*sic*] signed by the following, who endorsed them—

B. Van Horn	J. Hill
C. Cribbs	G. Carpenter
C. Blackburn	H. Cunningham
O. Kline	L. Smith
J. Dunn	W. McKee
J. Baxter	C. Gable
J. Blake	H. Nelson
C. Chaffee	J. Beardsley
P. Cummings	F. Hoffman
George Williams	

General Crook's Proclamation, 1875
Ordering the Miners to Leave
the Black Hills

Proclamation

Whereas the President of the United States has directed that No Miners or other unauthorized Citizens shall be allowed to remain in the Indian Reservation of the Black Hills, or in the unceded territory to the West, until some new treaty arrangements have been made with the Indians. And

x Whereas by the same authority the undersigned is directed to occupy Said Reservation and Territory with Troops and to remove all Miners or other unauthorized Citizens who may be now or May hereafter come into this Country in Violation of the treaty Obligations. Therefore the undersigned hereby requires every Miner or unauthorized Citizen to leave the Territory Known as the Black Hills, the Powder River, and Big Horn Country, by or before the 15th day of August Next.—He hopes that the good Sense and law-abiding disposition of the Miners will prompt them to obey this order without Compelling a resort to force.—

x It is Suggested that the Miners now in the Hills assemble at the Military Post, about to be established at Camp Harney Near the Stockade on French Creek, on or before the 10th day of August; that they there, and then, hold a meeting and take Such Steps as May Seem best to them, by organization and drafting of proper resolutions, to secure to each, when this Country shall

207

have been opened, the benefit of his discoveries, and the labor he has already expended.

(Sgd.) GEORGE CROOK
Brigadier General U.S.A.
Com'd'g Dept. of the Platte[1]

Camp Crook DT
July 29, 1875

[1] *The Black Hills Engineer*, Vol. XVIII (January, 1930), 42.

GLOSSARY OF MINING TERMS

Adit: a mine tunnel, especially one used to give access to other workings.

Amalgam: mixture of gold and mercury.

Ball mill: device used to grind ore to a powder by tumbling it in an enclosed container together with steel balls.

Bar down: to remove, with a long iron bar, the loose rock remaining overhead after a blast.

Bedrock: solid rock underneath the dirt and gravel.

Block-holing: breaking up large boulders and pieces of rock with dynamite.

Blower: a shallow metal tray into which gold dust was poured and the lighter dirt and sand blown from it.

Button: metallic residue remaining after the assaying process.

Cage: platform used to hoist men up a mine shaft.

Cap: a heavy timber cross-piece, supported by a "stull," and used to hold up the roof of a mine.

Cement ores: placer gravels bound together with iron oxide, which, although alluvial, often had to be mined like hard-rock deposits.

Chlorine process: a method of reducing refractory ore with salt and sulphuric acid.

Claim: (a) to lay claim to a definite piece of mining ground; (b) the ground so claimed, three hundred feet along a stream, or a claim three hundred by fifteen hundred feet along a mineral vein.

Colors: tiny flakes of gold, often not worth saving, but indicative of the presence of more valuable deposits nearby.

Cupel: a bone-ash cup, used in assaying.

Cyanide process: a method used to dissolve the gold out of refractory ores with sodium or potassium cyanide.

Drift: a mine tunnel, especially one with a working face at one end.

Flume: a wooden trough used to carry water.

Free-milling: ore from which the gold can be extracted by mechanical means.

Glory hole: a funnel-shaped shaft into which ore is thrown and drawn off through a tunnel below.

Gold pan: a shallow iron pan, about three inches deep and eighteen inches across, with a wide, flaring rim, used for washing gold.

Greenhorn: an inexperienced or youthful newcomer.

Grizzly: device made of iron bars, designed to keep out pieces of ore too large to pass through the machinery of a mill.

Hard-rock: a mining area other than placer, where the ore is composed not of gravel but of solid rock.

Headframe: the framework over a mine shaft used to hoist the men and ore from below.

Lagging: poles or boards braced against the walls and roof of a shaft or tunnel to keep loose rock or dirt from collapsing.

Locate: to lay claim to a mineral claim, mark it properly, and record the title.

Messenger: guard who accompanied gold shipments, either "riding shotgun" on the stage or on horseback beside it.

Miner's inch: the amount of water which will flow through a one-inch opening under six inches of water pressure.

Miner's spoon: a half-cylinder of metal, attached to a long rod, used for dipping pulverized rock out of a drill hole.

Mucking: loading broken rock into the ore cars.

Pan: to wash out gold from gravel in a gold pan; figuratively, to come to a conclusion, as in "to pan out well."

Patent: the title to land issued by the United States.

Placer: a place where alluvial gold is found in gravel, usually in a valley.

Pilgrim: a man headed for or just come to the mines; by extension, any miner.

Powder: in the early days, black gunpowder; now generally dynamite, which was at first known as "giant powder."

Quartz: a white, glassy rock, often containing gold. It was the most conspicuous surface indication of hard-rock gold deposits.

Raise: a shaft dug upward from a tunnel.

Refractory: ore from which the gold cannot be extracted by mechanical means, but requires smelting or chemical treatment.

Represent: to work a claim in order to continue possession.

Retort: (a) device for distilling off the mercury from a gold-mercury amalgam; (b) the lump of gold resulting from the distillation.

Rimrock: the exposed bedrock at the sides of a valley.

Rocker: hand-operated device used to agitate gravel and water to remove the gold from them.

Salt: to artificially enrich a mine or placer in order to sell it.

Shrinkage stoping: removing the ore from beneath, the miners standing on the broken rock as they dig their way upward.

Sink: to dig a mine shaft downward.

Sluice: a series of wooden troughs lined with obstructions, used for washing out large quantities of placer gravel.

Smelter: furnace for extracting metal from ores by the application of heat.

Spitter: a piece of fuse used to light other fuses.

Sponge: the porous gold remaining after the mercury had been distilled off a gold-mercury amalgam.

Stake out: to locate and properly mark a claim.

Stope: a drift or raise run upward into ore from beneath.

Stull: a heavy timber, placed vertically to support either the rock itself or other timbers, called "caps" which held up the roof.

Tailings: sand left after ore has been ground and the gold extracted from it.

Tram: a small wheeled car used to carry rock and ore, usually running on small tracks.

Winze: a shaft dug downward from a tunnel.

BIBLIOGRAPHY

Aids

COLLECTIONS

Adams Memorial Museum, Deadwood, South Dakota.
Deadwood Public Library, Deadwood, South Dakota.
Homestake Library, Lead, South Dakota.
Jennewein Western Collection, Dakota Wesleyan University, Mitchell, South Dakota.
Leedy Collection, Minnelusa Pioneers' Association, Rapid City, South Dakota.
Phillips Collection, Bizzell Memorial Library, University of Oklahoma, Norman, Oklahoma.
Rapid City Public Library, Rapid City, South Dakota.
South Dakota State Historical Society, Pierre, South Dakota.
South Dakota School of Mines & Technology Library, Rapid City, South Dakota.

BIBLIOGRAPHIES

Adams, Ramon F. *Burrs Under the Saddle: A Second Look at Books and Histories of the West.* Norman, University of Oklahoma Press, 1964.
Allen, Albert H. ed. *Dakota Imprints, 1858–1889.* New York, R. R. Bowker Company, 1947.
"Index Number," *The Black Hills Engineer*, Vol. XX (November, 1932).
"Index to the *Black Hills Mining Review*," typescript, South

Dakota School of Mines & Technology, Rapid City, South Dakota.

Jacobsen, Ethel Collins, comp. *Index to South Dakota Historical Collections, I–XVI.* Pierre, 1935.

Jennewein, J. Leonard. *Black Hills Booktrails.* Mitchell, Dakota Territory Centennial Commission, 1962.

———, and Jane Boorman. *Dakota Panorama.* Dakota Territory Centennial Commission, 1961.

O'Harra, Cleophas Cisney. *A Bibliography of the Geology and Mining Interests of the Black Hills Region. Bulletin Number 11,* South Dakota School of Mines, May, 1917.

Parmelee, Gertrude. *A South Dakota Bibliography.* Rapid City (?), South Dakota Library Association, 1961 (?).

Slouber, Joseph. *Bibliography of the Geology and Mining Interests of the Black Hills Region, Index to South Dakota State School of Mines Bulletin 11.* Rapid City, South Dakota State School of Mines, n.d.

South Dakota Library Association. *A Selected List of South Dakota Books.* N.p., South Dakota Library Association, 1943.

South Dakota Social Science Association. *Bibliography of South Dakota Social Science Research.* N.p., South Dakota Social Science Association, 1953.

U.S. Engineering Department. *Analytical and Topical Index to the Reports of the Chief of Engineers and Officers of the Corps of Engineers, United States Army, 1866–1900.* Washington, Government Printing Office, 1903.

Wagner, Henry R. *The Plains and Rockies.* Ed. by Charles L. Camp. Columbus, Long's College Book Company, 1953.

Ziegler, Victor. *The Minerals of the Black Hills. Bulletin Number 10,* South Dakota School of Mines, February, 1914.

ATLASES AND MAPS

Andreas, A. *Atlas of Dakota—Andreas' Historical Atlas of Dakota.* Chicago, A. T. Andreas, 1884.

Anonymous. "Map of the Mining Claims, 1878," *The Aurum,* Vol. II (November, 1902), 12–13.

————. *Prince Maximilian's Map of Travels in North America, 1832–1834.* London, 1843.

Clark, William. MS map, 1805 (?). Copy in Jennewein Western Collection, Dakota Wesleyan University, Mitchell, South Dakota.

Exline, Frank. *Map of Middle Section of Pennington County, South Dakota.* Rapid City, privately printed, 1907.

Fuller, C. L. *Pocket Map and Descriptive Outline History Accompanied by a Compendium of Statistics of the Black Hills of Dakota and Wyoming.* Rapid City, Black Hills Bed Spring Company, 1887.

Hulbert, Archer Butler. "The Deadwood Trails," *The Great Western Stage Routes, Crown Collection of American Maps.* Series V, Volume I. Colorado Springs, privately blueprinted, 1930.

Masi, William. *The Only Correct Guide to the Black Hills.* Cheyenne, 1876.

O'Harra, Cleophas Cisney. "School of Mines Map of the Black Hills Region," *Pahasapa Quarterly,* Vol. I (February, 1912), between 32 and 33.

Parker, Watson. *Black Hills Ghost Towns and Others: An Historical Gazetteer.* Norman, Oklahoma, privately published, 1964.

Paulin, Charles O. *Atlas of the Historical Geography of the United States.* Ed. by John K. Wright. Washington, Carnegie Institution of Washington, and New York: American Geographical Society of New York, 1932.

Peterson, E. Frank, comp. *Historical Atlas of South Dakota.* Vermillion, privately printed, 1904.

Scott, Samuel. *Map of the Black Hills of South Dakota and Wyoming with Full Descriptions of Mineral Resources, Etc.* Custer City, South Dakota, 1897.

Tucker, Francis C., and J. R. Hickox. *Mineralized Portion Black Hills of South Dakota, Prepared for Mining Men's Association.* N.p., n.d.

U.S., Department of the Interior, N. H. Darton and Sidney Page, comp. *Geologic Atlas of the United States: Central Black Hills Folio; South Dakota.* Washington, U.S. Geological Survey, 1925.

Primary Sources

MANUSCRIPTS

Bischoff, Herman. "Deadwood to the Big Horns, 1877." Translated by Edna LaMoore Waldo. Typescript, Jennewein Western Collection, Dakota Wesleyan University, Mitchell, South Dakota.

Brennan, John R. "Some Early History of the Black Hills of South Dakota." MS, n.d., Shelf 2, Tier 6, South Dakota Historical Society.

Carey, T. F., recorder. "Gold Run First Record Book, February 21, 1876." Adams Memorial Museum, Deadwood, South Dakota.

Custer, Brevet Brigadier-General George A. "Custer's Black Hills Order and Dispatch Book," Coe Collection, Yale University, New Haven, Connecticut.

Engle, P. M. "Sketches and Surveys Made During the Exploratory Tour of 1857 to Nebraska and Dakota under Lt. G. K. Warren." Coe Collection, Yale University, New Haven, Connecticut.

Falk, M. M. "The First Bull Train into the Black Hills." Copy of typescript, File B56–Black Hills, Coe Library, Hebard Room, University of Wyoming.

Grinnell, George Bird. Letters written from New York, July 22, 29, 1924, to Doane Robinson, Pierre, South Dakota. Stack 6, Shelf 1, South Dakota Historical Society, Pierre.

Manuel, Moses. "Forty-Eight Years in the West." Dictated to Mary Sheriff. Typescript, Helena, Montana, in the Homestake Library, Lead, South Dakota.

Mix, Captain John. "Report of Captain John Mix to the Post-Adjutant, Fort Laramie, Wyoming Territory, April 19, 1875."

Photostatic copy, File B, Drawer 3, South Dakota Historical Society, Pierre.

Peirce, Ellis Taylor. "Odd Characters and Incidents in the Black Hills During the '70's." MS, Box 6–3, South Dakota Historical Society, Pierre.

"Record Book — Early Miners — Custer — Dakota Ty., 1875." MS notebook and claim record, Tier 6, Shelf 5, South Dakota Historical Society, Pierre.

Russell, Thomas H. (?) Untitled MS on the Collins-Russell Black Hills Party of 1874. N.p., n.d. MS in possession of Don Clowser, 645½ Main Street, Deadwood, South Dakota.

———. Mining Laws Drafted at Gordon Stockade, February 23, 1878. MS, Adams Memorial Museum, Deadwood, South Dakota.

Smith, George Watson. Diary, January 1, 1878, to July 16, 1878. In possession of the writer.

Starbuck, Matilda White. "My Trip to the Black Hills, October 15, 1876," and "Don't You Remember." Typescripts, Stack 6, Shelf 1, South Dakota Historical Society, Pierre.

Townsend, A. C. Letter to I. C. Develling, 431 Main Street, Springfield, Mass., from Rapid City, September 1, 1876. Copied by Hazel N. Pendleton, Westfield, Mass. Black Hills File Cabinet, Drawer 3, Rapid City Public Library.

University of South Dakota, South Dakota W.P.A. Writers' Project. "Annals of Early Rapid City, 1878–87." N.p., n.d. Typescript, Rapid City Public Library, Rapid City, South Dakota.

Wood, W. H. "A Civilian with Custer in 1874." Typescript, Deadwood Public Library, Deadwood, South Dakota.

DOCUMENTS

Atkinson, General Henry. "Expedition Up the Missouri," 19 Cong., 1 sess., *House Doc. No. 117.*

Dakota Territory, Acting Governor Edwin Stanton McCook. "A Proclamation . . . Given at My Office in the City of Yankton, This 6th Day of April, A.D. 1872."

Dakota Territory, Legislative Assembly, Council Bill No. 10. "A Memorial to Congress Asking for a Geological Survey of the Black Hills and Badlands in Connection with the Military Forces under General Sully in this District," Yankton, Dakota Territory, 1866.

———. "Memorial Asking for a Scientific Exploration of the Territory," 42 Cong., 3 sess., *Senate Misc. Doc. No. 45.*

———. "Memorial in Reference to the Black Hills Country Serving as a Retreat for Hostile Indians," 42 Cong., 3 sess., *House Misc. Doc. No. 65.*

———. "Memorial of the Legislature of Dakota Praying that the Black Hills of Dakota Be Opened for Settlement, and the Indian Title to the same Be Extinguished," 43 Cong., 2 sess., *House Misc. Doc. No. 33.*

Harney, General William S. "Report on Sioux Expedition," 34 Cong., 1 sess., *Senate Exec. Doc. No. 1.*

Hinman, Samuel D. Letter to Rev. W. H. Hare, S. T. D., Chairman of the Sioux Commission, November 10, 1874. *Annual Report of the Commissioner of Indian Affairs—1874.* Washington, Government Printing Office, 1874.

Jenney, Walter P. "Report on the Mineral Wealth, Climate and Rain-Fall, and Natural Resources of the Black Hills of Dakota," 44 Cong., 1 sess., *Senate Exec. Doc. No. 51.*

Kappler, C. J. *Indian Affairs: Laws and Treaties.* 58 Cong., 2 sess., *Senate Exec. Doc. No. 310.* 2 vols. Washington, 1904.

Ludlow, William. "Report of a Reconnaissance of the Black Hills of Dakota, Made in the Summer of 1874, by Captain William Ludlow, Corps of Engineers," 44 Cong., 1 sess., *House Exec. Doc. No. 1.*

Mullan, Captain John. "Report on the Construction of a Military Road from Walla-Walla to Fort Benton," 37 Cong., 3 sess., *Senate Exec. Doc. No. 43.*

Raynolds, Captain William Franklin. "The Yellowstone Expedition," 36 Cong., 2 sess., *Senate Exec. Doc. No. 1.*

———. "Report of Brevet Brigadier General W. F. Raynolds, on

the Yellowstone and the country Drained by that River," 40
Cong., 1 sess., *Senate Exec. Doc. No. 77.*

Sawyer(s), James A. "Report on a Wagon Road from Niobrara
to Virginia City," 39 Cong., 1 sess., *House Exec. Doc. No. 58.*

The Sioux Tribe of Indians v. *The United States of America.*
Court of Claims of the United States, No. C–531–(7), Black
Hills.

Stanton, Captain William S. "Explorations and Surveys in the
Department of the Platte," *Annual Report of the Secretary of
War for the Year 1878,* Vol. II, Part III. Washington, Government Printing Office, 1878.

U.S., Department of the Interior. *Report of the Secretary of the
Interior, 1868–'69,* 40 Cong., 3 sess., *House Exec. Docs.,* II.

———. Department of the Interior, Office of Indian Affairs. *Annual
Report of the Commissioner of Indian Affairs, 1874.* Washington, Government Printing Office, 1874.

———. Department of the Interior, Office of Indian Affairs. *Annual
Report of the Commissioner of Indian Affairs, 1875.* Washington, Government Printing Office, 1875.

———. Department of the Interior, Office of Indian Affairs. *Annual
Report of the Commissioner of Indian Affairs, 1876.* Washington, Government Printing Office, 1876.

———. *Report and journal of the proceedings of the commission
appointed to obtain certain concessions from the Sioux Indians,*
44 Cong., 2 sess., *Senate Exec. Doc. No. 9.*

———. "Message from the President, Transmitting information in
relation to the Black Hills Country In the Sioux Reservation,"
43 Cong., special sess., *Senate Exec. Doc. No. 2.*

———. War Department. "Letter on the Exploration of the Black
Hills," 44 Cong., 1 sess., *House Exec. Doc. No. 125.*

———. War Department. *Reports of Explorations and Surveys, to
Ascertain the most Practicable and Economical Route for a
Railroad from the Mississippi River to the Pacific Ocean.* 12
vols. Washington, A. O. P. Nicholson, 1855–60.

———. War Department. *The War of Rebellion. A Compilation
of the Official Records of the Union and Confederate Armies.*

Four Series, 128 vols. Washington, Government Printing Office, 1880–1901.

Warren, Lieutenant Gouverneur Kemble. "Preliminary Report," 34 Cong., 1 sess., *Senate Exec. Doc. No. 76.*

Winchell, N. H. "Geological Report of a Reconnaissance of the Black Hills, Made in the Summer of 1874," *Annual Report of Chief of Engineers,* 1874–75, Vol. 2, Part 2, pp. 1113–1230.

NEWSPAPERS AND PERIODICALS

The Aurum. South Dakota State School of Mines, Rapid City.

Black Hills Central. Rochford.

Black Hills Champion. Deadwood.

Black Hills Daily and Weekly Times. Deadwood, April 7, 1877——.

The Black Hills Engineer. South Dakota State School of Mines, Rapid City, 1923–45.

Black Hills Herald. Central City.

The Black Hills Herald. Custer.

The Black Hills Industrial Review. 1911.

The Black Hills Journal. Rapid City, 1878——.

Black Hills Miner. Rockerville, March, 1879.

Black Hills Pioneer. Deadwood, June 8, 1878——.

The Black Hills Pioneer. Deadwood (Facsimile Edition), 1948.

Black Hills Tribune. Crook City, June 9, 1876.

Black Hills Weekly Journal. Rapid City, 1878——.

Carbonate Reporter. Carbonate Camp, circa 1881.

Cheyenne Daily Leader. Cheyenne, Wyoming, 1874–79.

Custer County Chronicle. 1880——.

Deadwood Miner.

Engineering and Mining Journal. 1874–79.

Golden Center Christian. Central City.

Lead City Daily Tribune. 1881.

Mining and Real Estate Journal. Deadwood, March 15, 1878.

The Monthly South Dakotan. 1898.

The Pahasapa Quarterly. South Dakota State School of Mines, Rapid City, 1911–21.

Register. Central City, 1878.

Report and Historical Collections. South Dakota State Historical Society, Pierre, 1901——.

The Rochford Miner. 1880.

Sharp Bits. Homestake Mining Company, Lead, South Dakota, February, 1950——.

Telegraph-Herald. Central and Lead Cities.

The Western Enterprise. Deadwood.

The Wi-Iyohi: Bulletin of the South Dakota Historical Society. 1947——.

BOOKS

Aken, David. *Pioneers of the Black Hills: Or, Gordon's Stockade Party of 1874.* (Milwaukee, 1920?).

Anonymous. *The Black Hills: Their Wonderful Mineral Wealth and Products.* Chicago, Poole Brothers, n.d.

——. *Constitution and By-Laws of the Society of Black Hills Pioneers Together with a Roll of Members.* Deadwood, Times Job Printing House, 1891.

——. *The Golden Land, History of the Black Hills Gold Region.* Chicago, 1875.

——. *Rapid City, South Dakota.* N.p., circa 1891.

Armstrong, Nelson. *Nuggets of Experience.* N.p., Times-Mirror P. and B. House, 1906.

Bandel, Eugene. *Frontier Life in the Army, 1854–1861.* Glendale, Arthur H. Clark Company, 1932.

Batchelder, George Alexander. *A Sketch of the History and Resources of Dakota Territory.* Yankton, Press Steam Power Printing Company, 1870.

Bennett, Estelline. *Old Deadwood Days.* New York, J. H. Sears & Company, Inc., 1928.

Black Hills Exploring and Mining Association. *The Black Hills Mining, Exploration, and Permanent Settlement Expedition.* Yankton, 1867.

——. *New and Short Route to the Gold Mines of the Black Hills, Montana and Idaho.* Yankton, April 18, 1865.

Black Hills Placer Mining Company. *Prospectus*. N.p., n.d., circa 1879.

Board of Trade, Deadwood, Dakota Territory. *The Black Hills of Dakota*. Deadwood, Daily Pioneer Book and Job Office, 1881.

Bourke, John G. *On the Border with Crook*. London, Sampson Low, Marston, Searle, and Rivington, 1892.

Bridwell, J. W. *The Life and Adventures of Robert McKimie*. Hillsboro, Hillsboro Gazette Office, 1878.

Brockett, L. P. *Our Western Empire* . . . . Philadelphia, Bradley & Company, 1881.

Brown, Jesse, and A. M. Willard. *The Black Hills Trails: A History of the Struggles of the Pioneers in the Winning of the West*. Rapid City, South Dakota, Rapid City Journal Company, 1924.

Bryan, Jerry. *An Illinois Gold Hunter in the Black Hills*. Springfield, Illinois, Illinois State Historical Society, 1960.

Burk, Mrs. M. (Calamity Jane). *Life and Adventures of Calamity Jane, by Herself*. N.p., 1896.

Carver, Jonathan. *Three Years' Travels Throughout the Interior Parts of North America* . . . . Walpole, N.H., Isaiah Thomas & Co., 1813.

Cheyenne Gold Mining Company of the Black Hills. *Prospectus*. New York, Mining Record Press, 1879.

Chittenden, H. M., and A. T. Richardson, eds. *Life, Letters and Travels of Father Pierre-Jean De Smet, S.J., 1801–1873*. 4 vols. New York, F. P. Harper, 1905.

Clippinger, C. T. *The Black Hills News Letter*. Deadwood, 1877.

Clyman, James. *James Clyman, Frontiersman, 1795–1881*. Ed. by Charles L. Camp. Portland, Oregon, Champoeg Press, 1960.

Collins, Charles. *Collins' History and Directory of the Black Hills*. Central City, Dakota Territory, Charles Collins, 1878.

Crawford, John Wallace. *The Broncho Book, Being Buck-Jumps in Verse*. East Aurora, New York, Roycrofters, 1908.

———. *The Poet Scout*. San Francisco, H. Keller, 1879.

Crawford, Lewis F. *Rekindling Camp Fires: The Exploits of Ben Arnold (Connor).* Bismarck, Capitol Book Co., 1926.

Crook, General George. *General George Crook: His Autobiography.* Ed. by Martin F. Schmidt. Norman, University of Oklahoma Press, 1946.

Culbertson, Thaddeus A., and John Francis McDermott. *Journal of an Expedition to the Mauvaises Terres and the Upper Missouri in 1850.* Smithsonian Institution, Bureau of American Ethnology, *Bulletin 147.* Washington, Government Printing Office, 1952.

Curley, Edwin A. *Glittering Gold, the True Story of the Black Hills.* New York, 1876.

———. *Guide to the Black Hills, Comprising the Travels of the Author and His Special Artist.* Chicago, privately printed, 1877.

Custer, Mrs. Elizabeth Bacon. *Boots and Saddles: or, Life in Dakota With General Custer.* New York, Harper & Brothers, 1885.

Deadwood Board of Trade. *The Black Hills of Dakota, 1881.* Deadwood, Dakota Territory, Daily Pioneer Book and Job Office, 1881.

Deadwood Gulch Hydraulic Mining Company. *Prospectus.* Deadwood, Pioneer Publishing Co., 1882.

Denig, Edwin Thompson. *Five Indian Tribes of the Upper Missouri.* Ed. by John C. Ewers. Norman, University of Oklahoma Press, 1961.

DeSmet, Pierre Jean, S. J. *Letters and Sketches: with a Narrative of a Year's Residence Among the Indian Tribes of the Rocky Mountains.* Philadelphia, 1843.

Dodge, Richard Irving. *The Black Hills.* New York, J. Miller, 1876.

Driscoll, Robert E. *The Black Hills of South Dakota: Its Pioneer Banking History.* New York, Newcomen Society in North America, 1951.

———. *Seventy Years of Banking in the Black Hills.* Rapid City, Gate City Guide, 1948.

Finerty, John F. *War-Path and Bivouac: The Big Horn and Yellowstone Expedition.* Chicago, R. R. Donnelly & Sons, 1955.

Grinnell, George B. *Two Great Scouts and Their Pawnee Battalion: The Experiences of Frank J. North and Luther H. North.* Cleveland, 1928.

Harney City Tin Mining, Milling, and Manufacturing Company. *Prospectus* . . . . Rapid City, 1886.

Hayden, Ferdinand V. *Contributions to the Ethnography and Philology of the Indian tribes of the Missouri Valley.* Philadelphia, C. Sherman & Son, Printers, 1862.

———. *Geological Report of the Exploration of the Yellowstone and Missouri Rivers.* Washington, Government Printing Office, 1869.

———. *The Great West.* Bloomington, Illinois, 1880.

Hazen, Colonel W. B. *Our Barren Lands.* Cincinnati, Robert Clarke & Co., 1875.

Hebert, Frank. *Forty Years Prospecting and Mining in the Black Hills of South Dakota.* Rapid City, Rapid City Daily Journal, 1921.

Holman, Albert M., and Constant R. Marks. *Pioneering in the Northwest: Niobrara–Virginia City Wagon Road.* Sioux City, Deitch and Lamar, 1924.

Holt, O. H. *Dakota.* Chicago, Rand, McNally & Co., 1885.

Howard, J. W. *"Doc" Howard's Memoirs.* Denver, 1931.

Hughes, Richard B. *Pioneer Years in the Black Hills.* Ed. by Agnes Wright Spring. Glendale, Arthur H. Clark Company, 1957.

Ingham, G. Thomas. *Digging Gold Among the Rockies* . . . . Philadelphia, Cottage Library Publishing House, 1881.

Irving, Washington. *Astoria.* Ed. by Edgeley W. Todd. Norman, University of Oklahoma Press, 1964.

Jones, James K. *The Black Hills of Dakota, Gold and Silver Mining.* Indianapolis, 1875.

Hafen, LeRoy R. and Ann W. Hafen. *Powder River Campaigns and Sawyer's Expedition of 1865.* Glendale, The Arthur H. Clark Company, 1961.

Kuykendall, William Littlebury. *Frontier Days: A True Narra-*

tive of Striking Events on the Western Frontier. N.p., J. M. and H. L. Kuykendall, 1917.

Lydston, G. Frank, M.D. *Trusty Five-Fifteen.* Kansas City, Missouri, Burton Publishing Company, 1921.

McClintock, John S. *Pioneer Days in the Black Hills: Accurate History and Facts, Related by One of the Early Day Pioneers.* Ed. by Edward L. Senn. New York, privately printed by J. J. Little and Ives Company, 1939.

McKeown, Martha Ferguson. *Them Was the Days: An American Saga of the '70's.* Lincoln, University of Nebraska Press, 1961.

Maguire, H. N. *The Black Hills and American Wonderland.* The Lakeside Library, IV, No. 82. Chicago, Donnelly, Loyd & Co., 1877.

———. *The Coming Empire.* Sioux City, Watkins & Smead, 1878.

———. *New Map and Guide to Dakota and the Black Hills.* Chicago, Rand McNally, 1877.

Mandat-Grancey, Edmond. *Cowboys and Colonels.* Trans. by William Conn. Philadelphia, J. B. Lippincott, 1963.

———. *La Breche Aux Buffles: Un Ranche Français Dans Le Dakota.* Paris, 1889.

———. *Dans Les Montagnes Rocheuses.* Paris, E. Plon, 1884.

Marcy, Colonel R. B. *Thirty Years of Army Life on the Border.* New York, Harper & Brothers, Publishers, 1866.

Margry, Pierre, comp. *Decouvertes et Établissements des Français dans L'ouest et dans le sud de L'Amérique Septentrionale.* 6 vols. Paris, Imprimerie D. Jouaust, 1875.

Nasatir, Abraham Phineas. *Before Lewis and Clark.* 2 vols. St. Louis Historical Documents Foundation, 1952.

Owen, David Dale. *Report of a Geological Survey of Wisconsin, Iowa, and Minnesota, and Incidentally a Portion of Nebraska Territory.* Philadelphia, 1852.

Parker, Rev. Samuel. *Journal of an exploring tour beyond the Rocky Mountains* . . . . Ithaca, published by the author, Mack, Andrus & Woodruff, printers, 1838.

Rhoads, William. *Recollections of Dakota Territory.* Fort Pierre, privately printed, 1931.

Richardson, James D., ed. *Messages and Papers of the Presidents, 1789–1897.* 10 vols. Washington, Government Printing Office, 1898.

Rollins, Philip Ashton, ed. *The Discovery of the Oregon Trail: Robert Stuart's Narratives.* New York, Charles Scribner's Sons, 1935.

Rosen, Rev. Peter. *Pa-Ha-Sa-Pah, or the Black Hills of Dakota.* St. Louis, Nixon-Jones Printing Co., 1895.

Ruxton, George Frederick. *Life in the Far West.* Ed. by Leroy R. Hafen. Norman, University of Oklahoma Press, 1951.

Saltiel, E. H. *Black Hills Guide.* St. Louis, 1875.

Schatz, A. H. *Opening a Cow Country: A History of the Pioneer's Struggle in Conquering the Prairies South of the Black Hills.* Ann Arbor, Edwards Brothers, 1939.

Smith, James E. *A Famous Battery and Its Campaigns.* Washington, W. H. Lowdermilk & Co., 1892.

Standing Bear, Chief. *Land of the Spotted Eagle.* New York, Houghton-Mifflin Company, 1933.

Stokes, George W., and Howard R. Driggs. *Deadwood Gold: A Story of the Black Hills.* Chicago, World Book Co., 1926.

Strahorn, Robert. *Handbook of Wyoming and Guide to the Black Hills and Big Horn Regions.* Cheyenne, privately printed, 1877.

———. *To the Rockies and Beyond.* Omaha, Omaha Republican Print., 1878.

Sutley, Zack T. *The Last Frontier.* New York, Macmillan Company, 1930.

Tabeau, Pierre Antoine. *Tabeau's Narrative of Loisel's Expedition to the Upper Missouri.* Ed. by Annie Heloise Abel. Norman, University of Oklahoma Press, 1939.

Tallent, Annie Donna Fraser. *The Black Hills: or The Last Hunting Grounds of the Dakotahs.* St. Louis, Nixon-Jones Printing Company, 1899.

Thwaites, Reuben Gold. *Early Western Travels, 1748–1846.* 32 vols. Cleveland, 1904–1907.

———, ed. *Original Journals of the Lewis and Clark Expedition, 1804–1806.* 7 vols. New York, Dodd, Mead and Co., 1904.

Triggs, J. H. *History of Cheyenne and Northern Wyoming Embracing the Gold Fields of the Black Hills.* Omaha, Herald Steam Book and Job Printing House, 1876.

U.S., Department of the Interior, Bureau of Mines. *Black Hills Mineral Atlas.* Bureau of Mines Information Circular 7688 (July, 1954) and Circular 7707 (May, 1955).

———, Department of the Interior, Newton, Henry, and Jenney, Walter P. *Report on the Geology and Resources of the Black Hills of Dakota with Atlas.* Washington, Department of Interior, 1880.

Wardner, Jim. *Jim Wardner, of Wardner, Idaho.* New York, Anglo-American Publishing Co., 1900.

Warren, Lieutenant Gouverneur Kemble. *Explorations in the Dakota Country in the Year 1855.* Washington, Government Printing Office, 1856.

Williams, Henry T. *The Pacific Tourist* . . . . New York, Henry T. Williams, Publisher, 1878.

Windolph, Charles A. *I Fought with Custer: The Story of Sergeant Windolph.* New York, Charles Scribner's Sons, 1947.

Wislizenus, F. A., M.D. *A Journey to the Rocky Mountains in the Year 1839.* Trans. by F. A. Wislizenus. St. Louis, Missouri Historical Society, 1912.

Wixson, Franklin. *The Black Hills Gold Mines.* Yankton, Taylor Brothers, 1875.

Young, Harry (Sam). *Hard Knocks: A Life Story of the Vanishing West.* Chicago, Laird & Lee, Inc., 1915.

ARTICLES

Anonymous. "Black Hills Expedition," *New York Daily Tribune,* August 1, September 4, 1874.

———. "The Black Hills—Their Value Regardless of Gold," *Potter's American Monthly,* Vol. V (August, 1875), 616–20.

———. "Custer's Expedition," *Harper's Weekly,* Vol. XLIX (September 12, 1874), 753.

———. "Facts About the Black Hills," *Engineering and Mining Journal*, Vol. XXIII (April 21, 1877), 251–52.

———. "Facts About the Black Hills," *The Daily Graphic* (New York), October 30, 1877.

———. "The Flora of the Black Hills," *Popular Science Monthly*, Vol. V (October, 1874), 760.

———. "General Custer's Expedition . . . ," *The Nation*, Vol. XIX (August 27, 1874), 130.

———. "Gold!" Bismarck Tribune, August 12, 1874.

———. "Gold," *The Inter Ocean* (Chicago), August 27, 1874.

———. "An Historic Stone," *Queen City Mail* (Spearfish, South Dakota), April 17, 1889. Typescript, Tier 6, Shelf 3, South Dakota Historical Society.

———. "Homestake," *Lead Daily Call*, May, 1953.

———. "Latest from the Black-Hills," *Engineering and Mining Journal*, Vol. XXIII (June 16, 1877), 414.

———. "The Medora-Deadwood Stage Route," *South Dakota Historical Collections*, Vol. XXV (1951), 368–84.

———. "Mining Notes—Mining Prospects in the Black Hills," *Engineering and Mining Journal*, Vol. XXIII (February 17, 1877), 108–109.

———. "Official Correspondence Pertaining to the War of the Outbreak, 1862–1865," *South Dakota Historical Collections*, Vol. VIII (1916), 100–588.

———. "Our Indian War," *Harper's Weekly*, Vol. XX (October 28, 1876), 875, 877.

———. "Souvenir Edition," *Lead Daily Call*, January 1, 1905.

———. "Struck it Rich," *Harper's Weekly*, Vol. XX (August 12, 1876), 650, 655.

Ayres, George V. "Early Transportation," *Black Hills Engineer*, Vol. XVIII (January, 1930), 12–18.

———. "Ayres Diary Authentic Hills Annal," *Deadwood Pioneer-Times*, n.d.

Briggs, H. E. "Black Hills Gold Rush," *North Dakota Historical Quarterly*, Vol. V (1930), 71.

Bullock, Seth. "An Account of Deadwood and the Northern

Black Hills in 1876" (ed. by Harry H. Anderson), *South Dakota Historical Collections*, Vol. XXXI (1962), 287–364.

Clarke, H. T. "Freighting—Denver and Black Hills," *Collections of the Nebraska State Historical Society*, Vol. V (1902), 299–312.

Custer, George Armstrong. "Opening the Black Hills: Custer's Report," *South Dakota Historical Collections*, Vol. VII (1914), 583–94.

D. Appleton and Company. "Dakota," *The American Annual Cyclopedia and Register of Important Events of the Year 1874*, Vol. XIV (1876).

———. "Dakota," *Appleton's Annual Cyclopedia and Register of Important Events of the Year 1877*, Vol. XVII (1878).

Donaldson, A. B. "The Black Hills Expedition," *South Dakota Historical Collections*, Vol. VII (1914), 554–80.

Finerty, John H. "Deadwood in 1876," *Motor Travel* (November, 1927), 17–18.

Forsyth, George A. "Diary of Custer Expedition," *Chicago Tribune*, August 26, 27, 1874.

Frost, W. H. "Diary, Gold Rush to Hills," *The Wi-Iyohi*, Vol. XIX (April, 1965), 1–8.

Gardner, C. V. "The First Quartz Mill in Deadwood Gulch," *Black Hills Engineer*, Vol. XVIII (January, 1930), 24–27.

H.H.B. "A Winter Campaign in the Black Hills," *McBride's Magazine*, Vol. XXXIII (March, 1884), 266–73.

Hayden, Ferdinand V. "Address on the Black Hills," *Proceedings of the American Philosophical Society*, Vol. X (1869), 322–26.

———. "Explanations of a Second Edition of a Geological Map ...," Philadelphia Academy of Natural Science, 1858.

Henry, Guy V. "Adventures of American Army and Navy Officers: A Winter March to the Black Hills," *Harper's Weekly*, Vol. XXXIX (July 27, 1895), 700.

Larsen, A. J., ed. "Black Hills Gold Rush," *North Dakota Historical Quarterly*, Vol. VI (1932), 302.

Maguire, H. N. "The Coming Empire [Extracts from]," *Rapid City Daily Journal*, February 20, 1926.

228

Meyers, Augustus. "Dakota in the Fifties," *South Dakota Historical Collections*, Vol. X (1920), 130–94.

Milner, Joe E. "California Joe Letter," *Middle Border Bulletin*, Vol. II (Spring, 1943), 1.

Nichols, George Ward. "Wild Bill," *Harper's New Monthly Magazine*, Vol. XXXIV (February, 1867), 273–385.

Peirce, Ellis T. "Log of a Trip to the Black Hills," *Second Biennial Report of the State Historian of Wyoming* (1922), 122–23.

Raddick, W. P. "Story of Lead's Inception, Building and Progress," *Lead Daily Call*, August 5, 1926.

Richardson, Leander P. "A Trip to the Black Hills," *Scribner's*, Vol. XIII (April, 1877), 748–56.

Scott, Samuel. "The Tin Mines of the Black Hills," *Frank Leslie's Popular Monthly*, Vol. XXX (August, 1890), 187–92.

Stokes, George W. "Deadwood Gold," *Motor Travel*, July, 1922.

———. "Echoes of the Old West," *Union Pacific Magazine* (November, 1923), 6–7.

Street, Margaret Frink. "Dakota Diary" (ed. by D. O. Collins), *The Westerners Brand Book* (Denver Posse, 1948), 77–100.

Two Strikes and Bear's Belly. "Of An Expedition Under Custer to the Black Hills in June, 1875," *North Dakota Historical Collections*, Vol. VI (1920), 163–70.

Vérendrye, François, Chevalier de la. "Journal," *South Dakota Historical Collections*, Vol. VII (1914), 349–58.

Warren, Lieutenant Gouverneur Kemble. "Preliminary Report of Explorations in Nebraska and Dakota in 1855–'56–'57," *South Dakota Historical Collections*, Vol. XI (1922), 134–219.

Wells, Philip F. "Ninety-Six Years Among the Indians," *North Dakota History*, Vol. XV (July, 1948), 169–215.

Secondary Sources

MANUSCRIPTS

Beckwith, Clarence G. "Early Settlements in the Black Hills,

1874–1884." Unpublished Doctoral Dissertation, University of Michigan, 1937.

Bleskelstad, Inga Theodosia. "Territorial School Days in Pennington County, 1876–1890." Unpublished Master's Thesis, University of Colorado, 1941.

Cash, Joseph H. "A History of Lead, South Dakota." Unpublished Master's Thesis, University of South Dakota, 1949.

Chase, Isaac H. "Our Fur Trader—The First White Man to Live in Pennington County." Unpublished manuscript re Thomas Sarpy, January 10, 1962, Isaac H. Chase, 911 St. Andrew Street, Rapid City, South Dakota.

Edwards, Mildred Margery Louise. "The Historical Geography of the Black Hills." Unpublished Master's Thesis, University of Oklahoma, 1958.

Korsgaard, Ross P. "A History of Rapid City, South Dakota, During Territorial Days." Unpublished Master's Thesis, University of South Dakota, 1955.

Martin, Harold E. "Gold Mining in the Black Hills." Manuscript, South Dakota School of Mines, 1937.

Olson, Lawrence E. "The Mining Frontier of South Dakota, 1874–1877." Unpublished Master's Thesis, University of Iowa, 1931.

Parker, Watson. "The Exploration of the Dakota Black Hills." Unpublished Master's Thesis, University of Oklahoma, 1962.

Stine, Lawrence Carl. "A History of Theater and Theatrical Activities in Deadwood, South Dakota, 1876–90." Unpublished Doctoral Dissertation, State University of Iowa, 1962.

BOOKS

Alter, J. Cecil. *James Bridger, Trapper, Frontiersman, Scout and Guide*. Salt Lake City, Shepard Book Company, 1925.

Anonymous. *The Black Hills: America's Land of Minerals: The Resources, Scenery, Commerce, Development and People of Dakota*. Omaha, Herald Job Printing Rooms, 1889.

———. *Authentic History of Sam Bass and His Gang*. Denton, Texas, Monitor, 1878.

——. *Life and Adventures of Sam Bass*. Dallas, Dallas Commercial Steam Print, 1878.

——. *Memorial and Biographical Record of the Black Hills Region*. Chicago, Geo. A. Ogle & Co., 1908.

Armstrong, M. K. *History and Resource of Dakota, Montana, and Idaho*. Yankton, Dakota Territory, Geo. W. Kingsbury, 1866.

Baldwin, George P. *The Black Hills Illustrated*. Deadwood, Black Hills Mining Men's Association, 1904.

Beebe, Lucius, and Charles Clegg. *The American West: A Pictorial Epic of a Continent*. New York, E. P. Dutton & Co., Inc., 1955.

Bennett, H. M. *The Truth About the Black Hills*. Deadwood, Pioneer Times, 1907.

Branch, E. Douglas. *The Hunting of the Buffalo*. Lincoln, University of Nebraska Press, 1962.

Briggs, Harold E. *Frontiers of the Northwest*. New York, D. Appleton-Century Co., 1940.

Brown, Mark H. *The Plainsmen of the Yellowstone: A History of the Yellowstone Basin*. New York, G. P. Putnam's Sons, 1961.

Burlington Route [Chicago, Burlington and Quincy Railroad]. *Mines and Mining in the Black Hills*. Omaha, Rees Print (1904).

Carr, Robert H. *Black Hills Ballads*. Denver, Reed Publishing Co., 1902.

Case, Lee [Leland]. *Lee's Official Guidebook to the Black Hills and Badlands*. Sturgis, South Dakota, Black Hills and Badlands Association, 1949.

Casey, Robert J. *The Black Hills and Their Incredible Characters*. Indianapolis, Bobbs-Merrill Company, Inc., 1949.

Castleman, Harvey N. *Sam Bass the Train Robber*. Girard, Kansas: Haldeman-Julius Publications, 1944.

Chicago and North-Western Railway. *Black Hills*. 8th edition. Chicago (?), Chicago and North-Western Railway, 1910.

Chittenden, Hiram Martin. *The American Fur Trade in the Far West*. 2 vols. New York, The Press of the Pioneers, 1935.

Clark, Badger. *Sun and Saddle Leather*. Boston, Richard G. Badger, 1920.

Connolly, Joseph P., and Cleophas C. O'Harra. *The Mineral Wealth of the Black Hills. Bulletin No. 16*, South Dakota School of Mines, May, 1929.

Crawford, Lewis F. *The Medora-Deadwood Stage Line*. Bismarck, Capitol Book Co., 1925.

———. *Ranching Days in Dakota*. Intro. by Usher L. Burdick. Baltimore, Wirth Brothers, 1950.

Crouse, Nellis M. *La Vérendrye, Fur Trader and Explorer*. Ithaca, Cornell University Press, 1956.

Dale, Harrison C. *The Ashley-Smith Explorations and the Discovery of a Central Route to the Pacific*. Glendale, Arthur H. Clark Company, 1941.

Danker, Donald F., ed. *Man of the Plains: Recollections of Luther North*. Lincoln, University of Nebraska Press, 1961.

Dunn, J. P. *Massacres of the Mountains: A History of the Indian Wars of the Far West, 1818–1875*. New York, Archer House, n.d.

El Comancho. *The Old-Timer's Tale*. Chicago, The Canterbury Press, 1929.

Fatout, Paul. *Ambrose Bierce and the Black Hills*. Norman, University of Oklahoma Press, 1956.

Fielder, Mildred. *Wild Bill and Deadwood*. Seattle, Superior Publishing Co., 1965.

Gard, Wayne. *Sam Bass*. Boston, Houghton Mifflin Co., 1936.

Goetzmann, William H. *Army Explorations in the American West, 1803–1863*. New Haven, Yale University Press, 1959.

Greever, William S. *The Bonanza West: The Story of the Western Mining Rushes, 1848–1900*. Norman, University of Oklahoma Press, 1963.

Grinnell, George Bird. *The Cheyenne Indians*. 2 vols. New Haven, Yale University Press, 1923.

———. *The Fighting Cheyennes*. Norman, University of Oklahoma Press, 1956.

Hebard, Grace Raymond, and E. A. Brininstool. *The Bozeman Trail.* 2 vols. Cleveland, 1922.

Heitman, Frances F. *Historical Register and Dictionary of the U. S. Army.* 2 vols. Washington, The Rare Book Shop, 1903.

Hoffman, H. O. *Gold Milling in the Black Hills.* Chicago, Fraser & Chalmers, Engineers, circa 1898.

Holley, Frances Chamberlain. *Once Their Home: Or, Our Legacy from the Dakotahs.* Chicago, Donohue and Henneberry, 1892.

Honig, Louis O. *James Bridger.* Kansas City, Missouri. Brown-White-Lowell Press, 1951.

Hosmer, James K., ed. *History of the Expedition of Captains Lewis and Clark.* 2 vols. Chicago, A. C. McClurg & Co., 1924.

Hunt, Frazier, and Robert Hunt. *I Fought with Custer: The Story of Sergeant Windolph.* New York, Scribner's Sons, 1947.

Hurt, Wesley R., and William E. Lass. *Frontier Photographer: Stanley J. Morrow's Dakota Years.* Lincoln, University of Nebraska Press, 1956.

Hyde, George E. *Red Cloud's Folk.* Norman, University of Oklahoma Press, 1937.

Jackson, Donald. *Custer's Gold.* New Haven, Yale University Press, 1966.

Jackson, William Turrentine. *Wagon Roads West.* Berkeley, University of California Press, 1952.

Jennewein, J. Leonard. *Calamity Jane of the Western Trails.* Huron, South Dakota, Dakota Books, 1953.

Kingsbury, George W. *History of Dakota Territory.* 5 vols. Chicago, The S. J. Clarke Publishing Co., 1915.

Lake, Stuart N. *Wyatt Earp: Frontier Marshal.* New York, Bantam Books, 1952.

Lawrence County Centennial Committee. *Lawrence County: For the Dakota Territorial Centennial.* Ed. by Mildred Fielder. Lead, South Dakota, Seaton Publishing Company, 1960.

Lee, Bob, and Dick Williams. *Last Grass Frontier: The South Dakota Stock Grower Heritage.* Sturgis, South Dakota, Black Hills Publishers, Inc., 1964.

Leedy, Carl H. *Golden Days in the Black Hills.* Rapid City, Holmgren's, Inc., 1961.

McClure, P. F., comp. *Dakota Territory: Resources of Dakota.* Sioux Falls, The Argus-Leader Company, Printers, 1887.

McFarling, Lloyd. *Exploring the Northern Plains, 1804–1876.* Caldwell, Caxton Printers, 1955.

McGillicuddy, Julia. *McGillicuddy, Agent.* Palo Alto, Stanford University Press, 1941.

McGregor, James H. *The Wounded Knee Massacre From the Viewpoint of the Sioux.* Minneapolis, The Lund Press, Inc., 1940.

McMurtrie, Douglas Crawford. *The Beginnings of the Press in South Dakota.* Iowa City, privately printed, 1933.

———. *Early Printing in Wyoming and the Black Hills.* Hattiesburg, Mississippi, The Book Farm, 1943.

———. *Pioneer Printing in Wyoming.* Cheyenne, privately printed, 1933.

Martin, Charles Lee. *A Sketch of Sam Bass, the Bandit.* Norman, University of Oklahoma Press, 1956.

Merington, Marguerite, ed. *The Custer Story.* New York, Devin-Adair Company, 1950.

Milner, Joe E. *California Joe.* Caldwell, The Caxton Printers, Ltd., 1935.

Mooney, James. *Calendar History of the Kiowa Indians.* Washington, Government Printing Office, 1898.

Morgan, Dale L. *Jedediah Smith and the Opening of the West.* Indianapolis, The Bobbs-Merrill Company, Inc., 1953.

———, and Carl Wheat. *Jedediah Smith and His Maps of the American West.* San Francisco, California Historical Society, 1954.

Mumey, Nolie. *Poker Alice: Alice Ivers, Duffield, Tubbs, Huckert (1851–1930): History of a Woman Gambler in the West.* Denver, Artcraft Press, 1951.

Neider, Charles, ed. *The Great West.* New York, Bonanza Books, 1958.

Odell, Thomas E. *Mato Paha: The Story of Bear Butte Black*

Hills Landmark and Indian Shrine, Its Scenic, Historic, and Scientific Uniqueness. Spearfish, South Dakota, privately printed, 1942.

O'Harra, Cleophas Cisney. *The Mineral Wealth of the Black Hills. Bulletin No. 6,* South Dakota School of Mines, January, 1902.

Paul, Rodman Wilson. *California Gold.* Lincoln, University of Nebraska Press, circa 1937.

———. *Mining Frontiers of the Far West, 1848–1880.* New York, Holt, Rinehart and Winston, 1963.

Peattie, Roderick, ed. *The Black Hills.* New York, Vanguard, 1952.

Popowski, Bert. *South Dakota Brags.* N.p., privately printed, 1953.

Remsburg, John E., and George J. Remsburg. *Charlie Reynolds: Soldier, Hunter, Scout and Guide.* Kansas City, Missouri, H. M. Sender, 1931.

Rickard, Thomas A. *A History of American Mining.* New York, McGraw Hill, 1932.

———. *Stamp Milling of Gold Ores.* New York, 1897.

Robinson, Doane. *Doane Robinson's Encyclopedia of South Dakota.* Pierre, privately printed, 1925.

Rosa, Joseph G. *They Called Him Wild Bill: The Life and Adventures of James Butler Hickok.* Norman, University of Oklahoma Press, 1964.

Ryder, David W. *The Merrill Story.* N.p., The Merrill Company, 1958.

Schell, Herbert S. *Dakota Territory During the Eighteen Sixties, Report No. 30,* Governmental Research Bureau. Vermillion, University of South Dakota, August, 1954.

———. *History of South Dakota.* Lincoln, University of Nebraska Press, 1961.

Schmidt, Martin F. and Dee Brown. *The Settler's West.* New York, Charles Scribner's Sons, 1955.

Senn, Edward L. *Deadwood Dick and Calamity Jane.* Deadwood, privately printed, 1939.

235

Shinn, Charles Howard. "Land Laws of Mining Districts," Johns Hopkins University *Studies in History and Political Science*, second series, Vol. II, No. 12. Baltimore, 1884.

Smith, George Martin. *South Dakota*. N.p., n.d.

Sorensen, Marie Thybo. *My Black Hills*. N.p., n.d.

South Dakota, State Planning Board. *Pegmatite Mining in South Dakota*. Brookings, South Dakota State Planning Board, 1937.

———. *Tin Deposits in South Dakota*. Brookings, South Dakota State Planning Board, 1936.

Spence, Clark C. *British Investments and the American Mining Frontier*. Ithaca, American Historical Association, Cornell University Press, 1958.

Spring, Agnes Wright. *Cheyenne and Black Hills Stage and Express Routes*. Glendale, Arthur H. Clark Co., 1949.

Stewart, Edgar I. *Custer's Luck*. Norman, University of Oklahoma Press, 1955.

Textor, Lucy E. *Official Relations Between the United States and the Sioux Indians*. Palo Alto, Stanford University, 1896.

Thwaites, Reuben Gold. *A Brief History of Rocky Mountain Exploration*. New York, D. Appleton and Company, 1914.

Todd, J. E. *Preliminary Report on the Geology of South Dakota*. South Dakota Geological Survey *Bulletin No. 1*. Sioux Falls, Brown & Saenger, 1894.

U.S., Department of Commerce, Bureau of the Census. *Historical Statistics of the United States*. Washington, U.S. Government Printing Office, 1960.

———, Department of the Interior, Bureau of Mines. Paul T. Allsman. *Reconnaissance of Gold-Mining Districts in the Black Hills, S. Dak.* Washington, U.S. Government Printing Office, 1940.

———, Department of the Interior, Nelson Horatio Darton. *Preliminary Description of the Geology and Water Resources of the Southern Half of the Black Hills and Adjoining Regions*. Washington, Government Printing Office, 1901.

———, Department of the Interior. *Preliminary Report on the*

Geology and Underground Water Resources of the Great Plains. Washington, Government Printing Office, 1905.

———, Department of the Interior. *Geology and Water Resources of the Northern Portion of the Black Hills and Adjoining Regions.* Washington, Government Printing Office, 1909.

———, Department of the Interior, Bureau of Mines, E. D. Gardner. *Information Circular 7069: Tin Deposits of the Black Hills, South Dakota.* Washington, Government Printing Office, April, 1939.

———, Department of the Interior, U.S. Geological Survey, S. D. Irving. *Economic Resources of the Northern Black Hills.* Washington, Government Printing Office, 1904.

———, Department of the Interior, T. A. Jaggar. *Economic Resources of the Northern Black Hills.* Washington, Government Printing Office, 1903.

Wedel, Waldo R. *Prehistoric Man on the Great Plains.* Norman, University of Oklahoma Press, 1961.

White, John M. *The Newer Northwest: A Description of the Health Resorts and Mining Camps of the Black Hills of South Dakota and Big Horn Mountains in Wyoming.* St. Louis, Self-Culture Publishing Co., 1894.

Wilstach, Frank J. *Wild Bill Hickok: The Prince of Pistoleers.* New York, Doubleday, Page & Co., 1926.

Wolle, Muriel Sibell. *The Bonanza Trail.* Bloomington, Indiana University Press, 1953.

ARTICLES

Adams, W. E. "A Few of the Early Leaders of Deadwood," *Black Hills Engineer,* Vol. XVIII (January, 1930), 43–51.

Anderson, H. H. "Gordon Stockade," *The Wi-Iyohi,* Vol. XV (February, 1962), 1–8.

Anonymous. "The Black Hills, Once Hunting Grounds of the Red Men," *National Geographic Magazine,* Vol. LII (September, 1927), 305–29.

———. "Brief Chronology of Early Deadwood," *Black Hills Engineer,* Vol. XVIII (January, 1930), 32–36.

——. "Cascade," *The Wi-Iyohi*, Vol. III (March 1, 1950), 1–7.

——. "First Settlers and First Laws" (re the Gordon Party), undated newspaper clipping, Deadwood Public Library.

——. "Gold Production of the Black Black Hills," *Black Hills Engineer*, Vol. XVIII (January, 1930), 77.

——. "The Medora-Deadwood Stage Route," *South Dakota Historical Collections*, Vol. XXV (1951), 368–84.

——. "Railroad to Denver," *Daily News* (Denver ?), November 26 (or December—copy mutilated), 1898, clipping. Deadwood Public Library.

——. "Souvenir Edition," *Lead Daily Call*, 1905.

——. "Stamp Mills in Operation in 1877–78, As Listed by the *Black Hills Times*," *Black Hills Engineer*, Vol. XVIII (January, 1930), 73.

Bates, Charles Francis. "The Redman and the Black Hills," *The Outlook*, Vol. 126 (July 27, 1927), 408–12.

Beadle, W. H. H. "Fremont in Dakota," *The Monthly South Dakotan*, Vol. II (September, 1899), 80–82.

Bishop, Coleman E. "The Black Hills of Dakota," *The Chautauquan*, Vol. VII (June, 1887), 538–41.

Blackburn, William Maxwell. "Historical Sketch of North and South Dakota" (ed. by De Lorme W. Robinson), *South Dakota Historical Collections*, Vol. I (1902), 21–162.

Bourne, Edward Gaylord. "The Travels of Jonathan Carver," *The American Historical Review*, Vol. XI (1906), 287–302.

Briggs, H. E. "Black Hills Gold Rush," *North Dakota Historical Quarterly*, Vol. V (1930), 71.

Brown, Mark H. "A New Focus on the Sioux War," *Montana*, Vol. XI (October, 1961), 76–85.

Case, Leland. "Back to the Historical Black Hills," *National Geographic Magazine*, Vol. CX (October, 1956), 479–509.

Crawford, Lewis F. "The Medora-Black Hills Stage Line," *Collections of the State Historical Society of North Dakota*, Vol. VII (1925), 309–23.

Crow, I. R. "Recollections of Black Hills Newspapers by Old Timer," *Lead Daily Call*, August 5, 1926.

Curran, Clay C. "Annie D. Tallent: Her Life Story and Contributions," *South Dakota Education Association Journal*, Vol. XXXVII (January, 1962), 25–29.

DeLand, Charles E., *et al.* "Vérendrye," *South Dakota Historical Collections*, Vol. VII (1914), 89–402.

Durrie, D. S. "Captain John Carver and 'Carver's Grant,'" *Report and Collections of the State Historical Society of Wisconsin for the Years 1869, 1870, 1871 and 1872*, 219–70. Madison, Atwood & Culver, 1872.

Eriksson, Erik McKinley. "Sioux City and the Black Hills Gold Rush, 1874–1877," *Iowa Journal of History and Politics*, Vol. XX (July, 1922), 319–47.

Fielder, Mildred. "Carbonate Camp," *South Dakota Historical Collections*, Vol. XXVIII (1956), 99–178.

———. "Railroads of the Black Hills," *South Dakota Historical Collections*, Vol. XXX (1960), 35–316.

Granberg, J. W. "Jim Wardner: Financial Wizard of the West," *The American West*, Vol. I (Fall, 1964), 32–37.

Guthe, Otto E. "The Black Hills of South Dakota and Wyoming," *Papers of the Academy of Science, Arts, and Letters*, Vol. XX. Ann Arbor, University of Michigan Press, 1935.

Hampton, H. D. "Powder River Indian Expedition of 1865," *Montana, The Magazine of Western History*, Vol. XIV (October, 1964), 2–15.

Haxby, Orpha Le Gros. "The Last Bull Train into Rapid City in 1876," *South Dakota Historical Collections*, Vol. XXV (1951), 306–15.

Heldt, F. G. *Montana, Historical Society, Contributions to the Historical Society of Montana*, Vol. I (1876).

Jennewein, J. Leonard. "Ben Ash and the Trail Blazers," *South Dakota Historical Collections*, Vol. XXV (1951), 300–305.

———. "Early Geographic Conceptions of the Black Hills," *The Denver Westerners Monthly Roundup*, Vol. XIII (October, 1957), 5–11.

Larsen, Arthur J. "The Northwestern Express and Transportation Company," *North Dakota Historical Quarterly*, Vol. VI (October, 1931), 42–62.

Mahnken, Norbert R. "The Sidney-Black Hills Trail," *Nebraska History*, Vol. XXX (September, 1949), 203–25.

Morford, Lee. "Newspapers of the Black Hills," *Black Hills Engineer*, Vol. XVIII (January, 1930), 61–66.

Naeseth, Henriette. "Drama in Early Deadwood, 1876–1879," *American Literature*, Vol. X (November, 1938), 289–312.

Nichol, Ralph E. "Steamboat Navigation on the Missouri River with Special Reference to Yankton and Vicinity," *South Dakota Historical Collections*, Vol. XXVI (1952), 181–221.

Odell, Thomas E. "Who Were Thoen Stone Victims?," *Rapid City Daily Journal*, November 12, 1950, pp. 11, 23.

O'Harra, Cleophas Cisney. "Custer's Black Hills Expedition of 1874," *Black Hills Engineer*, Vol. XVII (November, 1929), 220–286.

———. "The Discovery of Gold in the Black Hills," *Black Hills Engineer*, Vol. XVII (November, 1929), 286–99.

———. "An Early Magazine Article on the Black Hills," *Black Hills Engineer*, Vol. V (February, 1916), 11–15.

———. "Pahasapa—The Black Hills," *Pahasapa Quarterly*, Vol. I (December, 1911), 5–11.

Palais, Hyman. "Black Hills Miners' Folklore," *California Folklore Quarterly*, Vol. IV (1945), 255–69.

———. "A Study of the Trails to the Black Hills Gold Fields," *South Dakota Historical Collections*, Vol. XXV (1951), 215–62.

———. "A Survey of Early Black Hills History," *Black Hills Engineer*, Vol. XXVII (April, 1941), 3–101.

Philip, George. "James (Scotty) Philip," *South Dakota Historical Review*, Vol. I (October, 1935), 3–48.

Robinson, Doane. "The Astorians in South Dakota," *South Dakota Historical Collections*, Vol. X (1920), 196–247.

———. "Black Hills Bygones," *South Dakota Historical Collections*, Vol. XII (1924), 198–207.

———. "A Comprehensive History of the Dakota or Sioux Indians," *South Dakota Historical Collections*, Vol. II (1904), 1–523.

Robinson, Will G. "Hayward City: The County Seat Without a County," *The Wi-Iyohi*, Vol. IV (January, 1951), 1–4.

———. "Tinton," *The Wi-Iyohi*, Vol. V (December, 1951).

———. "Vérendrye Plate," *Bulletin South Dakota State Historical Society* (July, 1955).

Russell, William H. "Promoters and Promotion Literature of Dakota Territory," *South Dakota Historical Collections*, Vol. XXVI (1952), 434–55.

Simpich, Frederick. "South Dakota Keeps Its West Wild," *National Geographic Magazine*, Vol. XCI (May, 1947), 555–88.

Snow, E. A., and J. Roeser, Jr. "The National Forests of the Black Hills," *Black Hills Engineer*, Vol. XXVI (December, 1940), 245–59.

Storms, W. H. "The Early History of the Black Hills, South Dakota," *Mining World* (February, 1906).

Recorders, claim: 61, 67, 73, 80, 91
Red Angry Bear (Custer's Scout): 25
Red Canyon: 108, 111, 114, 135–36, 179
Red Cloud (Sioux Chief): 128
Red Cloud Agency, D.T.: 13, 35–36, 47, 54, 116, 121, 127, 138
"Red Dan": *see* Red Dan McDonald
Red Dog (Sioux Chief): 139
Ree scouts, on Custer Expedition: 24
Refractory ores: 186, 192, 194
Register (Central City): 159
Renshaw, Thomas: 13
Reporter (Carbonate): 159
Restaurants, in Deadwood: 146
Retort gold: 192
Reynolds, Charlie: 26
Reynold's Ranch Stage Station: 114
Rich, Charles: 165
Richardson, Leander P. ("L. Putty-head"): 42
Richmond mine: 194
Riffles, in placer mining: 57–58
Rivers, crossing: 108; *see also* bridges
Rio Que Corré: see Niobrara River
Robinson, Jim: 22
Ross, Horatio Nelson: 25, 42
Rochford, D.T.: 49, 63, 160, 193, 201
Rochford, Michael D.: 193
Rocker, used in placer mining: 57, 87
Rockerville, D.T.: 60n., 63, 72, 87, 201
Rosebud, D.T.: 86
Rosengarden: *see* Frank Miller
Rothrock, G. W.: 77
Roughlocks, used going into Deadwood: 109
Ruhlen, Camp: *see* Camp Ruhlen
Rumney, Reverend W. L.: 160
Running Bear (Sioux Chief): 139
Rush, Cortland: 87
Russell, Thomas H.: 22–23, 28, 30, 33–34, 37
Ruxton, George Frederick: 10

Saint Elmo mine: 80
Saint Joseph Valley, Michigan: 13
St. Louis, Missouri: 34
St. Paul, Minnesota: 29
Salamander (treasure coach): 120
Saloon Number Ten: 165
Saloons: 73, 76–77, 86, 92, 95, 97, 101, 151–53, 160, 165, 172
Salt: 186, 793

Salting a claim: 103–104, 187
Saltiel, E. H.: 117
Sand Creek: 99–100, 185
Sander, J.: 67
Sandhill route (Sioux City to the Black Hills): 45, 111, 126
Santo Domingo: 142
Sarpy, Thomas L.: 10
Sasse, Charles: 151
Sawmills: 57, 74, 81, 92, 97
Sawyers, Colonel James A.: 17, 117
Scales, for gold: 150
Schools: 77
Scientific American: 41
Scooptown, D.T. (Sturgis): 98
Scott, Miss Carrie (Nellie?): 77 & n.
Scott, Dan: 23
Scott, Sam: 83
Scout, Calamity Jane as: 168
Scribners: 42
Second U.S. Cavalry Regiment: 35, 70, 136
Seventh U.S. Cavalry Regiment: 25, 102, 131n.
Seymour and Utter Pony Express: 121
Shankland, Samuel: 67
Shannon County, South Dakota: 10
Shannon, C. P.: 166
Shannon, Don: 45
Shannon, Jim: 163
Shaunessey, Ed.: 157
Shaw, Alex: 163
Sheridan, D.T.: 59, 72, 80–81, 87, 113–14, 181, 201
Sheridan Dam: 82
Sheridan, General Philip Henry: 23, 28–29, 34, 40, 66, 71, 124, 130
Sheriffs: 182
Sheriff, Mary: 197n.
Sherman, James C.: 82
Sherman, Maj. Gen. William T.: 21, 34, 66
Shining Mountains: 7
Short, Thomas: 94
Shoudy, Jacob: 151
Shoun, V. P.: 70
"Shrinkage stoping" in mining: 189
Sidney, Nebraska: 37, 40, 42, 46–48, 111; stage and freight lines: 85, 112, 118–19
Sidney-Black Hills trail: 47
Sidney *Telegraph: see Telegraph* (Sidney)

255